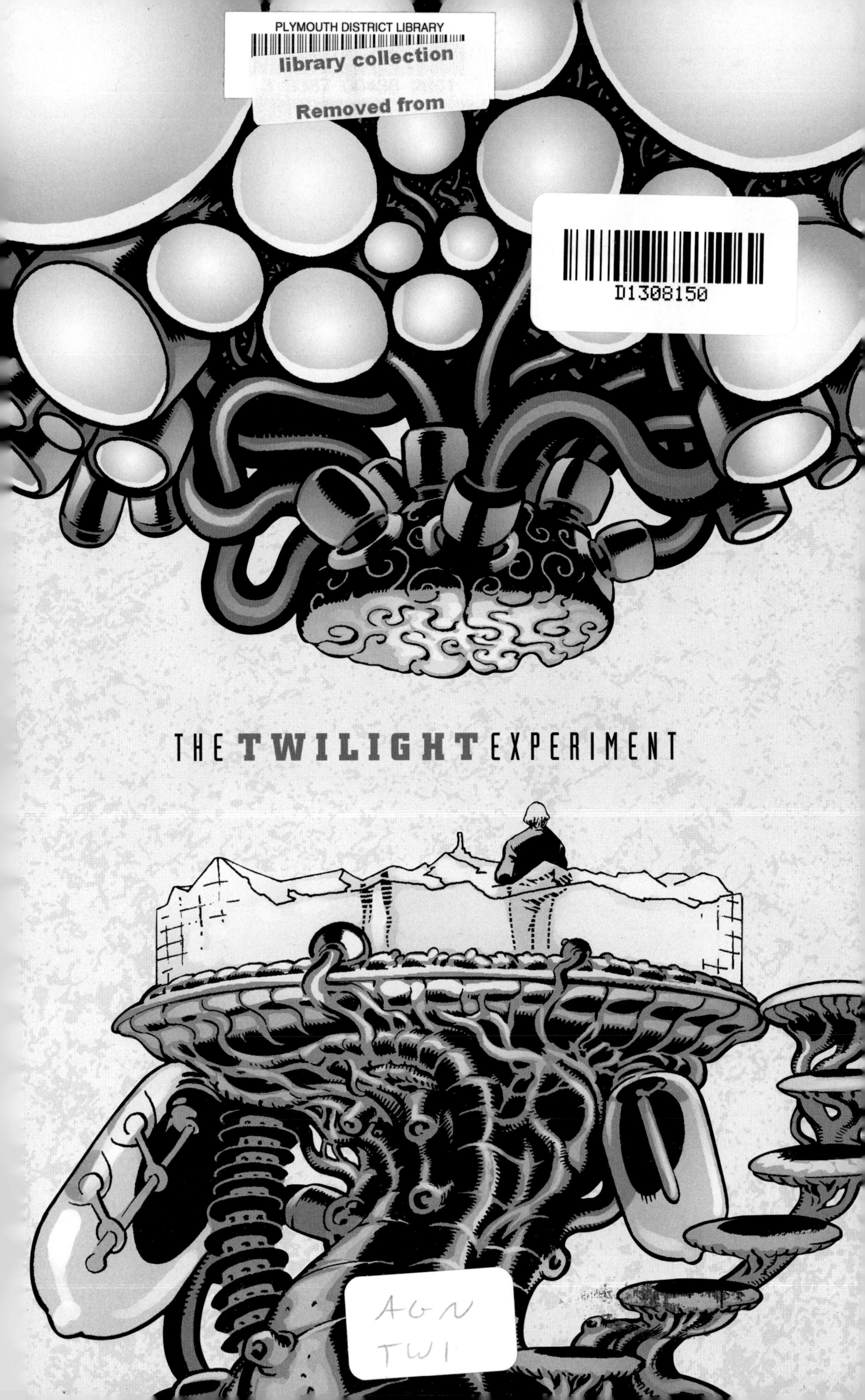
THE TWILIGHT EXPERIMENT

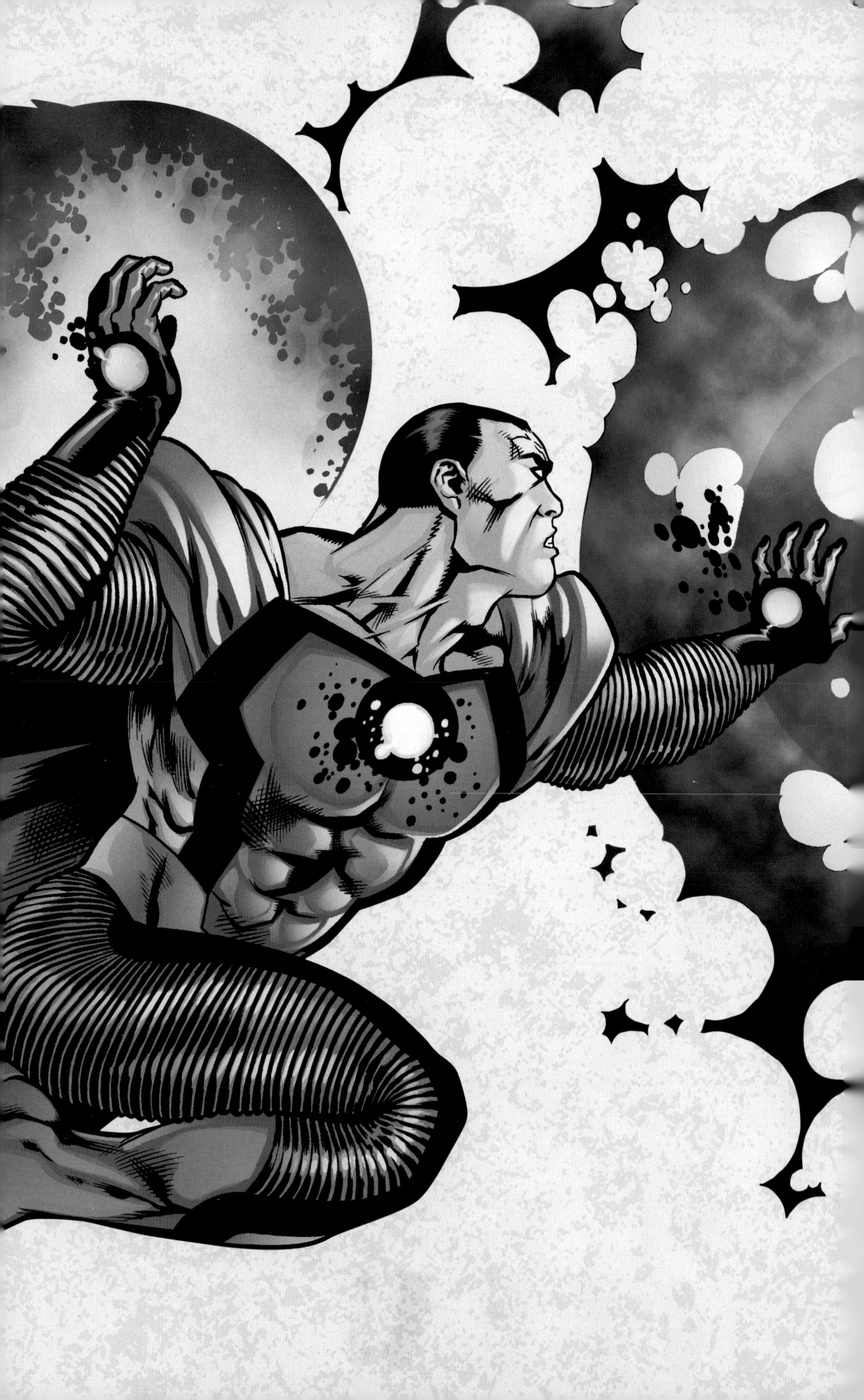

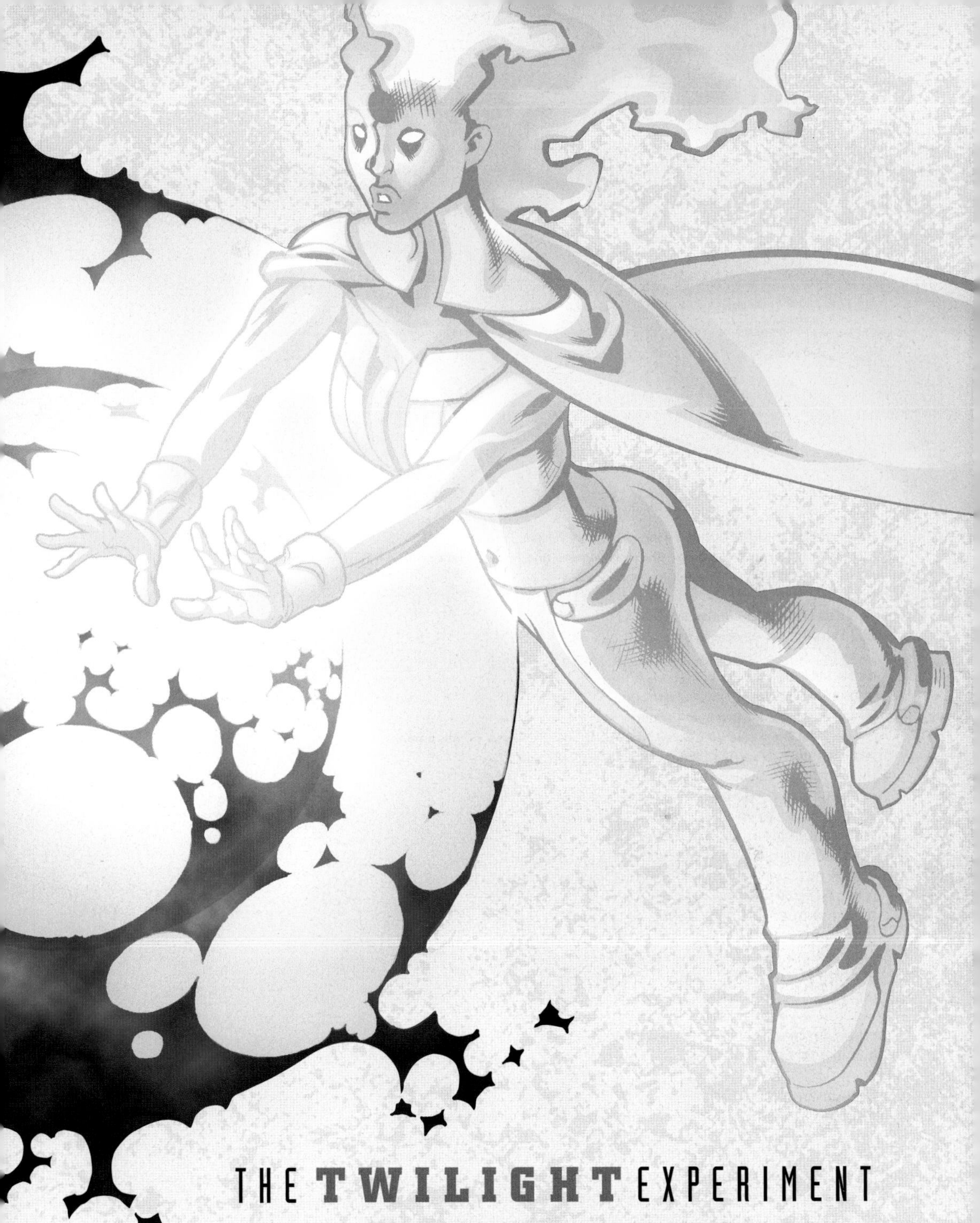

THE TWILIGHT EXPERIMENT

JIMMY PALMIOTTI and JUSTIN GRAY
writers

JUAN SANTACRUZ
artist

JOSÉ LUIS ROGER (parts 1-2) CARRIE STRACHAN (parts 3-6)
colors

PHIL BALSMAN
letters

JUAN SANTACRUZ
cover art and original series covers

The Twilight Experiment created by
JUSTIN GRAY, JIMMY PALMIOTTI and JUAN SANTACRUZ.

BOB HARRAS KRISTY QUINN Editors - Original Series
IAN SATTLER Director Editorial, Special Projects and Archival Editions
ROBBIN BROSTERMAN Design Director - Books

EDDIE BERGANZA Executive Editor
BOB HARRAS VP - Editor in Chief

DIANE NELSON President
DAN DIDIO and JIM LEE Co-Publishers
GEOFF JOHNS Chief Creative Officer
JOHN ROOD Executive VP - Sales, Marketing and Business Development
AMY GENKINS Senior VP - Business and Legal Affairs
NAIRI GARDINER Senior VP - Finance
JEFF BOISON VP - Publishing Operations
MARK CHIARELLO VP - Art Direction and Design
JOHN CUNNINGHAM VP - Marketing
TERRI CUNNINGHAM VP - Talent Relations and Services
ALISON GILL Senior VP - Manufacturing and Operations
DAVID HYDE VP - Publicity
HANK KANALZ Senior VP - Digital
JAY KOGAN VP - Business and Legal Affairs, Publishing
JACK MAHAN VP - Business Affairs, Talent
NICK NAPOLITANO VP - Manufacturing Administration
RON PERAZZA VP - Online
SUE POHJA VP - Book Sales
COURTNEY SIMMONS Senior VP - Publicity
BOB WAYNE Senior VP - Sales

THE TWILIGHT EXPERIMENT

DC Comics
1700 Broadway, New York, NY 10019. A Warner Bros. Entertainment Company.
Printed by Quad/Graphics, Dubuque, IA, USA 5/6/11. First Printing.
ISBN: 978-1-4012-3055-5

SUSTAINABLE
FORESTRY
INITIATIVE
Certified Chain of Custody
Promoting Sustainable
Forest Management
www.sfiprogram.org

Fiber used in this product line meets the
sourcing requirements of the SFI program.
www.sfiprogram.org SGS-SFICOC-0130

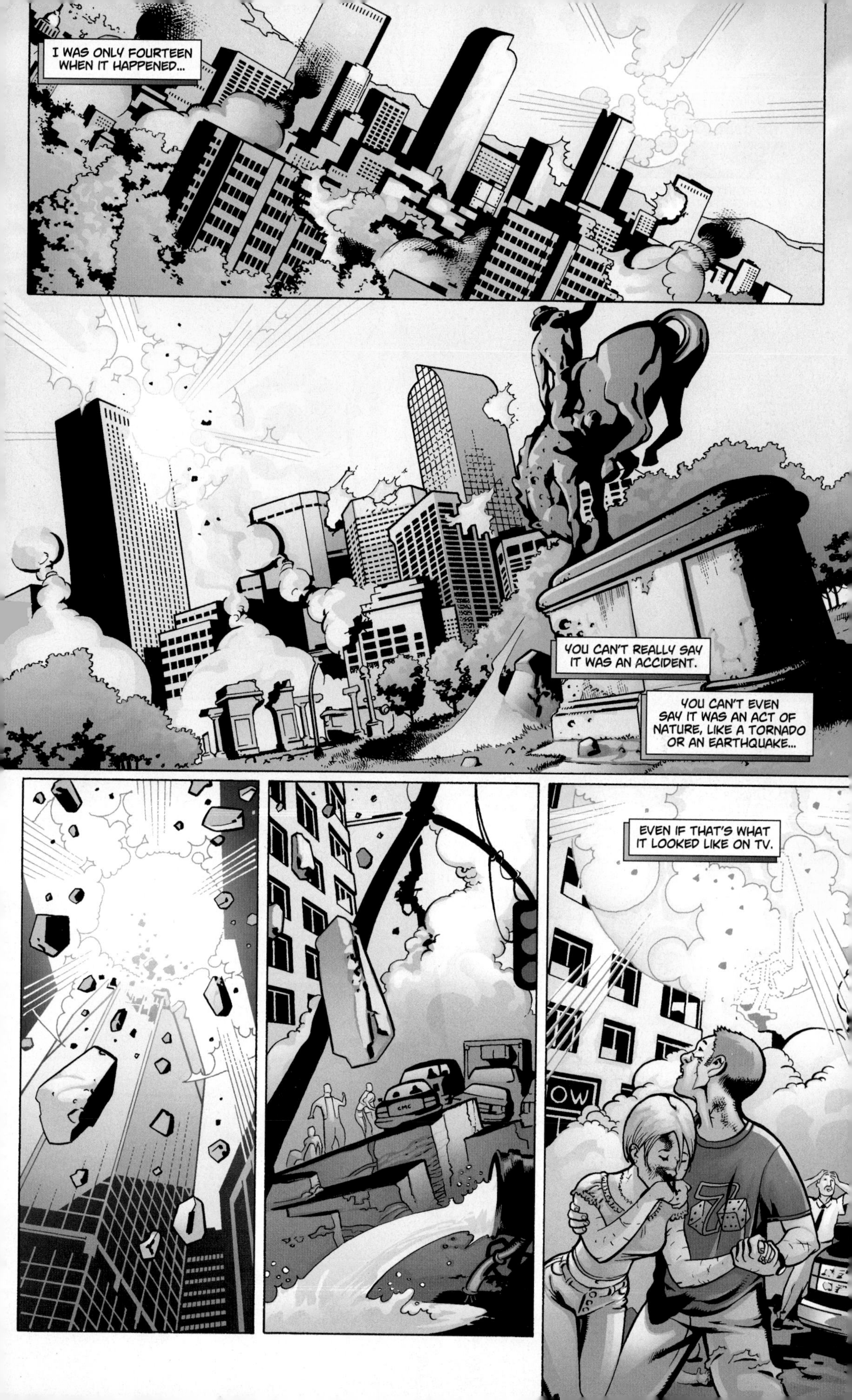
I WAS ONLY FOURTEEN WHEN IT HAPPENED...
YOU CAN'T REALLY SAY IT WAS AN ACCIDENT.
YOU CAN'T EVEN SAY IT WAS AN ACT OF NATURE, LIKE A TORNADO OR AN EARTHQUAKE...
EVEN IF THAT'S WHAT IT LOOKED LIKE ON TV.

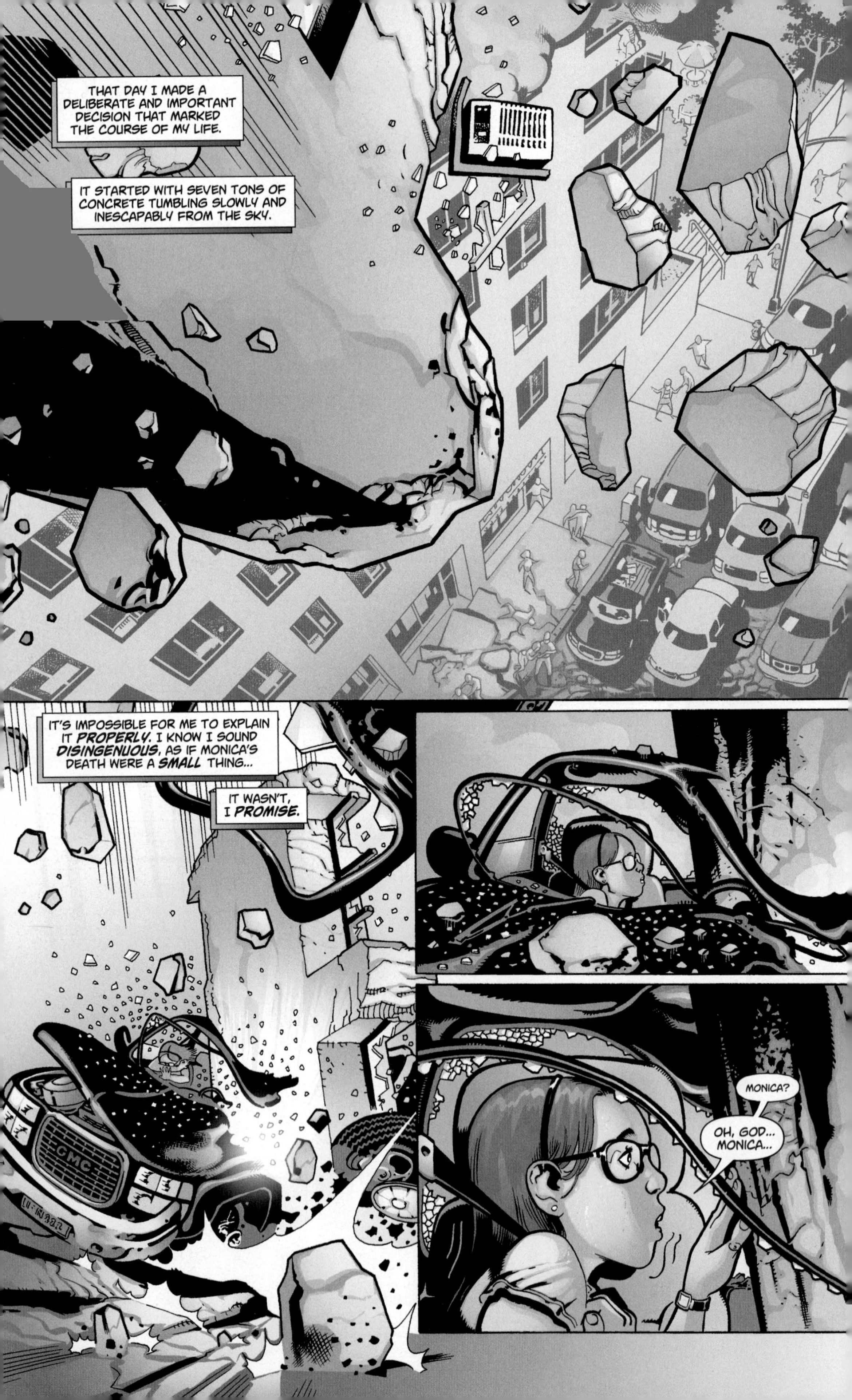
THAT DAY I MADE A DELIBERATE AND IMPORTANT DECISION THAT MARKED THE COURSE OF MY LIFE.
IT STARTED WITH SEVEN TONS OF CONCRETE TUMBLING SLOWLY AND INESCAPABLY FROM THE SKY.
IT'S IMPOSSIBLE FOR ME TO EXPLAIN IT PROPERLY. I KNOW I SOUND DISINGENUOUS, AS IF MONICA'S DEATH WERE A SMALL THING...
IT WASN'T, I PROMISE.
GMC
MONICA?
OH, GOD... MONICA...

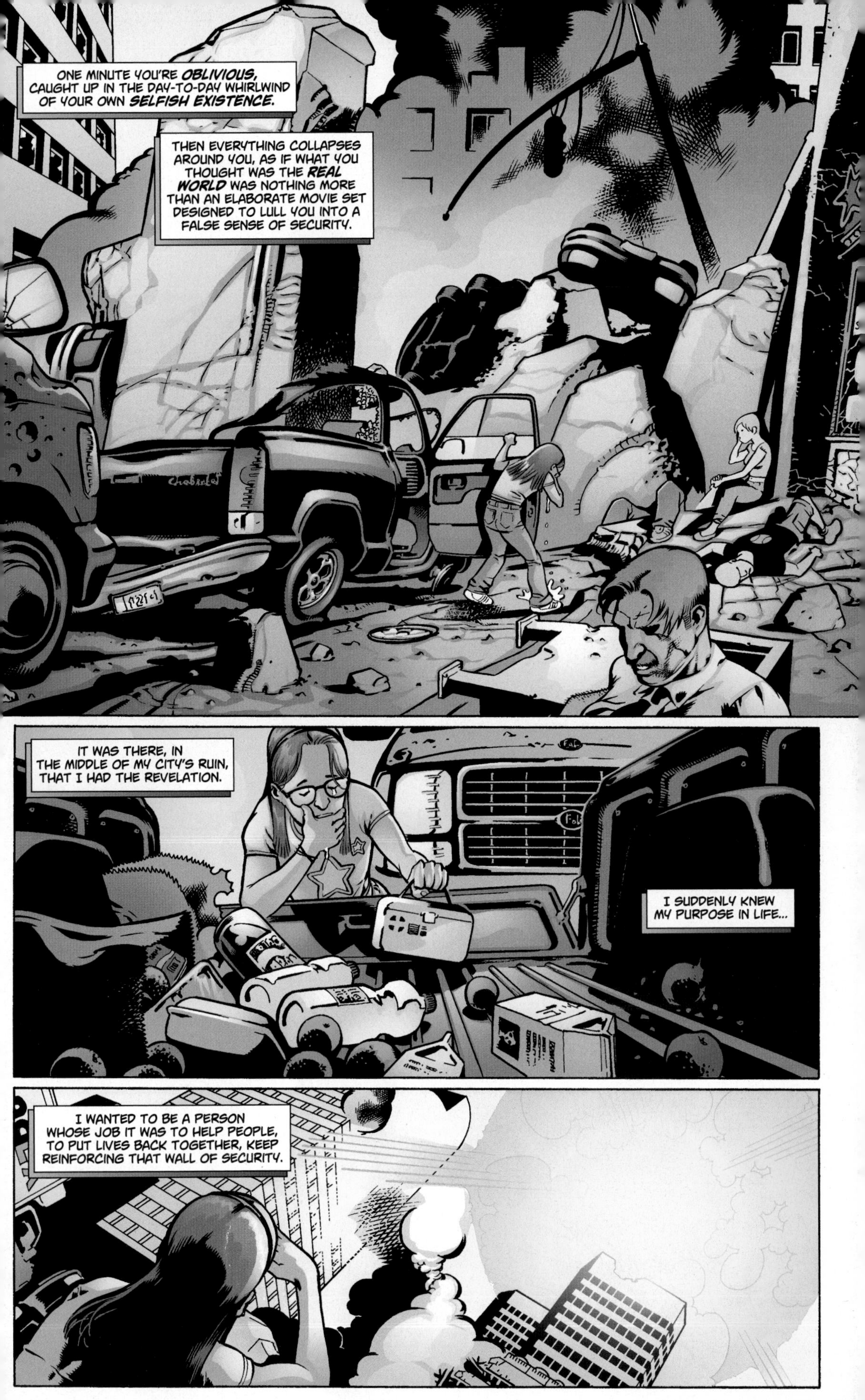

ONE MINUTE YOU'RE *OBLIVIOUS*, CAUGHT UP IN THE DAY-TO-DAY WHIRLWIND OF YOUR OWN *SELFISH EXISTENCE*.
THEN EVERYTHING COLLAPSES AROUND YOU, AS IF WHAT YOU THOUGHT WAS THE *REAL WORLD* WAS NOTHING MORE THAN AN ELABORATE MOVIE SET DESIGNED TO LULL YOU INTO A FALSE SENSE OF SECURITY.
IT WAS THERE, IN THE MIDDLE OF MY CITY'S RUIN, THAT I HAD THE REVELATION.
I SUDDENLY KNEW MY PURPOSE IN LIFE...
I WANTED TO BE A PERSON WHOSE JOB IT WAS TO HELP PEOPLE, TO PUT LIVES BACK TOGETHER, KEEP REINFORCING THAT WALL OF SECURITY.

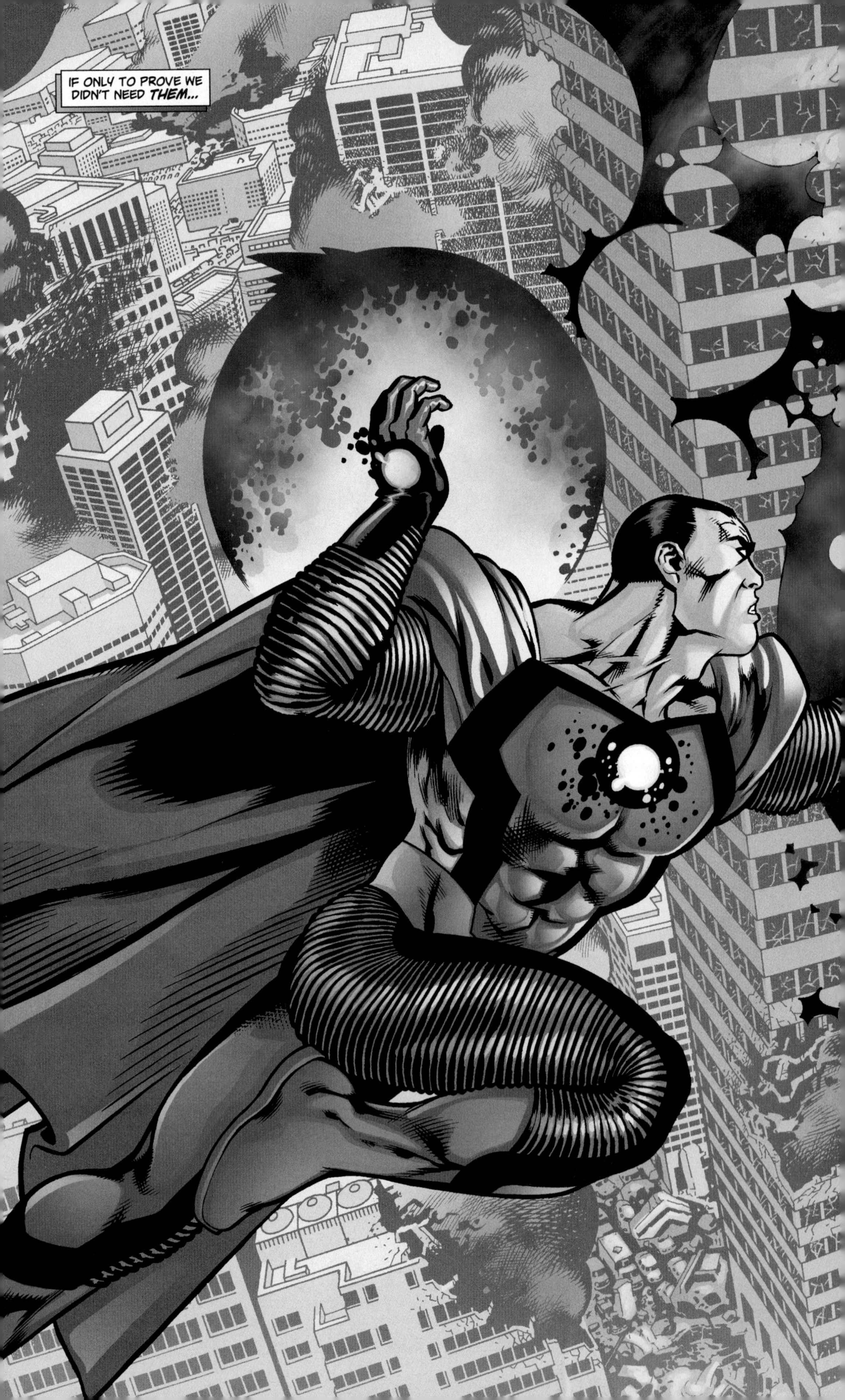
IF ONLY TO PROVE WE DIDN'T NEED *THEM*...

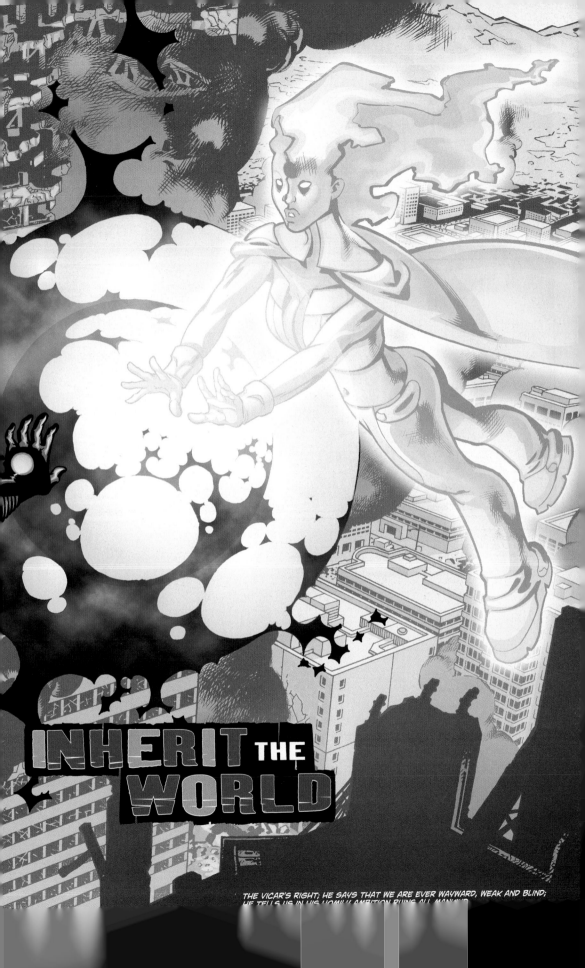

INHERIT THE WORLD

THE VICAR'S RIGHT; HE SAYS THAT WE ARE EVER WAYWARD, WEAK AND BLIND;
HE TELLS US IN HIS HOMILY AMBITION RUINS ALL MANKIND

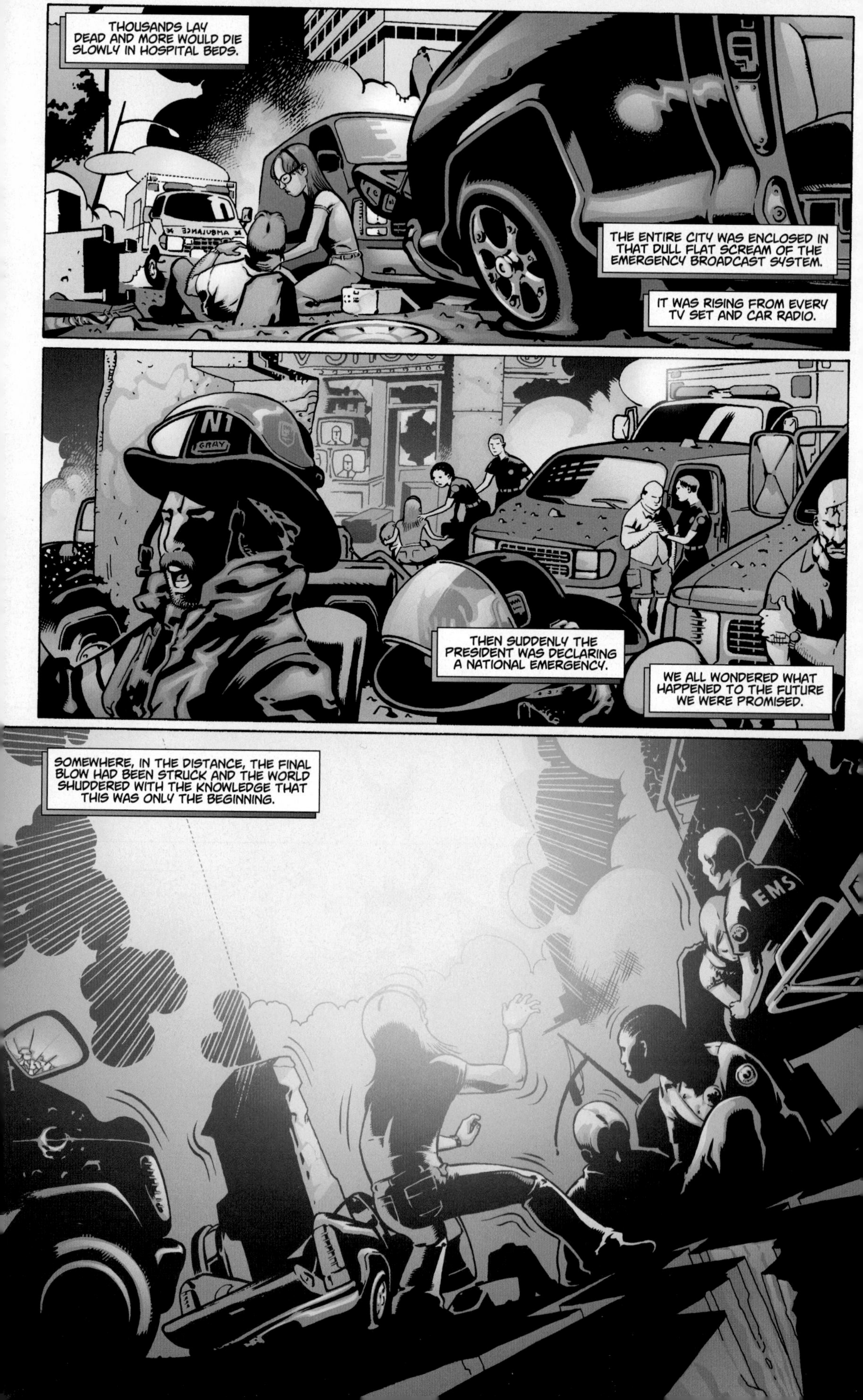
THOUSANDS LAY DEAD AND MORE WOULD DIE SLOWLY IN HOSPITAL BEDS.
AMBULANCE
THE ENTIRE CITY WAS ENCLOSED IN THAT DULL FLAT SCREAM OF THE EMERGENCY BROADCAST SYSTEM.
IT WAS RISING FROM EVERY TV SET AND CAR RADIO.
N1
GRAY
THEN SUDDENLY THE PRESIDENT WAS DECLARING A NATIONAL EMERGENCY.
WE ALL WONDERED WHAT HAPPENED TO THE FUTURE WE WERE PROMISED.
SOMEWHERE, IN THE DISTANCE, THE FINAL BLOW HAD BEEN STRUCK AND THE WORLD SHUDDERED WITH THE KNOWLEDGE THAT THIS WAS ONLY THE BEGINNING.
EMS

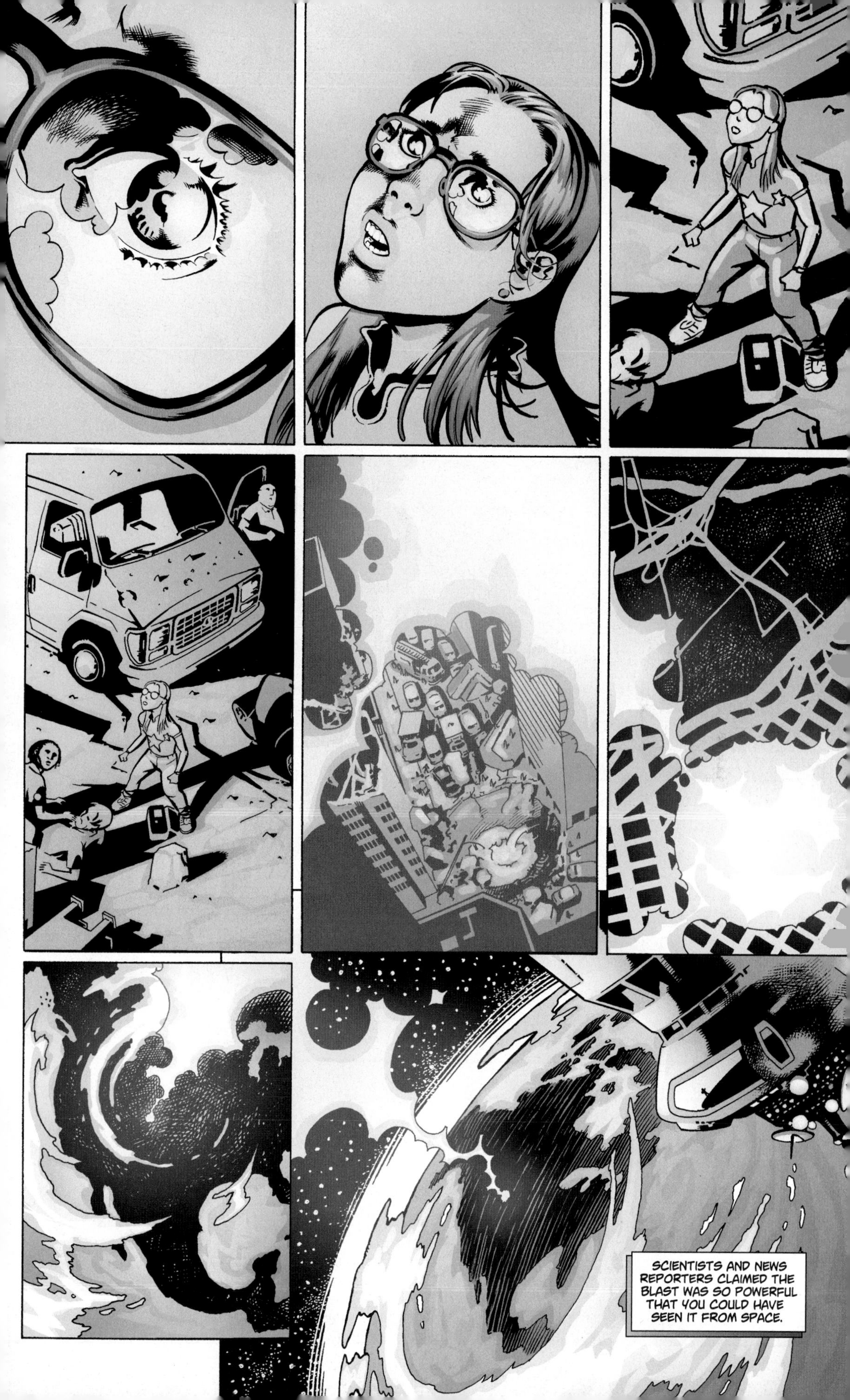
SCIENTISTS AND NEWS REPORTERS CLAIMED THE BLAST WAS SO POWERFUL THAT YOU COULD HAVE SEEN IT FROM SPACE.

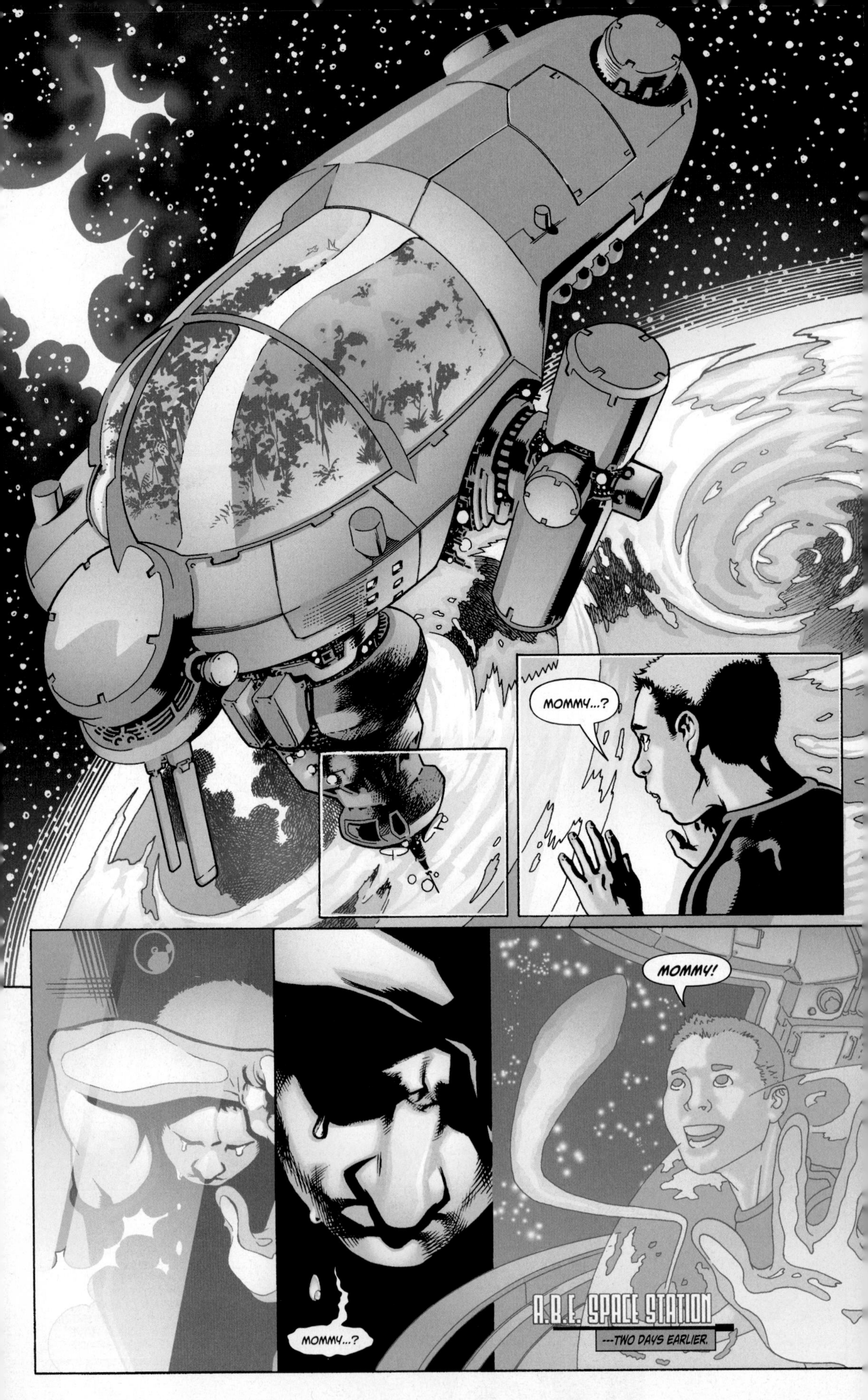
MOMMY...?
MOMMY...?
MOMMY!
A.B.E. SPACE STATION
---TWO DAYS EARLIER.

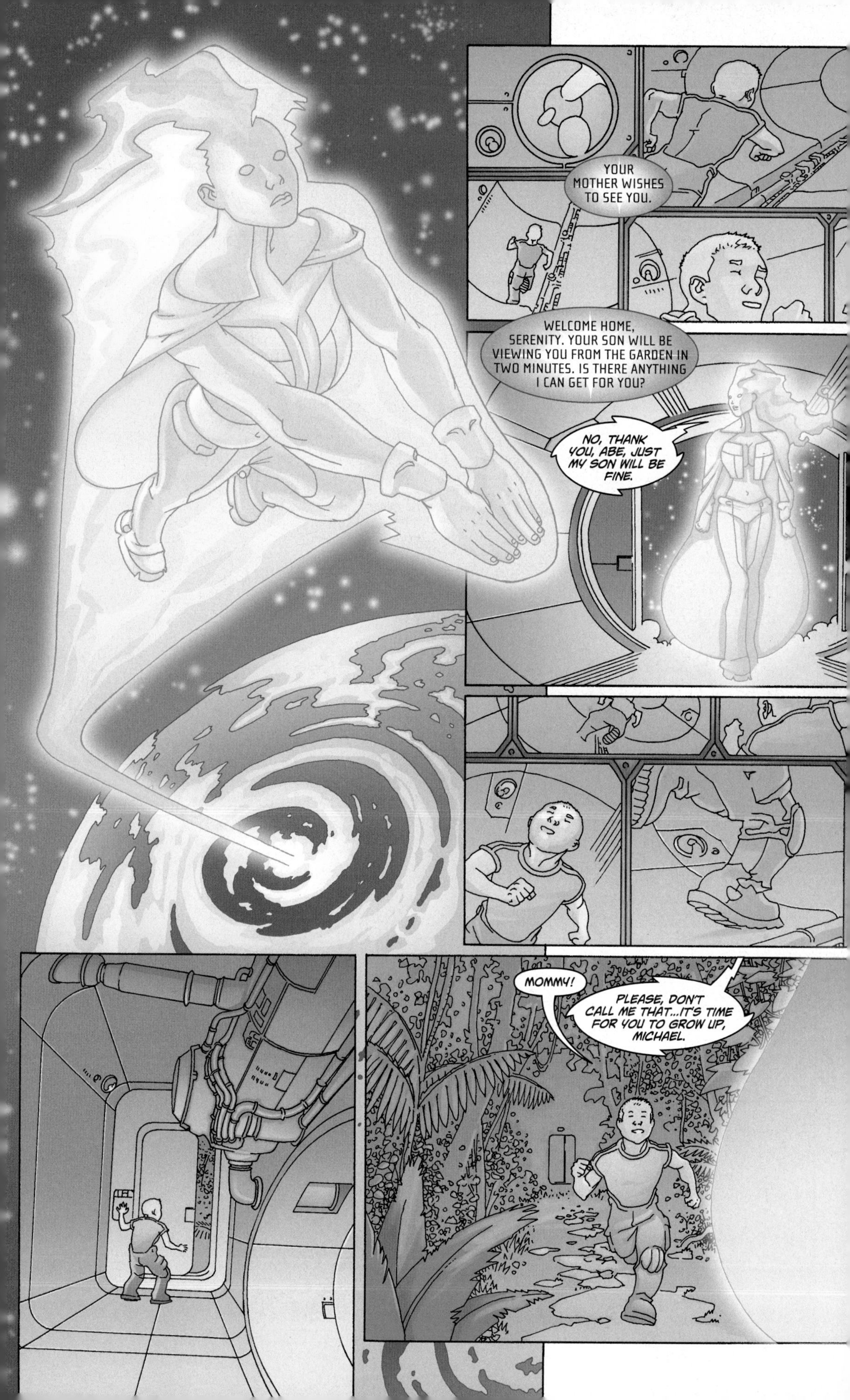
YOUR MOTHER WISHES TO SEE YOU.
WELCOME HOME, SERENITY. YOUR SON WILL BE VIEWING YOU FROM THE GARDEN IN TWO MINUTES. IS THERE ANYTHING I CAN GET FOR YOU?
NO, THANK YOU, ABE, JUST MY SON WILL BE FINE.
MOMMY!
PLEASE, DON'T CALL ME THAT...IT'S TIME FOR YOU TO GROW UP, MICHAEL.

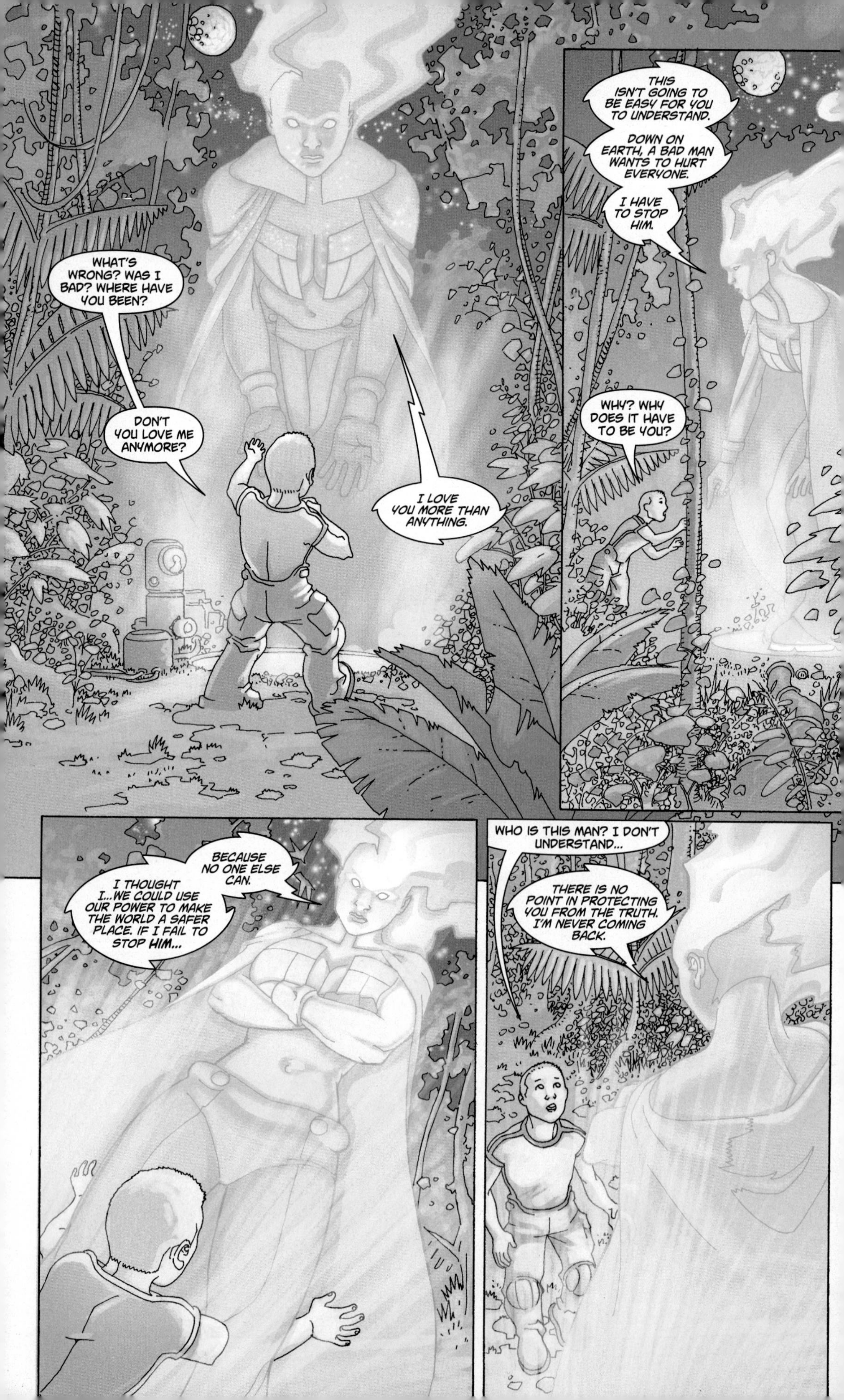
WHAT'S WRONG? WAS I BAD? WHERE HAVE YOU BEEN?
DON'T YOU LOVE ME ANYMORE?
I LOVE YOU MORE THAN ANYTHING.
THIS ISN'T GOING TO BE EASY FOR YOU TO UNDERSTAND.
DOWN ON EARTH, A BAD MAN WANTS TO HURT EVERYONE.
I HAVE TO STOP HIM.
WHY? WHY DOES IT HAVE TO BE YOU?
BECAUSE NO ONE ELSE CAN.
I THOUGHT I...WE COULD USE OUR POWER TO MAKE THE WORLD A SAFER PLACE. IF I FAIL TO STOP HIM...
WHO IS THIS MAN? I DON'T UNDERSTAND...
THERE IS NO POINT IN PROTECTING YOU FROM THE TRUTH. I'M NEVER COMING BACK.

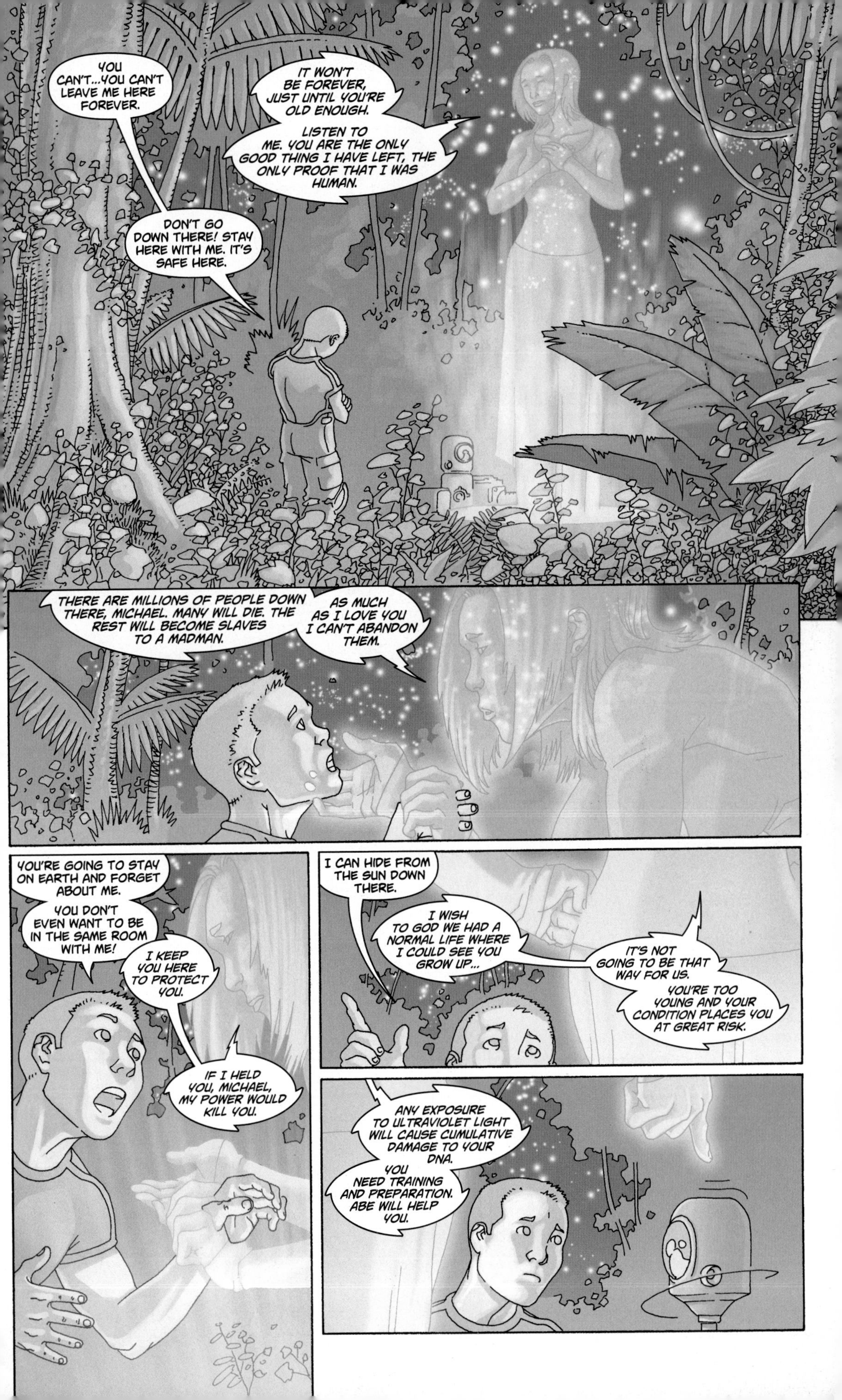
YOU CAN'T...YOU CAN'T LEAVE ME HERE FOREVER.
IT WON'T BE FOREVER, JUST UNTIL YOU'RE OLD ENOUGH.
LISTEN TO ME. YOU ARE THE ONLY GOOD THING I HAVE LEFT, THE ONLY PROOF THAT I WAS HUMAN.
DON'T GO DOWN THERE! STAY HERE WITH ME. IT'S SAFE HERE.
THERE ARE MILLIONS OF PEOPLE DOWN THERE, MICHAEL. MANY WILL DIE. THE REST WILL BECOME SLAVES TO A MADMAN.
AS MUCH AS I LOVE YOU I CAN'T ABANDON THEM.
YOU'RE GOING TO STAY ON EARTH AND FORGET ABOUT ME.
YOU DON'T EVEN WANT TO BE IN THE SAME ROOM WITH ME!
I KEEP YOU HERE TO PROTECT YOU.
IF I HELD YOU, MICHAEL, MY POWER WOULD KILL YOU.
I CAN HIDE FROM THE SUN DOWN THERE.
I WISH TO GOD WE HAD A NORMAL LIFE WHERE I COULD SEE YOU GROW UP...
IT'S NOT GOING TO BE THAT WAY FOR US.
YOU'RE TOO YOUNG AND YOUR CONDITION PLACES YOU AT GREAT RISK.
ANY EXPOSURE TO ULTRAVIOLET LIGHT WILL CAUSE CUMULATIVE DAMAGE TO YOUR DNA.
YOU NEED TRAINING AND PREPARATION. ABE WILL HELP YOU.

WHEN YOU'RE OLD ENOUGH, YOU'LL GO TO EARTH. YOU'LL UNDERSTAND WHY I HAVE TO DO THIS.

MICHAEL, I AM SORRY.

A.B.E. SPACE STATION

---TWO DAYS LATER.

YOU CAN'T BE SORRY. YOU'RE JUST A DUMB MACHINE.

I'M TRYING TO CONSOLE YOU AS BEST I CAN.

I'M GOING TO EARTH TO BE WITH MY MOTHER!

YOUR MOTHER IS DEAD.

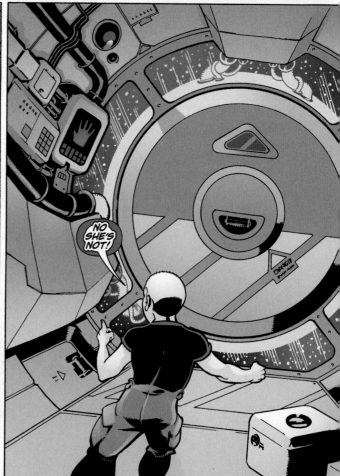

NO SHE'S NOT!

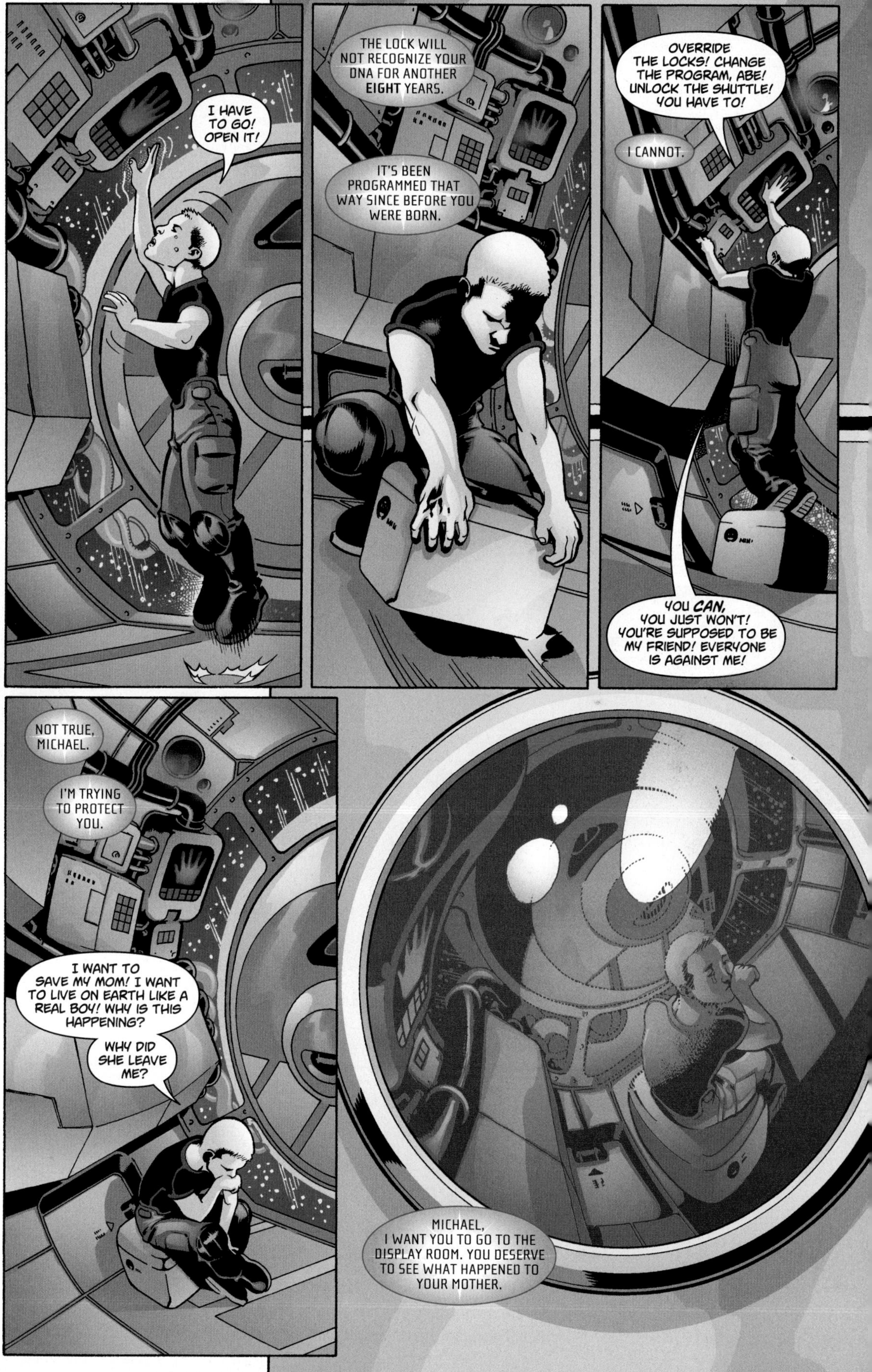
I HAVE TO GO! OPEN IT!
THE LOCK WILL NOT RECOGNIZE YOUR DNA FOR ANOTHER EIGHT YEARS.
IT'S BEEN PROGRAMMED THAT WAY SINCE BEFORE YOU WERE BORN.
OVERRIDE THE LOCKS! CHANGE THE PROGRAM, ABE! UNLOCK THE SHUTTLE! YOU HAVE TO!
I CANNOT.
YOU CAN, YOU JUST WON'T! YOU'RE SUPPOSED TO BE MY FRIEND! EVERYONE IS AGAINST ME!
NOT TRUE, MICHAEL.
I'M TRYING TO PROTECT YOU.
I WANT TO SAVE MY MOM! I WANT TO LIVE ON EARTH LIKE A REAL BOY! WHY IS THIS HAPPENING?
WHY DID SHE LEAVE ME?
MICHAEL, I WANT YOU TO GO TO THE DISPLAY ROOM. YOU DESERVE TO SEE WHAT HAPPENED TO YOUR MOTHER.

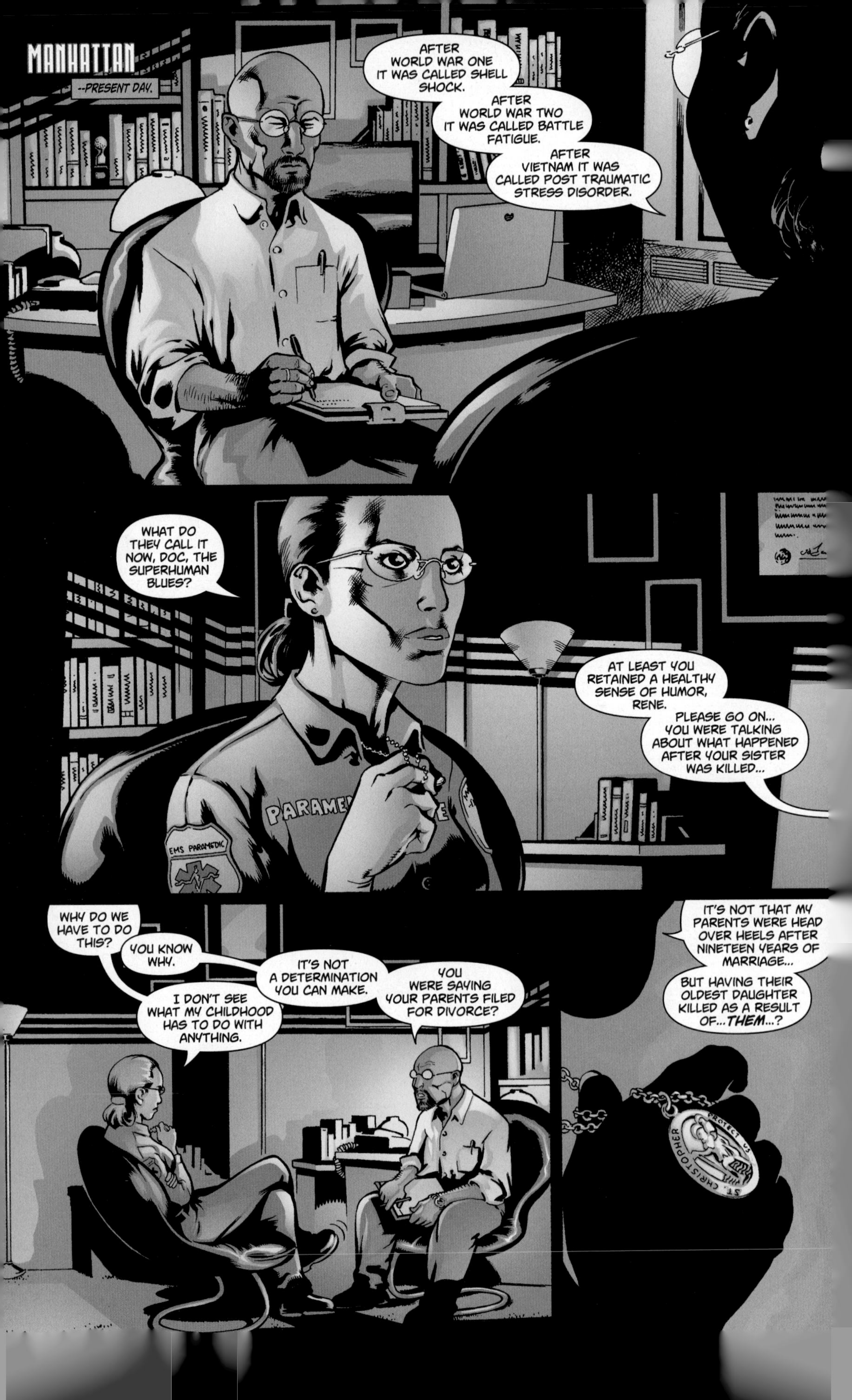
MANHATTAN
--PRESENT DAY.
AFTER WORLD WAR ONE IT WAS CALLED SHELL SHOCK.
AFTER WORLD WAR TWO IT WAS CALLED BATTLE FATIGUE.
AFTER VIETNAM IT WAS CALLED POST TRAUMATIC STRESS DISORDER.
WHAT DO THEY CALL IT NOW, DOC, THE SUPERHUMAN BLUES?
AT LEAST YOU RETAINED A HEALTHY SENSE OF HUMOR, RENE.
PLEASE GO ON... YOU WERE TALKING ABOUT WHAT HAPPENED AFTER YOUR SISTER WAS KILLED...
PARAMEDIC
EMS PARAMEDIC
WHY DO WE HAVE TO DO THIS?
YOU KNOW WHY.
I DON'T SEE WHAT MY CHILDHOOD HAS TO DO WITH ANYTHING.
IT'S NOT A DETERMINATION YOU CAN MAKE.
YOU WERE SAYING YOUR PARENTS FILED FOR DIVORCE?
IT'S NOT THAT MY PARENTS WERE HEAD OVER HEELS AFTER NINETEEN YEARS OF MARRIAGE...
BUT HAVING THEIR OLDEST DAUGHTER KILLED AS A RESULT OF...*THEM*...?
ST. CHRISTOPHER PROTECT US

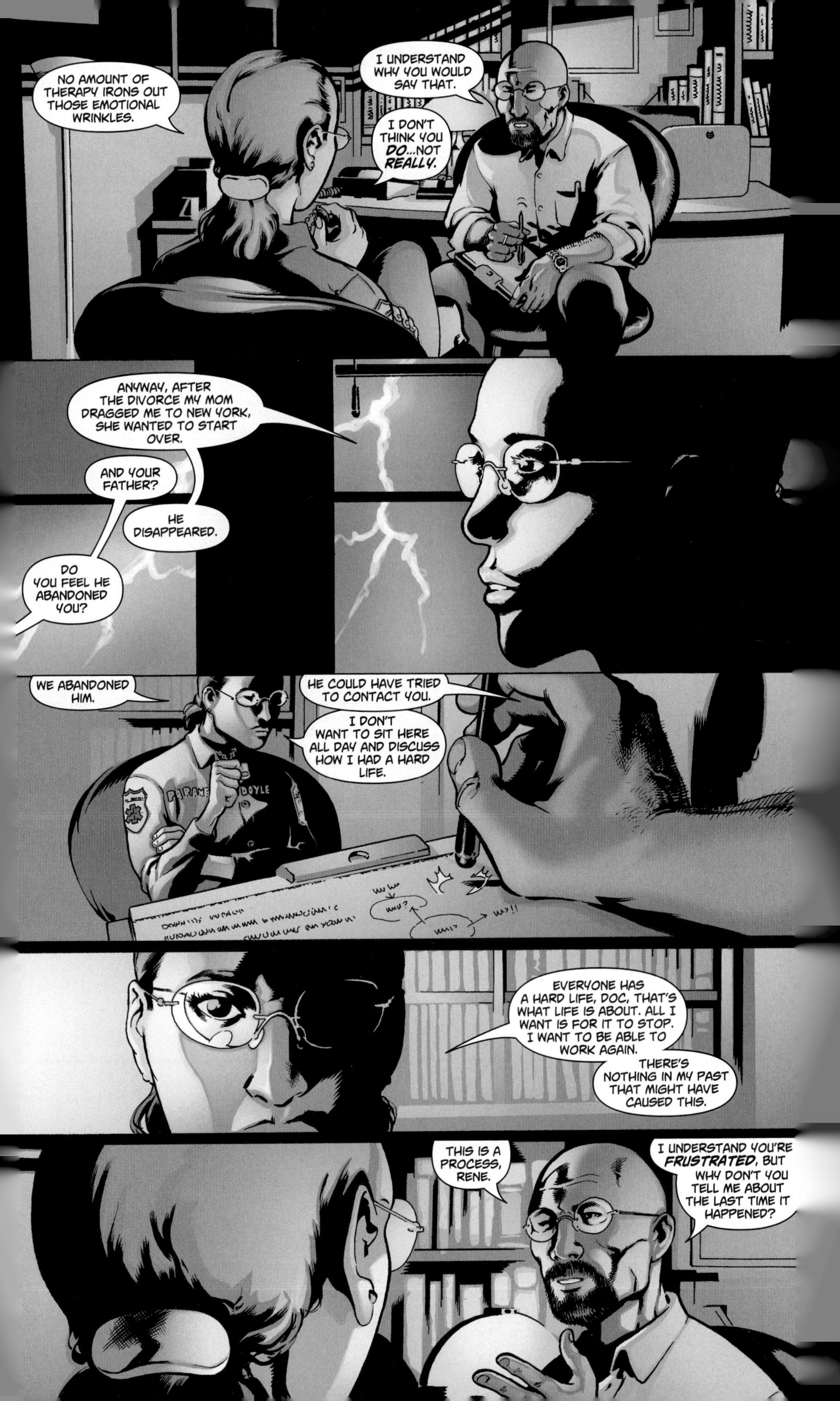

NO AMOUNT OF THERAPY IRONS OUT THOSE EMOTIONAL WRINKLES.
I UNDERSTAND WHY YOU WOULD SAY THAT.
I DON'T THINK YOU DO...NOT REALLY.
ANYWAY, AFTER THE DIVORCE MY MOM DRAGGED ME TO NEW YORK, SHE WANTED TO START OVER.
AND YOUR FATHER?
HE DISAPPEARED.
DO YOU FEEL HE ABANDONED YOU?
WE ABANDONED HIM.
HE COULD HAVE TRIED TO CONTACT YOU.
I DON'T WANT TO SIT HERE ALL DAY AND DISCUSS HOW I HAD A HARD LIFE.
PARAMEDIC
DOYLE
EVERYONE HAS A HARD LIFE, DOC, THAT'S WHAT LIFE IS ABOUT. ALL I WANT IS FOR IT TO STOP. I WANT TO BE ABLE TO WORK AGAIN.
THERE'S NOTHING IN MY PAST THAT MIGHT HAVE CAUSED THIS.
THIS IS A PROCESS, RENE.
I UNDERSTAND YOU'RE FRUSTRATED, BUT WHY DON'T YOU TELL ME ABOUT THE LAST TIME IT HAPPENED?

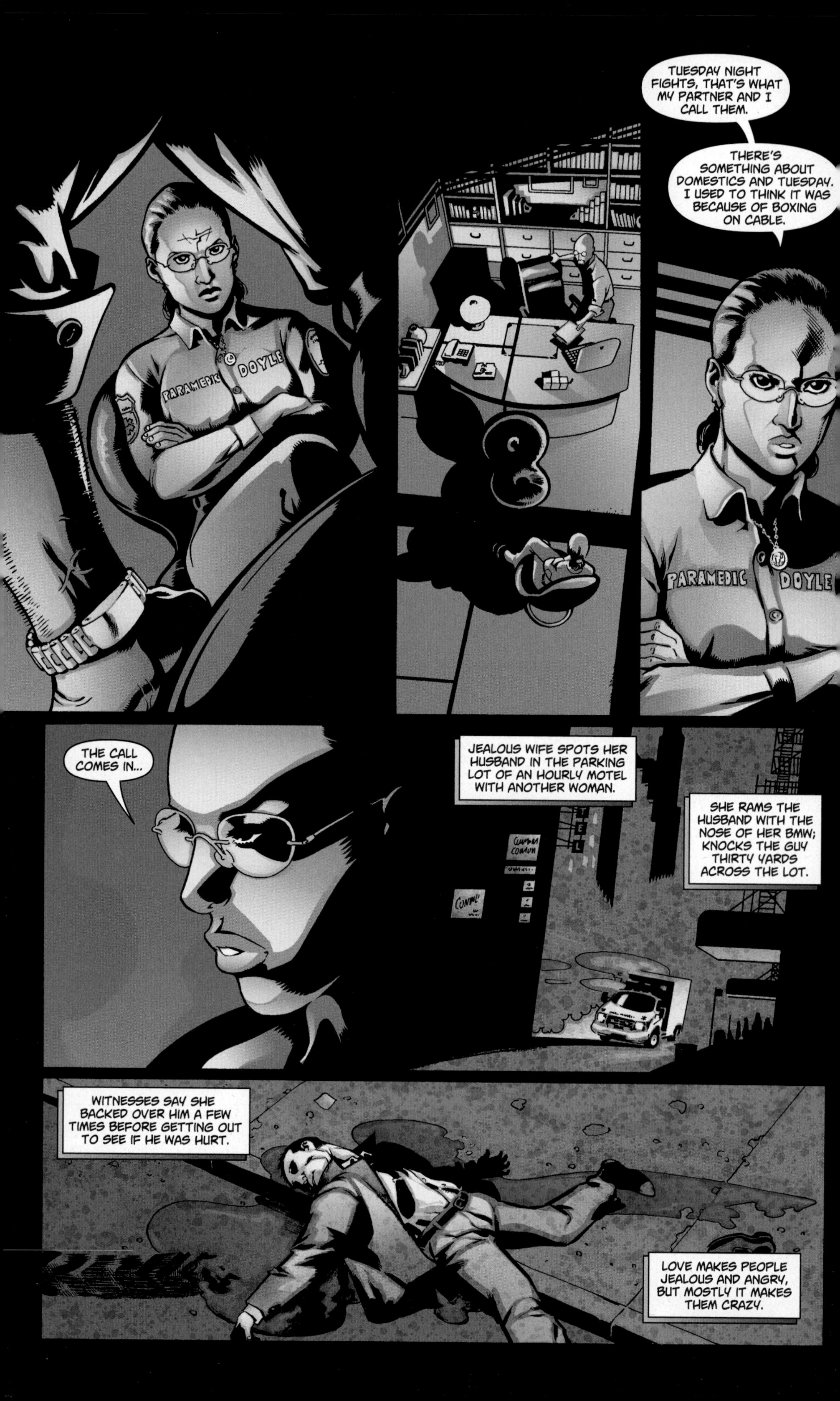

TUESDAY NIGHT FIGHTS, THAT'S WHAT MY PARTNER AND I CALL THEM.
THERE'S SOMETHING ABOUT DOMESTICS AND TUESDAY. I USED TO THINK IT WAS BECAUSE OF BOXING ON CABLE.
PARAMEDIC DOYLE
THE CALL COMES IN...
JEALOUS WIFE SPOTS HER HUSBAND IN THE PARKING LOT OF AN HOURLY MOTEL WITH ANOTHER WOMAN.
SHE RAMS THE HUSBAND WITH THE NOSE OF HER BMW; KNOCKS THE GUY THIRTY YARDS ACROSS THE LOT.
WITNESSES SAY SHE BACKED OVER HIM A FEW TIMES BEFORE GETTING OUT TO SEE IF HE WAS HURT.
LOVE MAKES PEOPLE JEALOUS AND ANGRY, BUT MOSTLY IT MAKES THEM CRAZY.

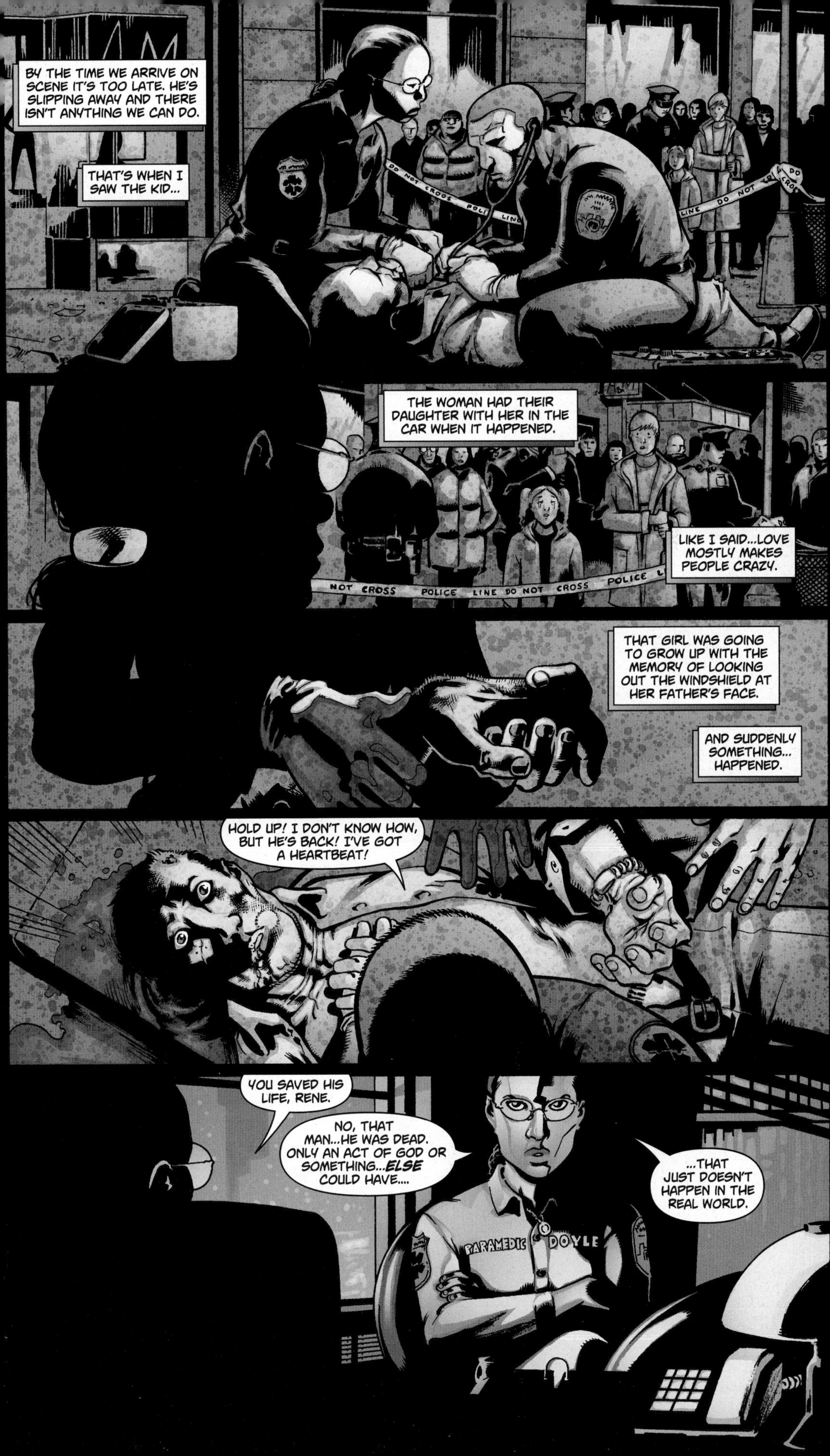
BY THE TIME WE ARRIVE ON SCENE IT'S TOO LATE. HE'S SLIPPING AWAY AND THERE ISN'T ANYTHING WE CAN DO.
THAT'S WHEN I SAW THE KID...
THE WOMAN HAD THEIR DAUGHTER WITH HER IN THE CAR WHEN IT HAPPENED.
LIKE I SAID...LOVE MOSTLY MAKES PEOPLE CRAZY.
NOT CROSS POLICE LINE DO NOT CROSS POLICE
THAT GIRL WAS GOING TO GROW UP WITH THE MEMORY OF LOOKING OUT THE WINDSHIELD AT HER FATHER'S FACE.
AND SUDDENLY SOMETHING... HAPPENED.
HOLD UP! I DON'T KNOW HOW, BUT HE'S BACK! I'VE GOT A HEARTBEAT!
YOU SAVED HIS LIFE, RENE.
NO, THAT MAN...HE WAS DEAD. ONLY AN ACT OF GOD OR SOMETHING...*ELSE* COULD HAVE....
...THAT JUST DOESN'T HAPPEN IN THE REAL WORLD.
PARAMEDIC DOYLE

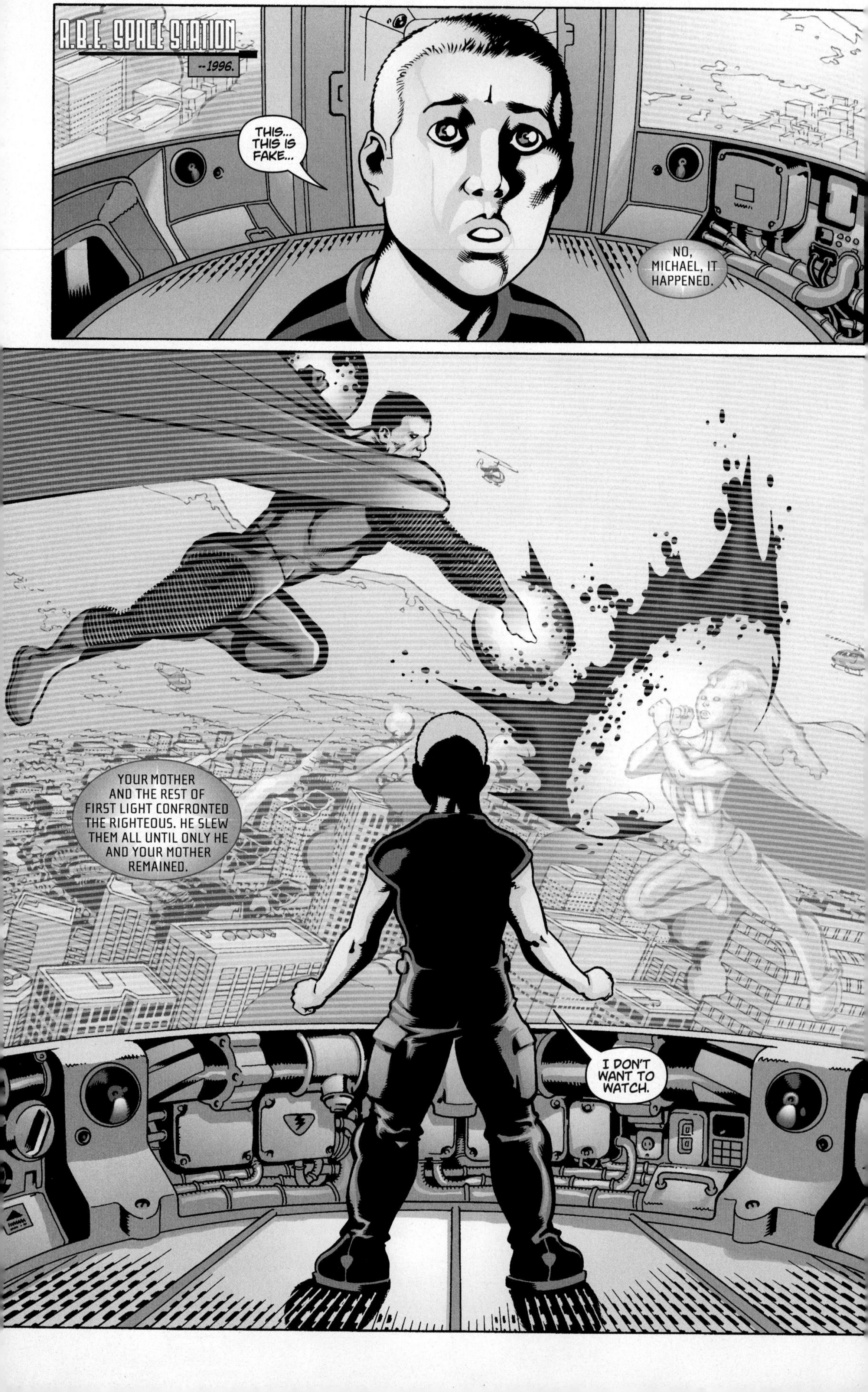
A.B.E. SPACE STATION
--1996.
THIS... THIS IS FAKE...
NO, MICHAEL, IT HAPPENED.
YOUR MOTHER AND THE REST OF FIRST LIGHT CONFRONTED THE RIGHTEOUS. HE SLEW THEM ALL UNTIL ONLY HE AND YOUR MOTHER REMAINED.
I DON'T WANT TO WATCH.

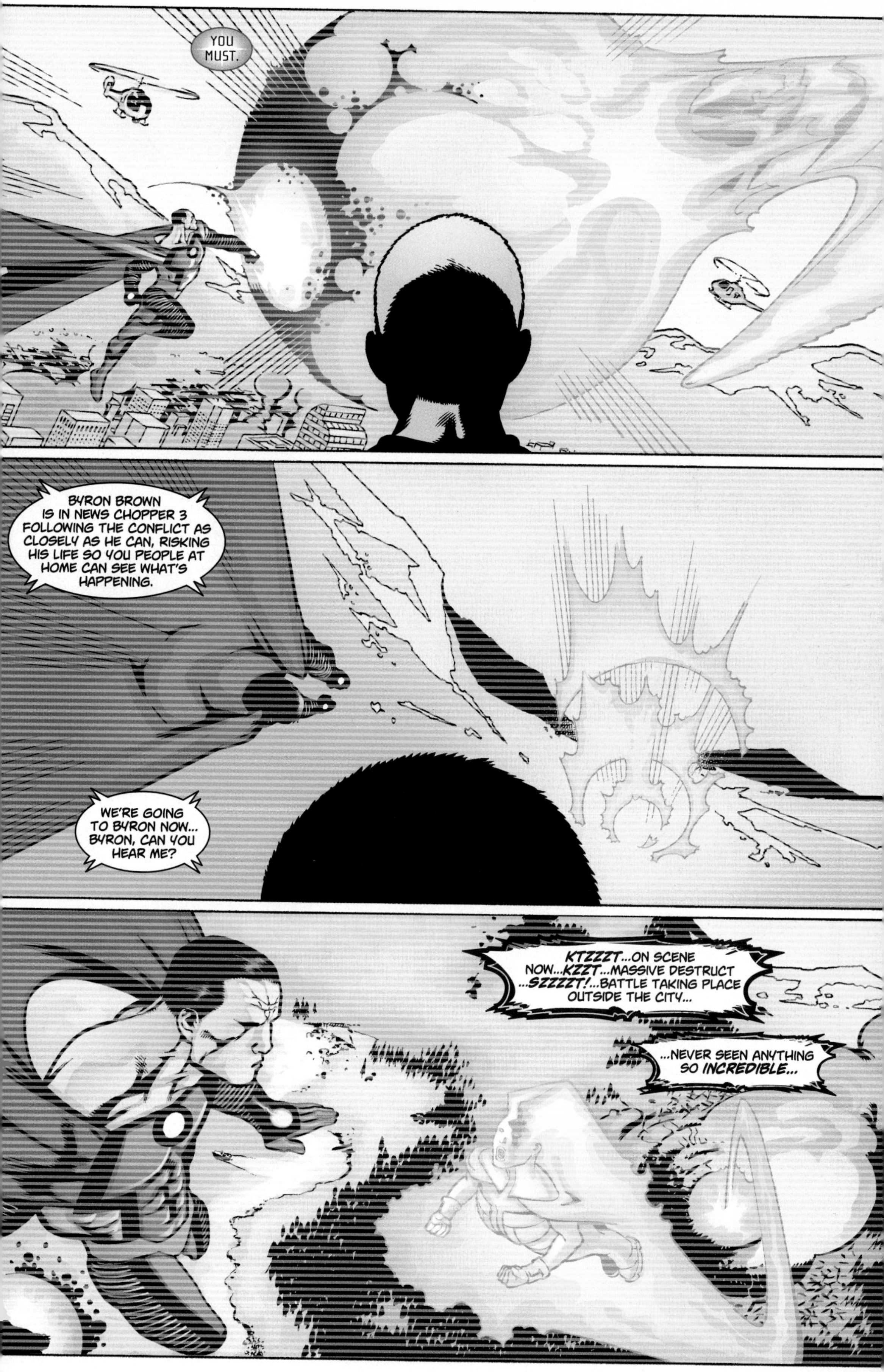
YOU MUST.
BYRON BROWN IS IN NEWS CHOPPER 3 FOLLOWING THE CONFLICT AS CLOSELY AS HE CAN, RISKING HIS LIFE SO YOU PEOPLE AT HOME CAN SEE WHAT'S HAPPENING.
WE'RE GOING TO BYRON NOW... BYRON, CAN YOU HEAR ME?
KTZZZT...ON SCENE NOW...KZZT...MASSIVE DESTRUCT ...SZZZZT!...BATTLE TAKING PLACE OUTSIDE THE CITY...
...NEVER SEEN ANYTHING SO INCREDIBLE...

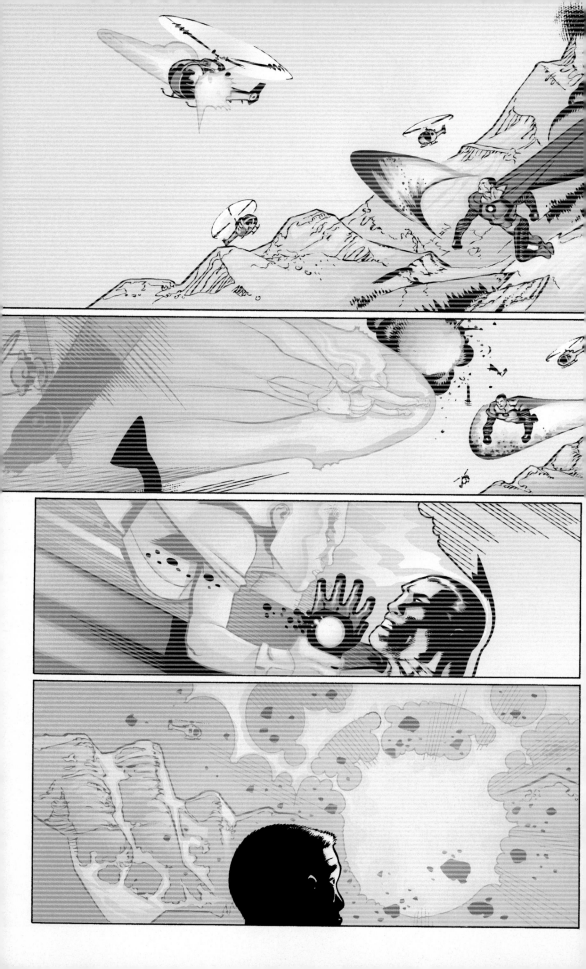

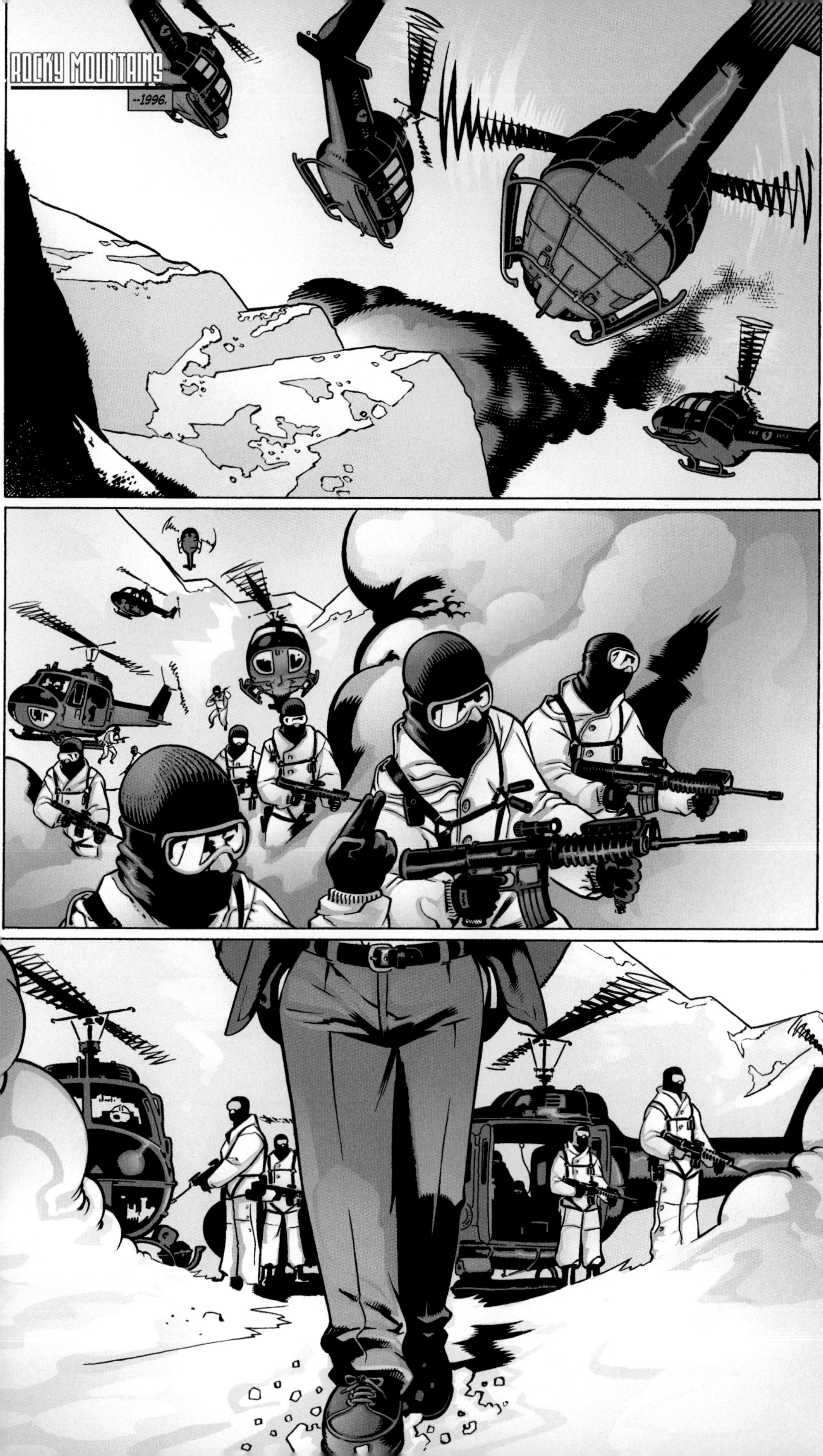
ROCKY MOUNTAINS
--1996.

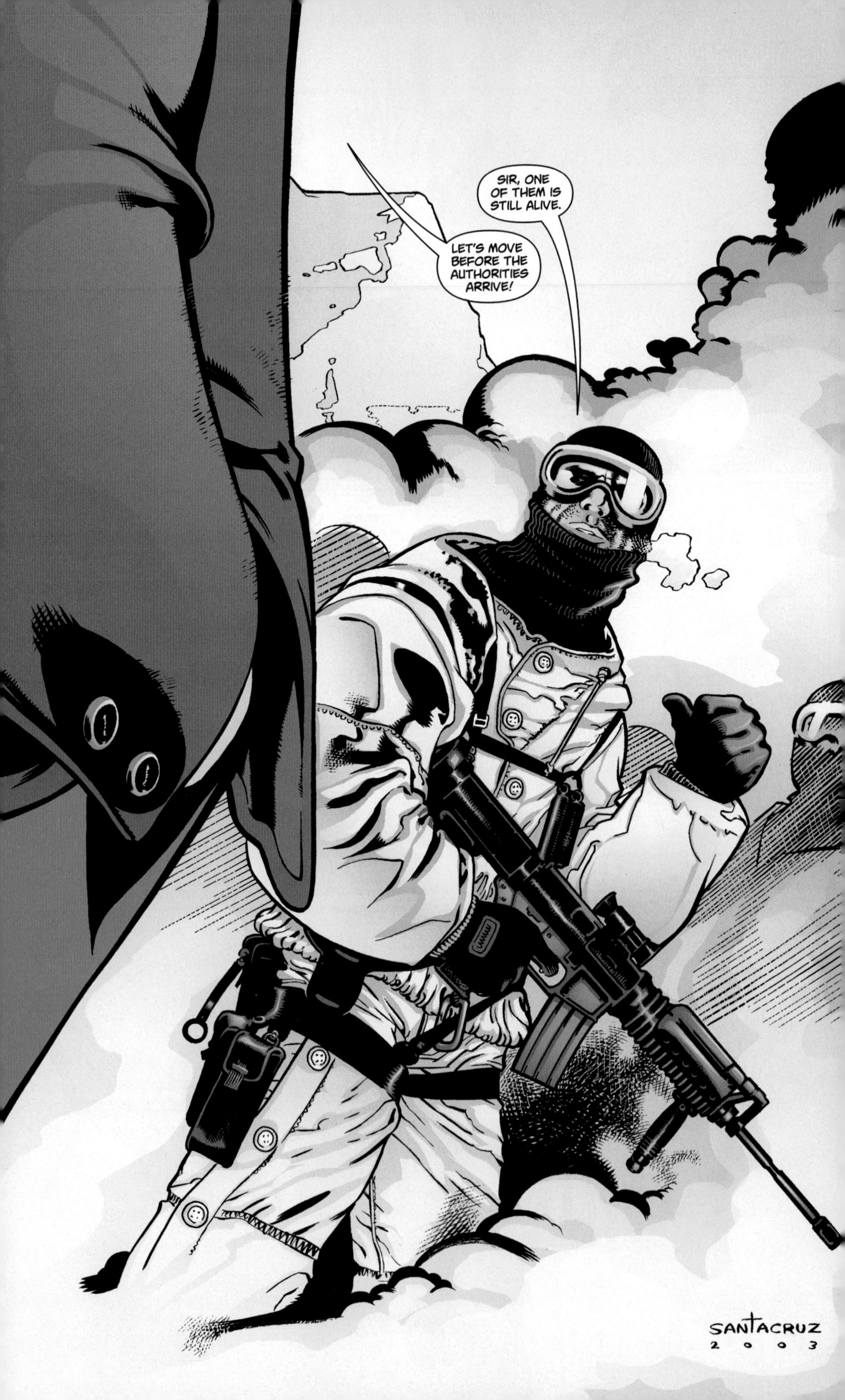
SIR, ONE OF THEM IS STILL ALIVE.
LET'S MOVE BEFORE THE AUTHORITIES ARRIVE!
SANTACRUZ 2003

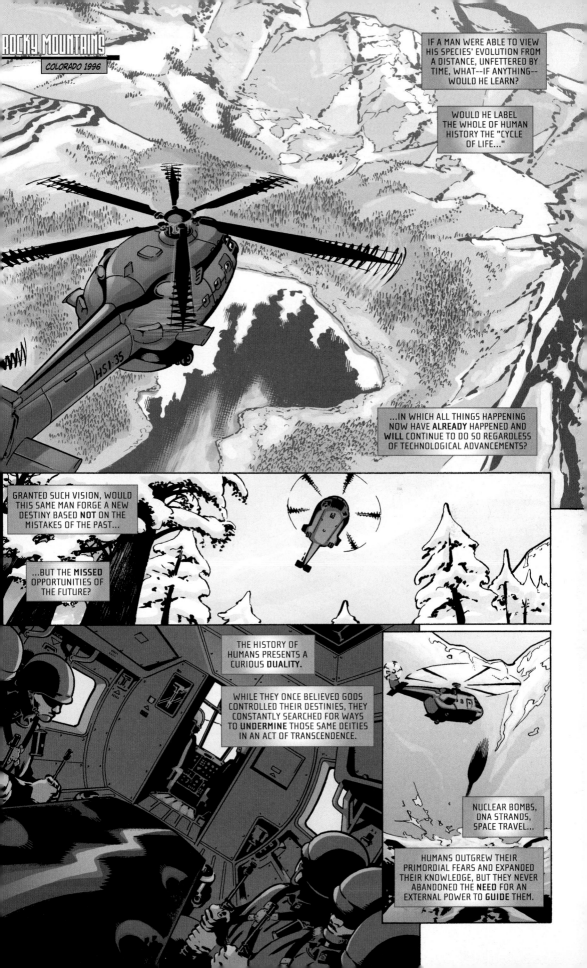

ROCKY MOUNTAINS

COLORADO 1996

IF A MAN WERE ABLE TO VIEW HIS SPECIES' EVOLUTION FROM A DISTANCE, UNFETTERED BY TIME, WHAT--IF ANYTHING-- WOULD HE LEARN?

WOULD HE LABEL THE WHOLE OF HUMAN HISTORY THE "CYCLE OF LIFE..."

...IN WHICH ALL THINGS HAPPENING NOW HAVE **ALREADY** HAPPENED AND **WILL** CONTINUE TO DO SO REGARDLESS OF TECHNOLOGICAL ADVANCEMENTS?

GRANTED SUCH VISION, WOULD THIS SAME MAN FORGE A NEW DESTINY BASED **NOT** ON THE MISTAKES OF THE PAST...

...BUT THE **MISSED** OPPORTUNITIES OF THE FUTURE?

THE HISTORY OF HUMANS PRESENTS A CURIOUS **DUALITY**.

WHILE THEY ONCE BELIEVED GODS CONTROLLED THEIR DESTINIES, THEY CONSTANTLY SEARCHED FOR WAYS TO **UNDERMINE** THOSE SAME DEITIES IN AN ACT OF TRANSCENDENCE.

NUCLEAR BOMBS, DNA STRANDS, SPACE TRAVEL...

HUMANS OUTGREW THEIR PRIMORDIAL FEARS AND EXPANDED THEIR KNOWLEDGE, BUT THEY NEVER ABANDONED THE **NEED** FOR AN EXTERNAL POWER TO **GUIDE** THEM.

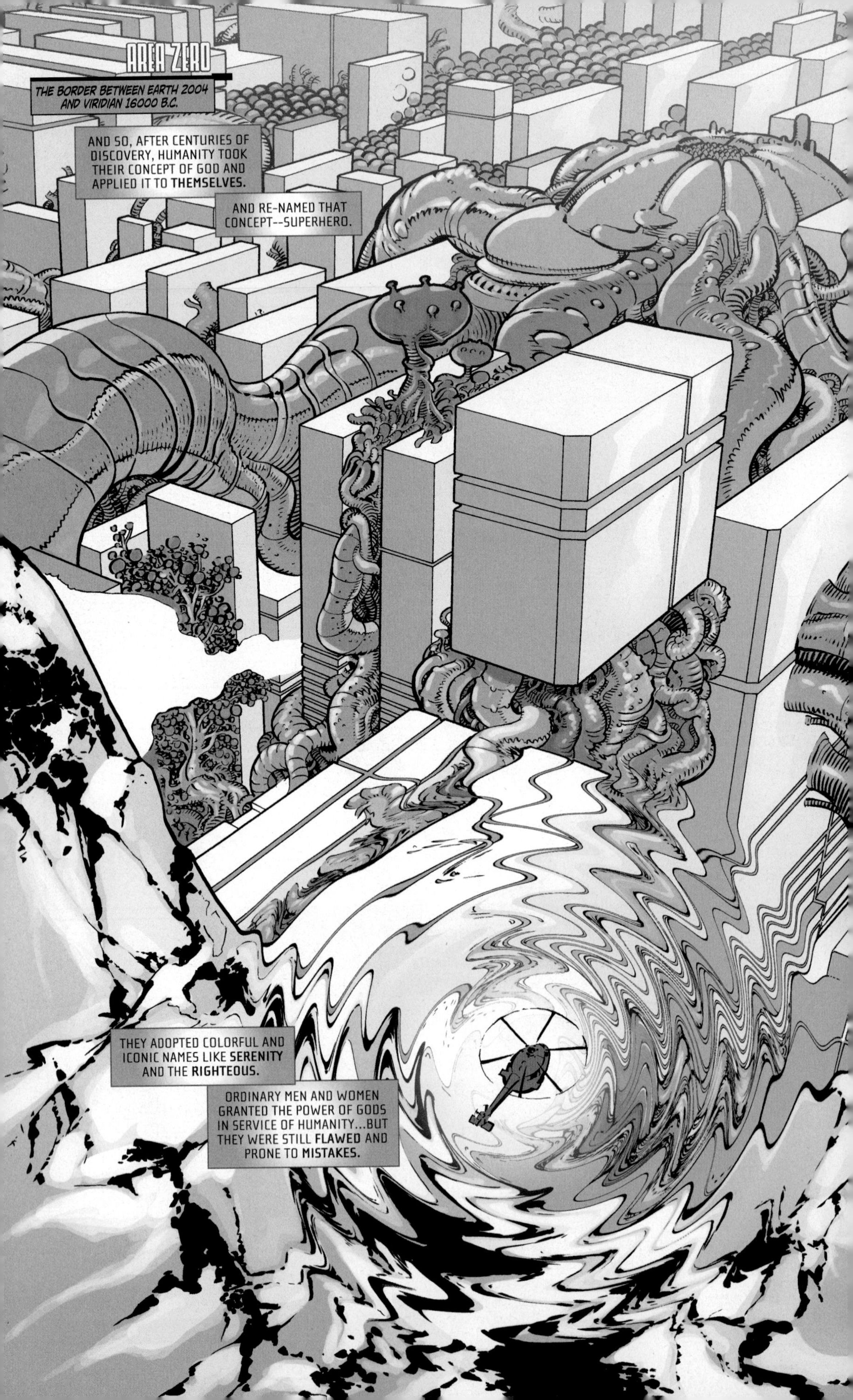
AREA ZERO
THE BORDER BETWEEN EARTH 2004 AND VIRIDIAN 16000 B.C.
AND SO, AFTER CENTURIES OF DISCOVERY, HUMANITY TOOK THEIR CONCEPT OF GOD AND APPLIED IT TO THEMSELVES.
AND RE-NAMED THAT CONCEPT--SUPERHERO.
THEY ADOPTED COLORFUL AND ICONIC NAMES LIKE SERENITY AND THE RIGHTEOUS.
ORDINARY MEN AND WOMEN GRANTED THE POWER OF GODS IN SERVICE OF HUMANITY...BUT THEY WERE STILL FLAWED AND PRONE TO MISTAKES.

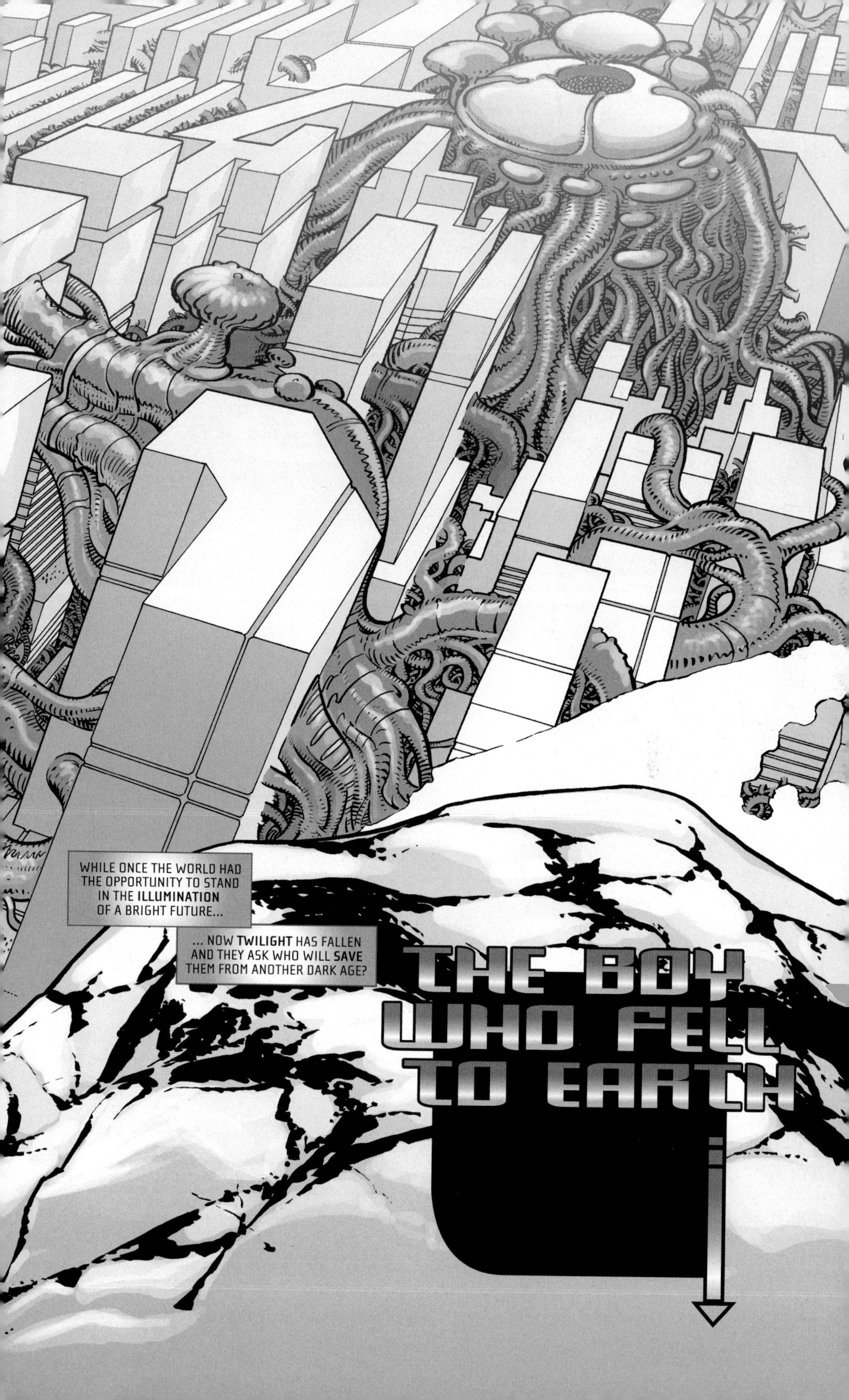
WHILE ONCE THE WORLD HAD THE OPPORTUNITY TO STAND IN THE ILLUMINATION OF A BRIGHT FUTURE...
... NOW TWILIGHT HAS FALLEN AND THEY ASK WHO WILL SAVE THEM FROM ANOTHER DARK AGE?
THE BOY WHO FELL TO EARTH

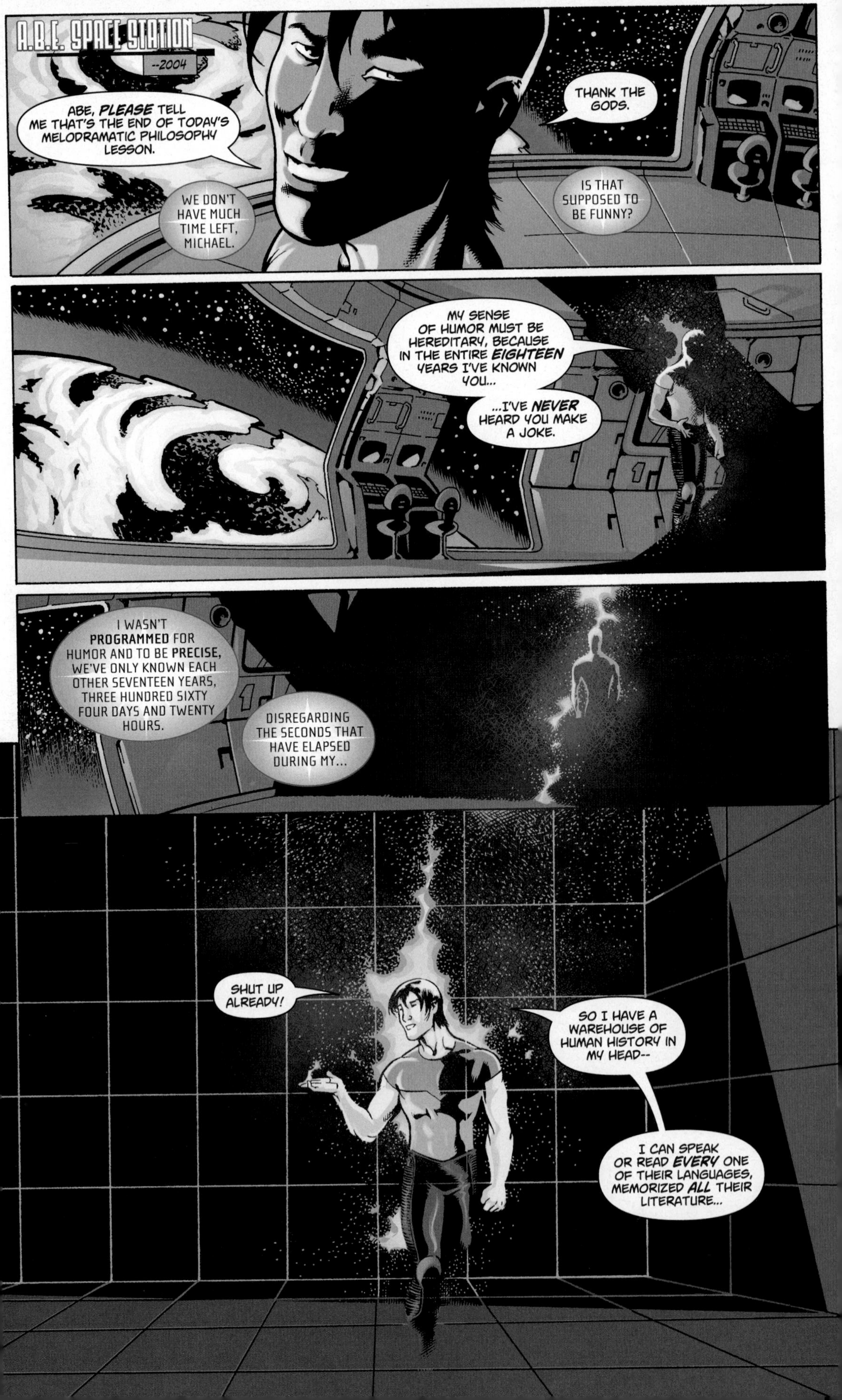
A.B.E. SPACE STATION
--2004
ABE, PLEASE TELL ME THAT'S THE END OF TODAY'S MELODRAMATIC PHILOSOPHY LESSON.
WE DON'T HAVE MUCH TIME LEFT, MICHAEL.
THANK THE GODS.
IS THAT SUPPOSED TO BE FUNNY?
MY SENSE OF HUMOR MUST BE HEREDITARY, BECAUSE IN THE ENTIRE EIGHTEEN YEARS I'VE KNOWN YOU...
...I'VE NEVER HEARD YOU MAKE A JOKE.
I WASN'T PROGRAMMED FOR HUMOR AND TO BE PRECISE, WE'VE ONLY KNOWN EACH OTHER SEVENTEEN YEARS, THREE HUNDRED SIXTY FOUR DAYS AND TWENTY HOURS.
DISREGARDING THE SECONDS THAT HAVE ELAPSED DURING MY...
SHUT UP ALREADY!
SO I HAVE A WAREHOUSE OF HUMAN HISTORY IN MY HEAD--
I CAN SPEAK OR READ EVERY ONE OF THEIR LANGUAGES, MEMORIZED ALL THEIR LITERATURE...

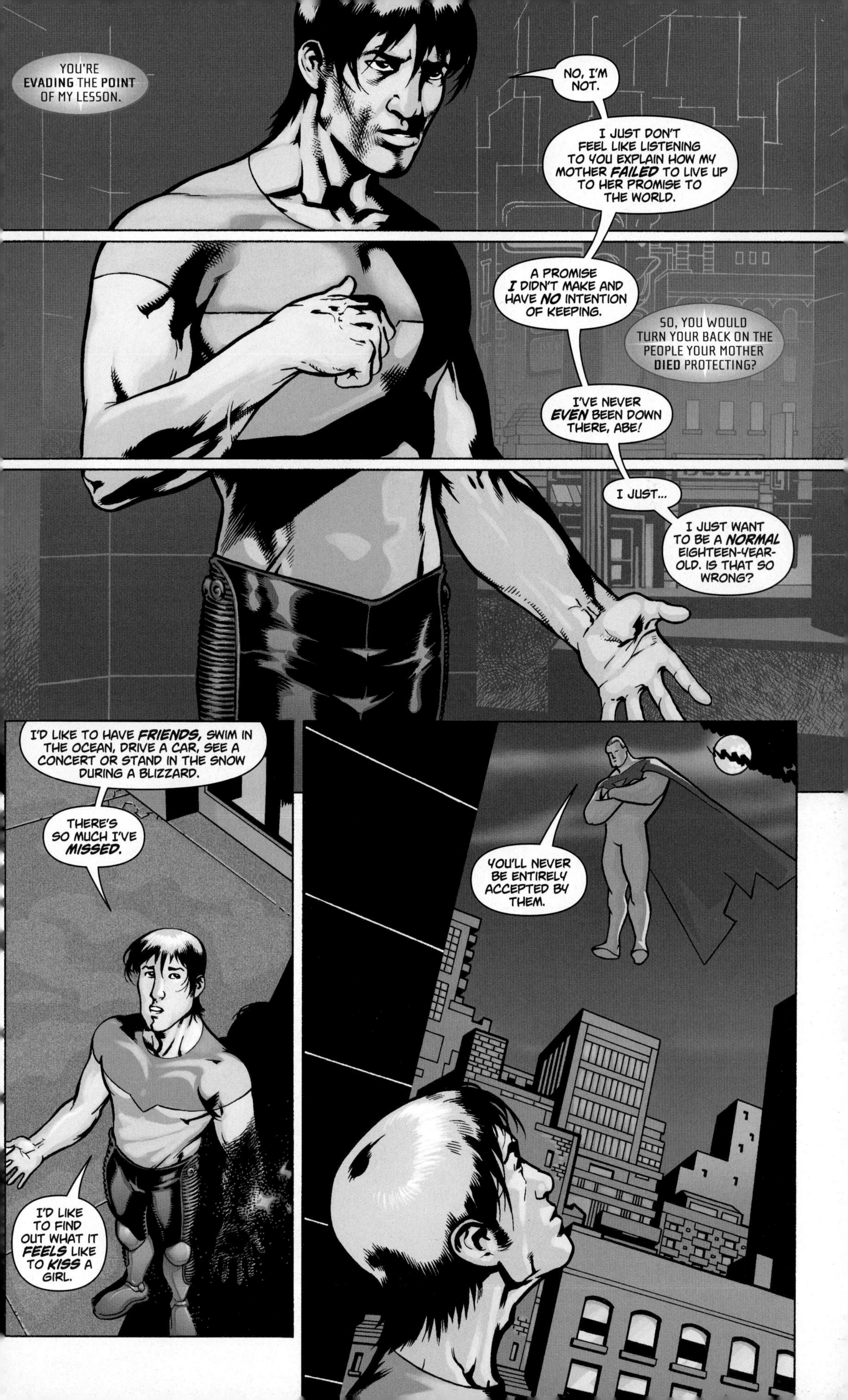
YOU'RE EVADING THE POINT OF MY LESSON.
NO, I'M NOT.
I JUST DON'T FEEL LIKE LISTENING TO YOU EXPLAIN HOW MY MOTHER FAILED TO LIVE UP TO HER PROMISE TO THE WORLD.
A PROMISE I DIDN'T MAKE AND HAVE NO INTENTION OF KEEPING.
SO, YOU WOULD TURN YOUR BACK ON THE PEOPLE YOUR MOTHER DIED PROTECTING?
I'VE NEVER EVEN BEEN DOWN THERE, ABE!
I JUST...
I JUST WANT TO BE A NORMAL EIGHTEEN-YEAR-OLD. IS THAT SO WRONG?
I'D LIKE TO HAVE FRIENDS, SWIM IN THE OCEAN, DRIVE A CAR, SEE A CONCERT OR STAND IN THE SNOW DURING A BLIZZARD.
THERE'S SO MUCH I'VE MISSED.
I'D LIKE TO FIND OUT WHAT IT FEELS LIKE TO KISS A GIRL.
YOU'LL NEVER BE ENTIRELY ACCEPTED BY THEM.

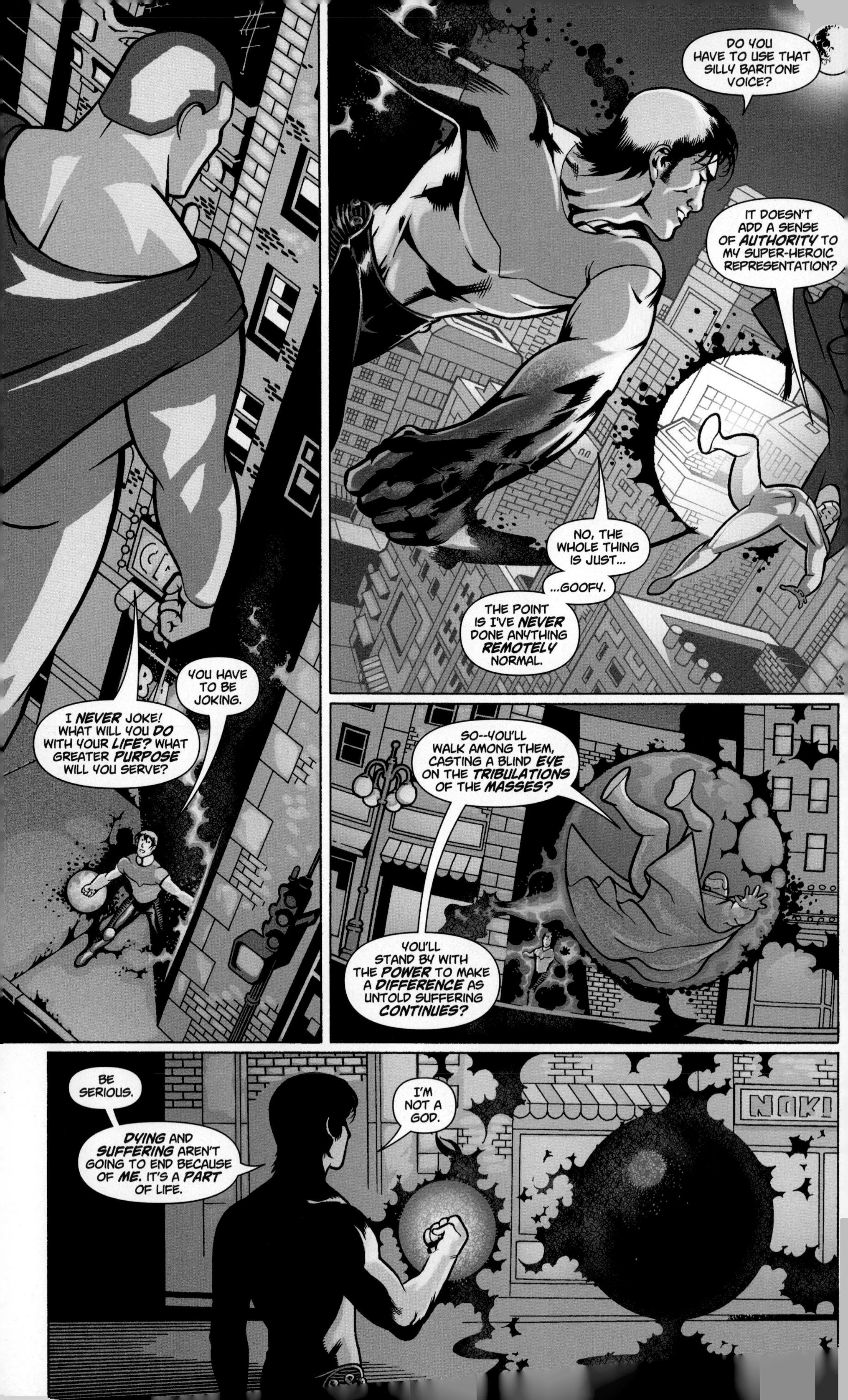

DO YOU HAVE TO USE THAT SILLY BARITONE VOICE?
IT DOESN'T ADD A SENSE OF AUTHORITY TO MY SUPER-HEROIC REPRESENTATION?
NO, THE WHOLE THING IS JUST...
...GOOFY.
THE POINT IS I'VE NEVER DONE ANYTHING REMOTELY NORMAL.
YOU HAVE TO BE JOKING.
I NEVER JOKE! WHAT WILL YOU DO WITH YOUR LIFE? WHAT GREATER PURPOSE WILL YOU SERVE?
SO--YOU'LL WALK AMONG THEM, CASTING A BLIND EYE ON THE TRIBULATIONS OF THE MASSES?
YOU'LL STAND BY WITH THE POWER TO MAKE A DIFFERENCE AS UNTOLD SUFFERING CONTINUES?
BE SERIOUS.
DYING AND SUFFERING AREN'T GOING TO END BECAUSE OF ME. IT'S A PART OF LIFE.
I'M NOT A GOD.
NOKI

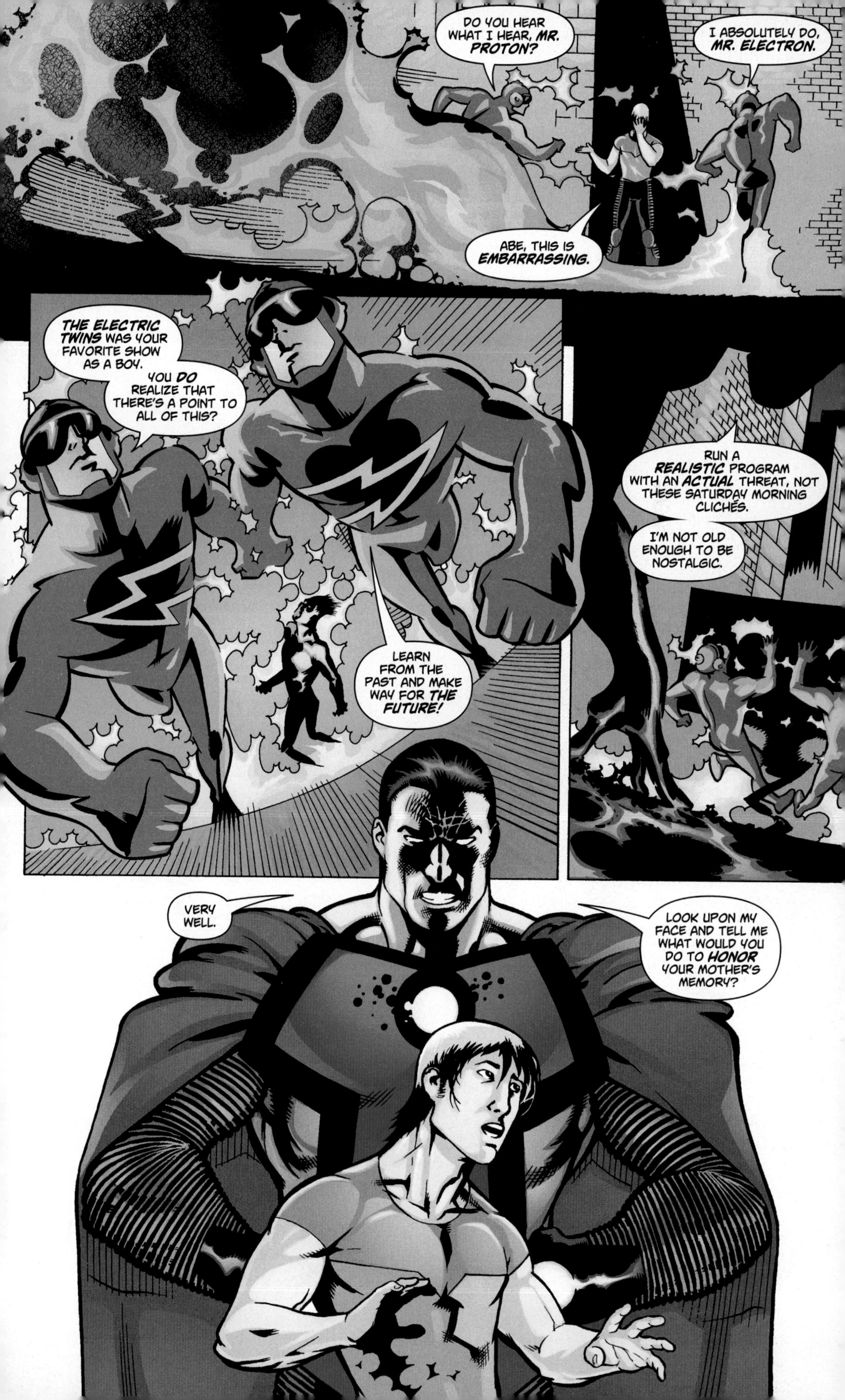
DO YOU HEAR WHAT I HEAR, MR. PROTON?
I ABSOLUTELY DO, MR. ELECTRON.
ABE, THIS IS EMBARRASSING.
THE ELECTRIC TWINS WAS YOUR FAVORITE SHOW AS A BOY.
YOU DO REALIZE THAT THERE'S A POINT TO ALL OF THIS?
LEARN FROM THE PAST AND MAKE WAY FOR THE FUTURE!
RUN A REALISTIC PROGRAM WITH AN ACTUAL THREAT, NOT THESE SATURDAY MORNING CLICHÉS.
I'M NOT OLD ENOUGH TO BE NOSTALGIC.
VERY WELL.
LOOK UPON MY FACE AND TELL ME WHAT WOULD YOU DO TO HONOR YOUR MOTHER'S MEMORY?

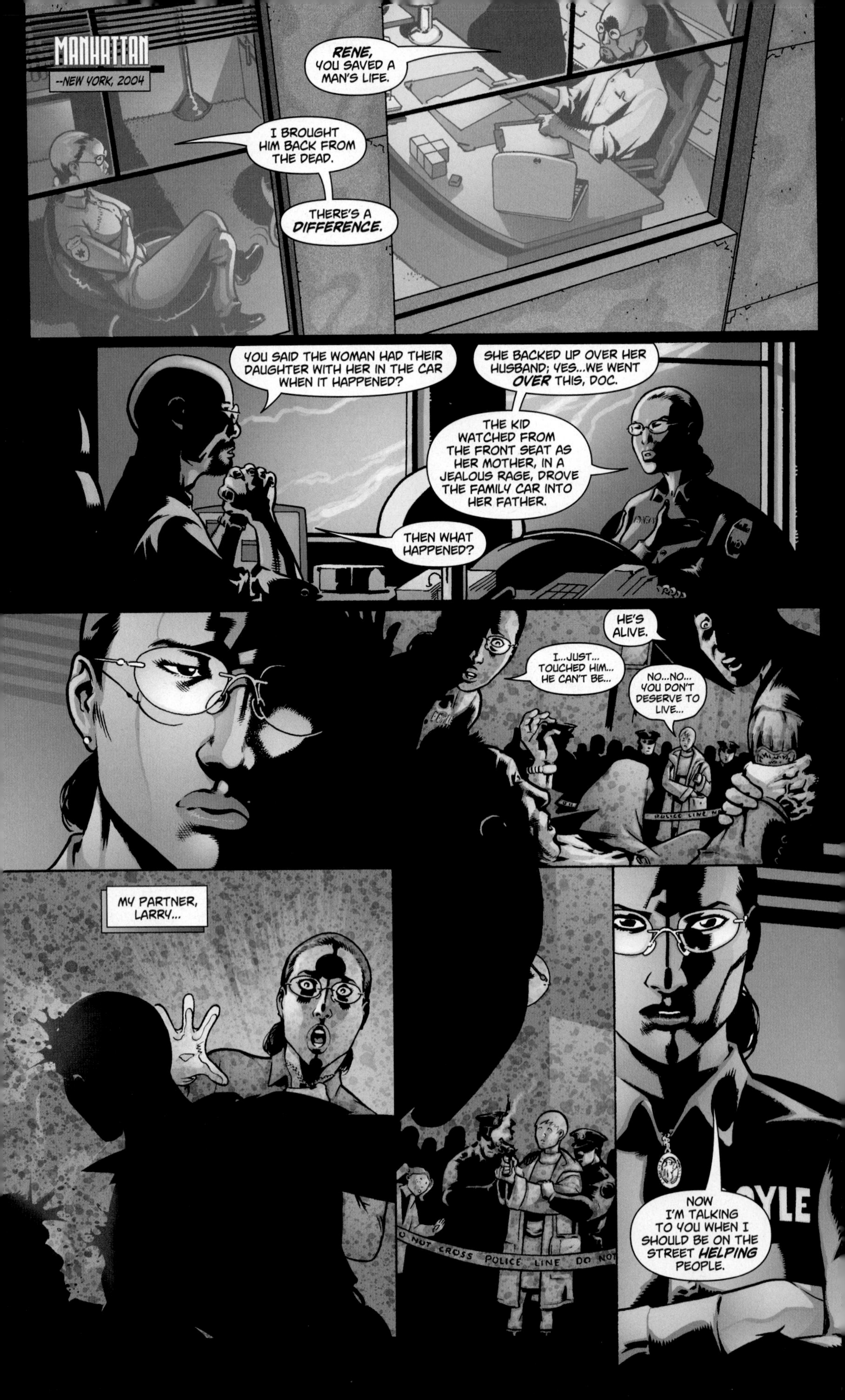
MANHATTAN
--NEW YORK, 2004
RENE, YOU SAVED A MAN'S LIFE.
I BROUGHT HIM BACK FROM THE DEAD.
THERE'S A DIFFERENCE.
YOU SAID THE WOMAN HAD THEIR DAUGHTER WITH HER IN THE CAR WHEN IT HAPPENED?
SHE BACKED UP OVER HER HUSBAND; YES...WE WENT OVER THIS, DOC.
THE KID WATCHED FROM THE FRONT SEAT AS HER MOTHER, IN A JEALOUS RAGE, DROVE THE FAMILY CAR INTO HER FATHER.
THEN WHAT HAPPENED?
HE'S ALIVE.
I...JUST... TOUCHED HIM... HE CAN'T BE...
NO...NO... YOU DON'T DESERVE TO LIVE...
POLICE LINE
MY PARTNER, LARRY...
DO NOT CROSS POLICE LINE DO NO
NOW I'M TALKING TO YOU WHEN I SHOULD BE ON THE STREET HELPING PEOPLE.

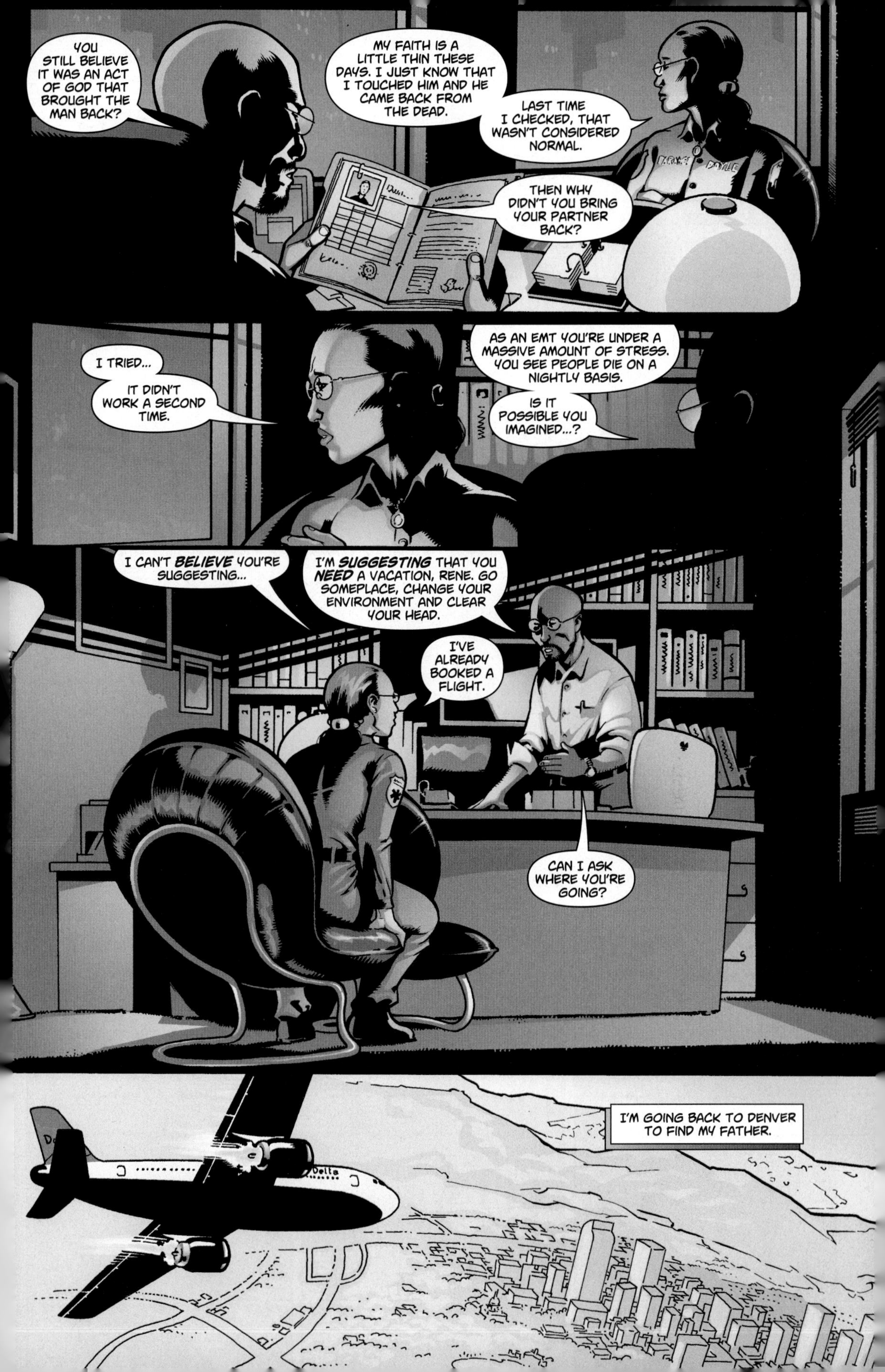
YOU STILL BELIEVE IT WAS AN ACT OF GOD THAT BROUGHT THE MAN BACK?
MY FAITH IS A LITTLE THIN THESE DAYS. I JUST KNOW THAT I TOUCHED HIM AND HE CAME BACK FROM THE DEAD.
LAST TIME I CHECKED, THAT WASN'T CONSIDERED NORMAL.
THEN WHY DIDN'T YOU BRING YOUR PARTNER BACK?
I TRIED...
IT DIDN'T WORK A SECOND TIME.
AS AN EMT YOU'RE UNDER A MASSIVE AMOUNT OF STRESS. YOU SEE PEOPLE DIE ON A NIGHTLY BASIS.
IS IT POSSIBLE YOU IMAGINED...?
I CAN'T BELIEVE YOU'RE SUGGESTING...
I'M SUGGESTING THAT YOU NEED A VACATION, RENE. GO SOMEPLACE, CHANGE YOUR ENVIRONMENT AND CLEAR YOUR HEAD.
I'VE ALREADY BOOKED A FLIGHT.
CAN I ASK WHERE YOU'RE GOING?
I'M GOING BACK TO DENVER TO FIND MY FATHER.
Delta

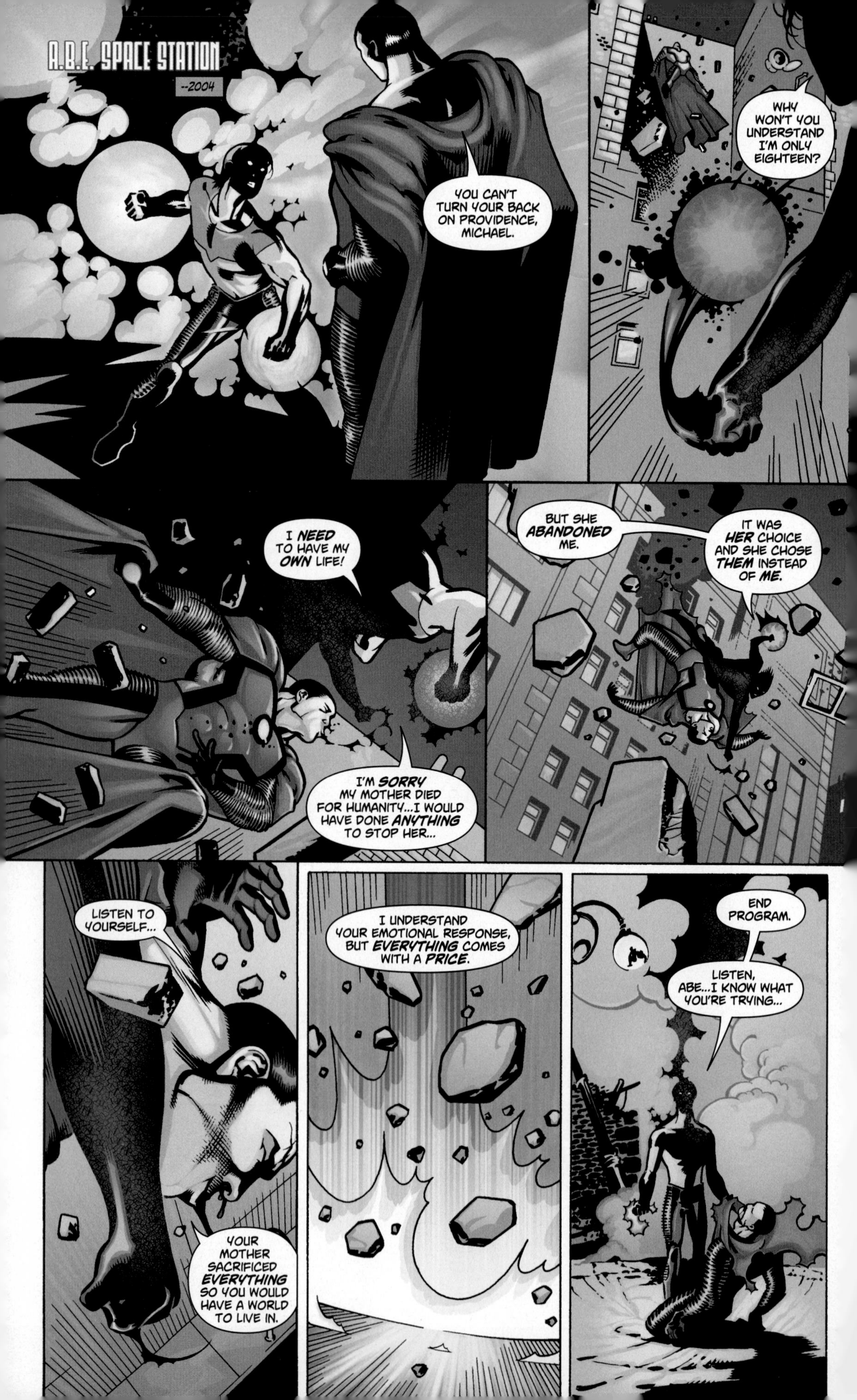
A.B.E. SPACE STATION
--2004
YOU CAN'T TURN YOUR BACK ON PROVIDENCE, MICHAEL.
WHY WON'T YOU UNDERSTAND I'M ONLY EIGHTEEN?
I NEED TO HAVE MY OWN LIFE!
I'M SORRY MY MOTHER DIED FOR HUMANITY...I WOULD HAVE DONE ANYTHING TO STOP HER...
BUT SHE ABANDONED ME.
IT WAS HER CHOICE AND SHE CHOSE THEM INSTEAD OF ME.
LISTEN TO YOURSELF...
YOUR MOTHER SACRIFICED EVERYTHING SO YOU WOULD HAVE A WORLD TO LIVE IN.
I UNDERSTAND YOUR EMOTIONAL RESPONSE, BUT EVERYTHING COMES WITH A PRICE.
END PROGRAM.
LISTEN, ABE...I KNOW WHAT YOU'RE TRYING...

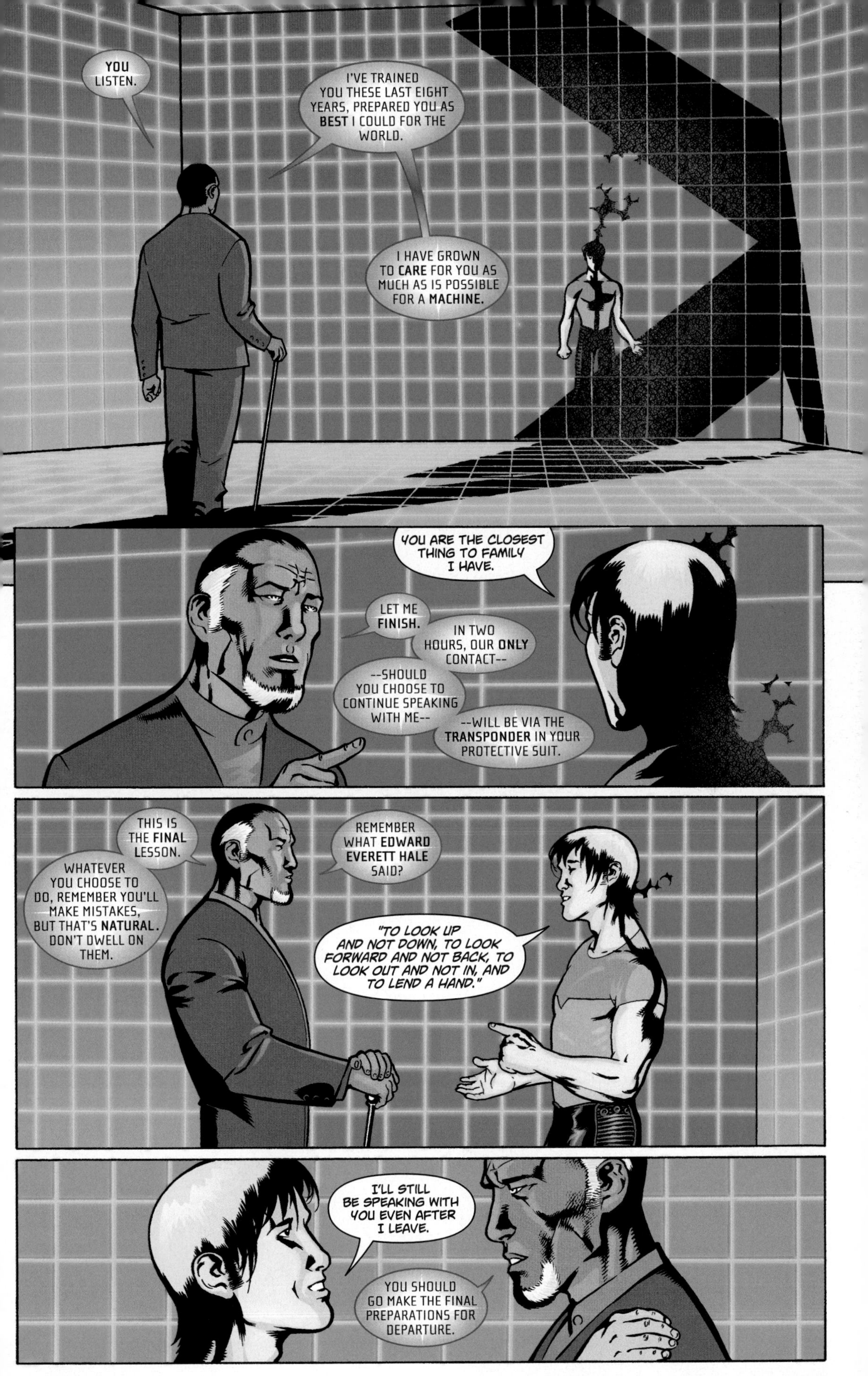
YOU LISTEN.
I'VE TRAINED YOU THESE LAST EIGHT YEARS, PREPARED YOU AS BEST I COULD FOR THE WORLD.
I HAVE GROWN TO CARE FOR YOU AS MUCH AS IS POSSIBLE FOR A MACHINE.
YOU ARE THE CLOSEST THING TO FAMILY I HAVE.
LET ME FINISH.
IN TWO HOURS, OUR ONLY CONTACT--
--SHOULD YOU CHOOSE TO CONTINUE SPEAKING WITH ME--
--WILL BE VIA THE TRANSPONDER IN YOUR PROTECTIVE SUIT.
THIS IS THE FINAL LESSON.
WHATEVER YOU CHOOSE TO DO, REMEMBER YOU'LL MAKE MISTAKES, BUT THAT'S NATURAL. DON'T DWELL ON THEM.
REMEMBER WHAT EDWARD EVERETT HALE SAID?
"TO LOOK UP AND NOT DOWN, TO LOOK FORWARD AND NOT BACK, TO LOOK OUT AND NOT IN, AND TO LEND A HAND."
I'LL STILL BE SPEAKING WITH YOU EVEN AFTER I LEAVE.
YOU SHOULD GO MAKE THE FINAL PREPARATIONS FOR DEPARTURE.

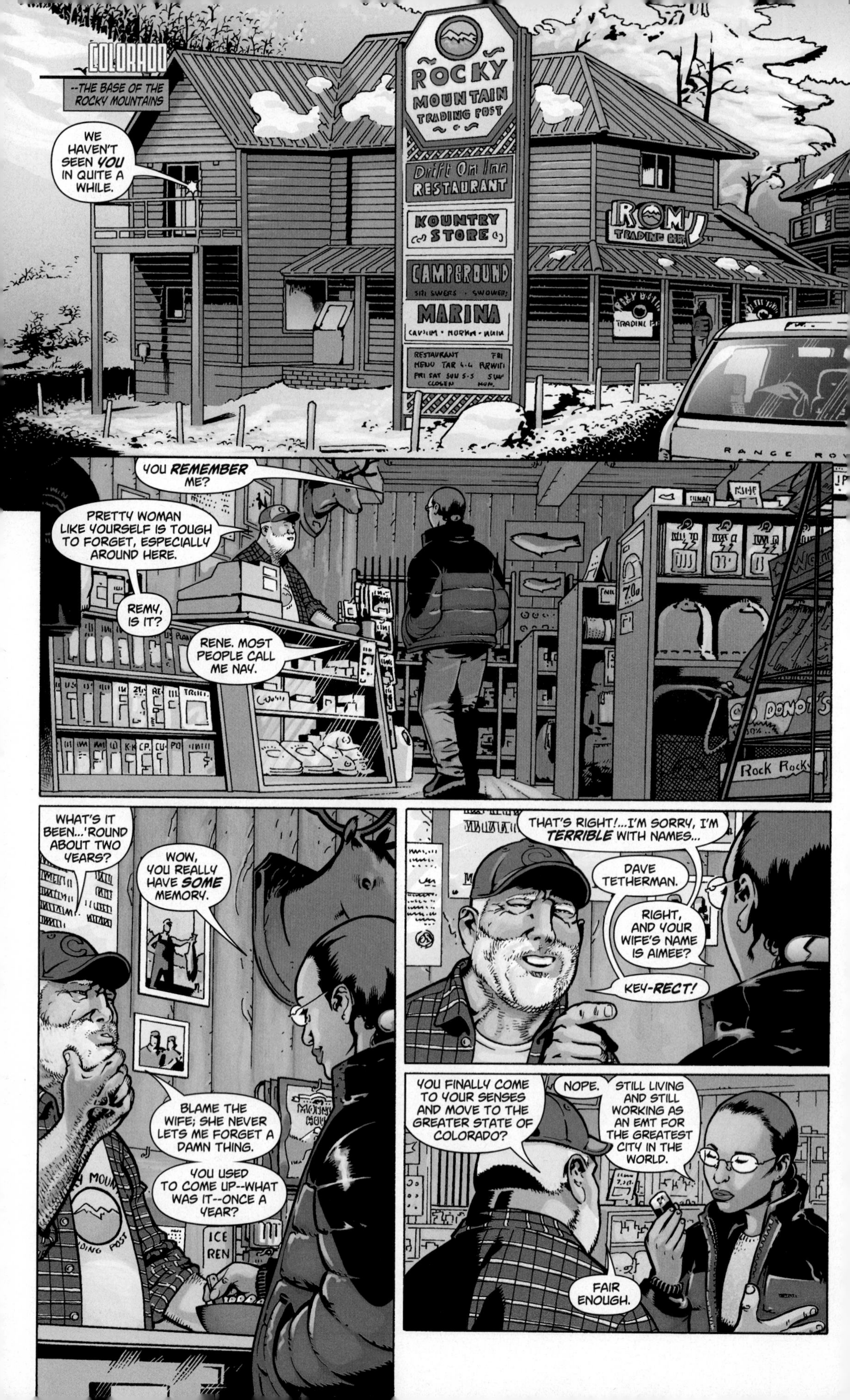
COLORADO
--THE BASE OF THE ROCKY MOUNTAINS
ROCKY MOUNTAIN TRADING POST
Drift On Inn RESTAURANT
KOUNTRY STORE
CAMPGROUND
MARINA
WE HAVEN'T SEEN YOU IN QUITE A WHILE.
YOU REMEMBER ME?
PRETTY WOMAN LIKE YOURSELF IS TOUGH TO FORGET, ESPECIALLY AROUND HERE.
REMY, IS IT?
RENE. MOST PEOPLE CALL ME NAY.
WHAT'S IT BEEN...'ROUND ABOUT TWO YEARS?
WOW, YOU REALLY HAVE SOME MEMORY.
BLAME THE WIFE; SHE NEVER LETS ME FORGET A DAMN THING.
YOU USED TO COME UP--WHAT WAS IT--ONCE A YEAR?
THAT'S RIGHT!...I'M SORRY, I'M TERRIBLE WITH NAMES...
DAVE TETHERMAN.
RIGHT, AND YOUR WIFE'S NAME IS AIMEE?
KEY-RECT!
YOU FINALLY COME TO YOUR SENSES AND MOVE TO THE GREATER STATE OF COLORADO?
NOPE.
STILL LIVING AND STILL WORKING AS AN EMT FOR THE GREATEST CITY IN THE WORLD.
FAIR ENOUGH.

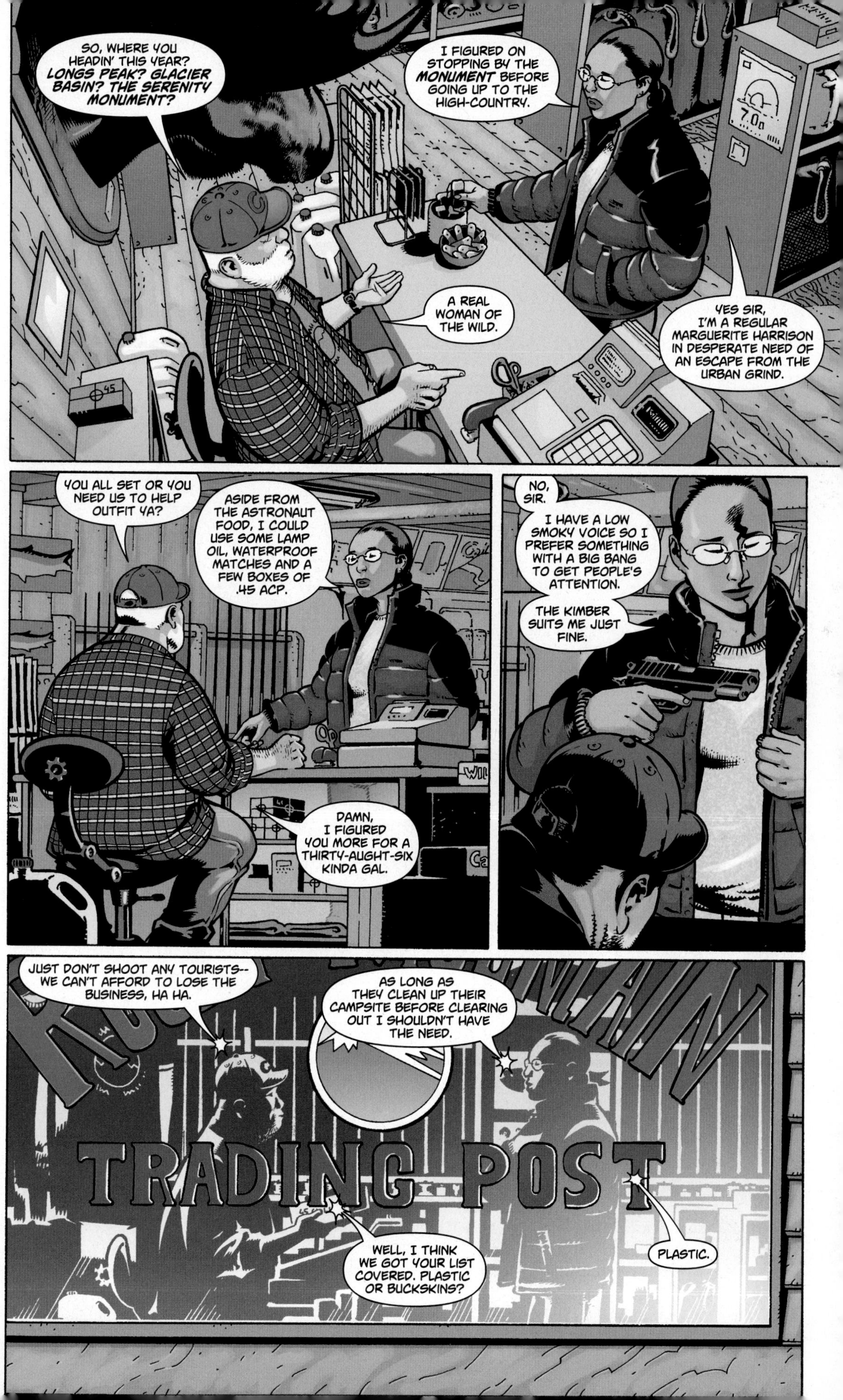
SO, WHERE YOU HEADIN' THIS YEAR? LONGS PEAK? GLACIER BASIN? THE SERENITY MONUMENT?
I FIGURED ON STOPPING BY THE MONUMENT BEFORE GOING UP TO THE HIGH-COUNTRY.
A REAL WOMAN OF THE WILD.
YES SIR, I'M A REGULAR MARGUERITE HARRISON IN DESPERATE NEED OF AN ESCAPE FROM THE URBAN GRIND.
YOU ALL SET OR YOU NEED US TO HELP OUTFIT YA?
ASIDE FROM THE ASTRONAUT FOOD, I COULD USE SOME LAMP OIL, WATERPROOF MATCHES AND A FEW BOXES OF .45 ACP.
DAMN, I FIGURED YOU MORE FOR A THIRTY-AUGHT-SIX KINDA GAL.
NO, SIR.
I HAVE A LOW SMOKY VOICE SO I PREFER SOMETHING WITH A BIG BANG TO GET PEOPLE'S ATTENTION.
THE KIMBER SUITS ME JUST FINE.
JUST DON'T SHOOT ANY TOURISTS-- WE CAN'T AFFORD TO LOSE THE BUSINESS, HA HA.
AS LONG AS THEY CLEAN UP THEIR CAMPSITE BEFORE CLEARING OUT I SHOULDN'T HAVE THE NEED.
TRADING POST
WELL, I THINK WE GOT YOUR LIST COVERED. PLASTIC OR BUCKSKINS?
PLASTIC.

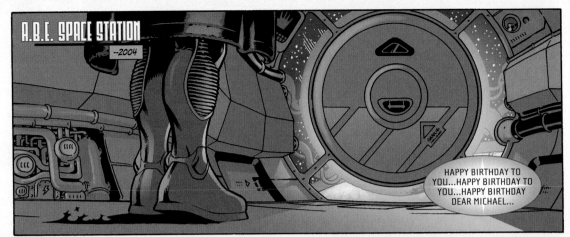

A.B.E. SPACE STATION
--2004

HAPPY BIRTHDAY TO YOU...HAPPY BIRTHDAY TO YOU...HAPPY BIRTHDAY DEAR MICHAEL...

CUT IT OUT, ABE.

IT'S TRADITION TO SING.

THIS IS AS *NON*-TRADITIONAL AS IT GETS.

ARE YOU FRIGHTENED?

YEAH.

THAT'S NATURAL.

SAID THE LIVING SPACE STATION TO THE DEPARTING SON OF A GODDESS.

REMEMBER TO WEAR YOUR SUNBLOCK.

WAS THAT A JOKE?

I BELIEVE IT WAS.

GO ON... THE WORLD IS WAITING.

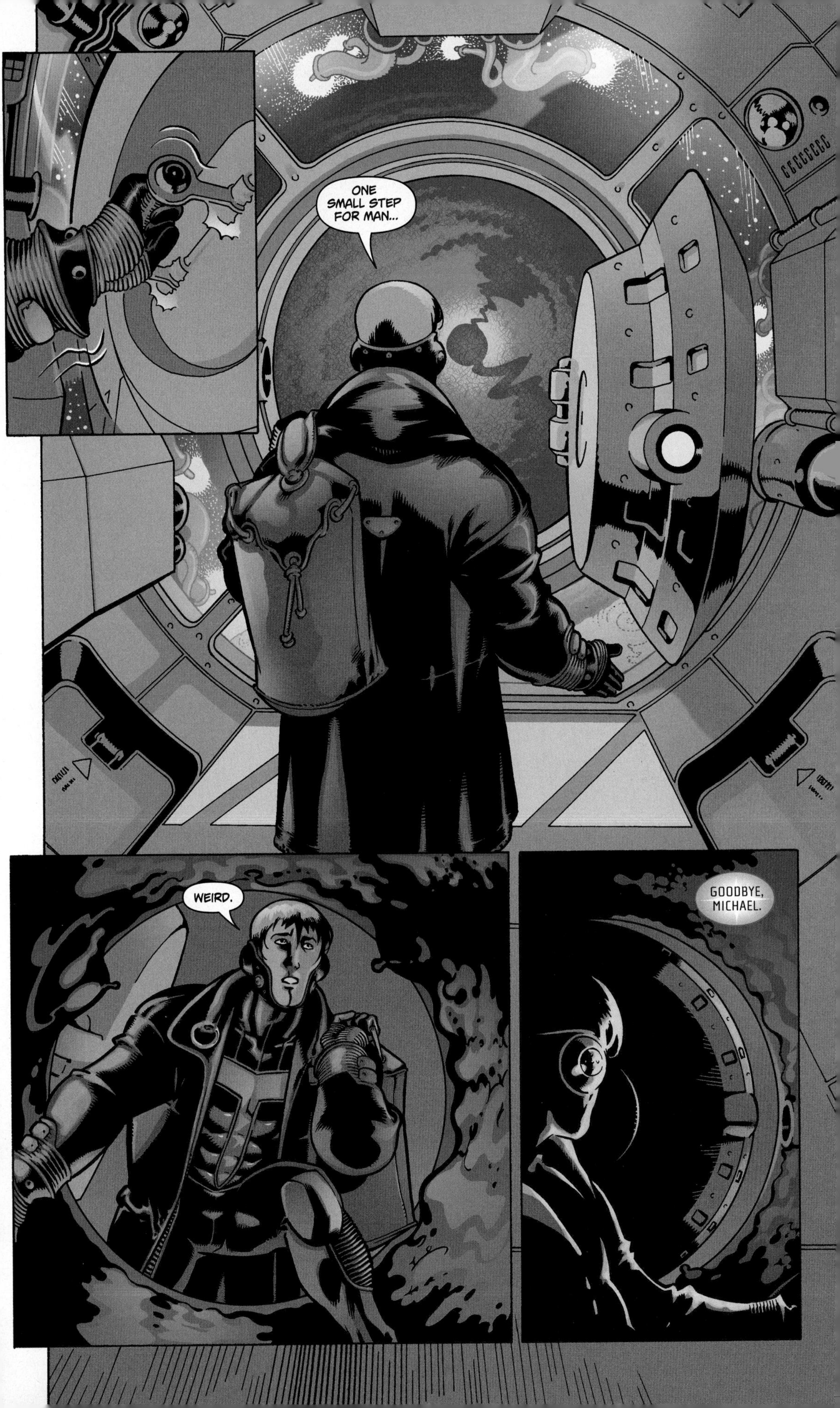
ONE SMALL STEP FOR MAN...
WEIRD.
GOODBYE, MICHAEL.

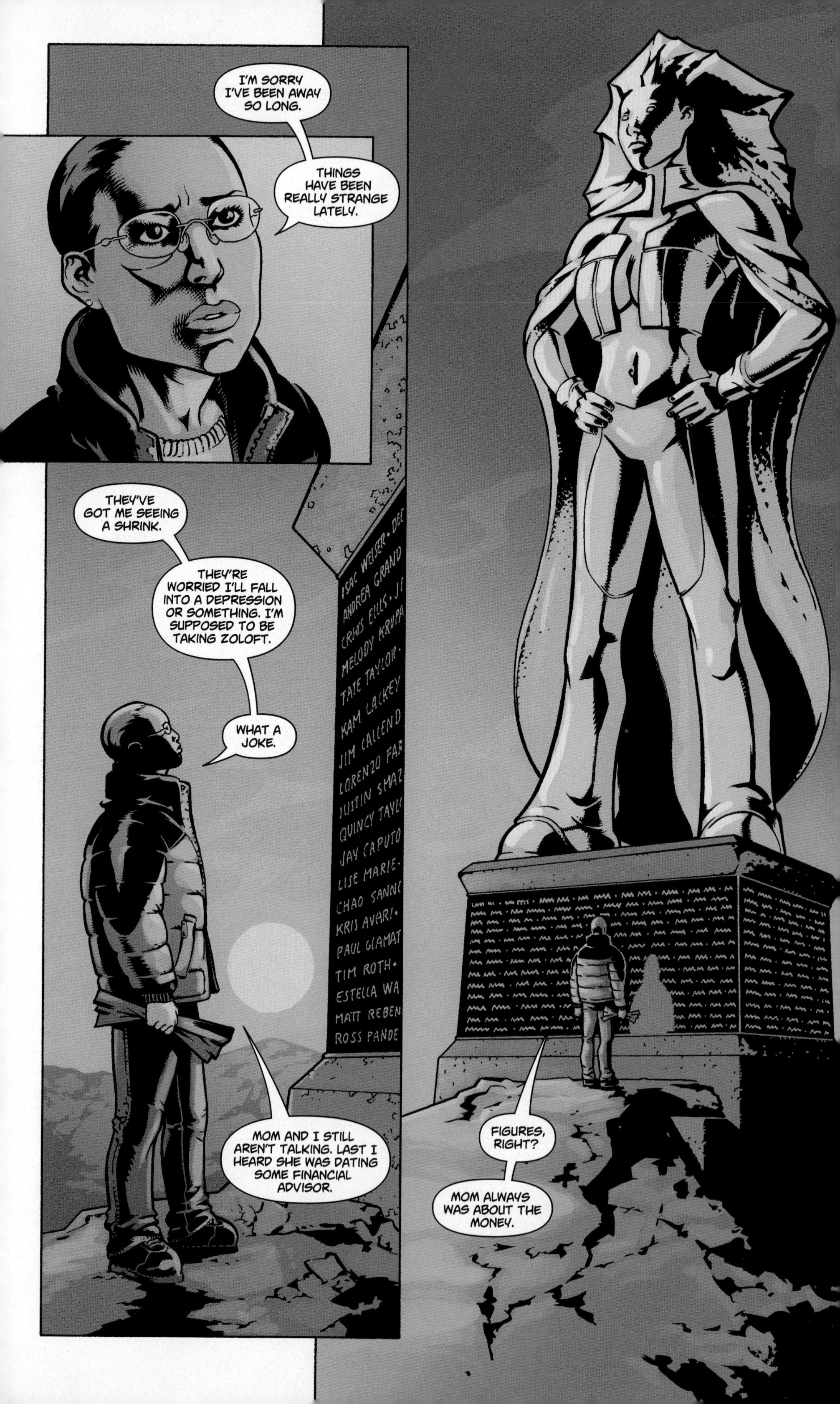
I'M SORRY I'VE BEEN AWAY SO LONG.
THINGS HAVE BEEN REALLY STRANGE LATELY.
THEY'VE GOT ME SEEING A SHRINK.
THEY'RE WORRIED I'LL FALL INTO A DEPRESSION OR SOMETHING. I'M SUPPOSED TO BE TAKING ZOLOFT.
WHAT A JOKE.
MOM AND I STILL AREN'T TALKING. LAST I HEARD SHE WAS DATING SOME FINANCIAL ADVISOR.
FIGURES, RIGHT?
MOM ALWAYS WAS ABOUT THE MONEY.

DAD'S BEEN MISSING FOR SEVEN YEARS NOW AND SO HE'S OFFICIALLY LISTED AS DEAD.

IF THAT'S TRUE THEN YOU PROBABLY DON'T NEED ME TO TELL YOU.

I'M NOT READY TO GIVE UP JUST YET.

• THOMAS MORON • MARI FE LACION • ROGER STEVENS • KATHERINE
DON JONES • WILLIAM ACKERMAN • ROSS PALMER • ESTELLA GIAMAT
CHAEL CARTER • JIM CALENDE • TIM REBENKOFF • MARK PANDER • CA
MARIANO DE LA TORRE • ERICK AVARI • LUKE COCAL • EVAN DEXTER
DIX • FREDA FOHSHEN • MARC IZAGUIRRE • CHRIS ELLIS • JAVIER CASAR
K KURBY • SCOTT RIDLEY • ANNE RAMSAY • ANDREA GRAND • ORLAND
LIAMS • PHIL NOWLAN • CHAO SANNON • ISAAC C. SINGLETON JR. • LI
MSEY • DEREC CASEY • JOE KRAMER • ROBERT PARONTINI • MARCO VI
JONATHAN DICKERSON • MICHAEL PROVOLONE • DEEP ROY • EILEEN
REVIOUX • QUINCY TAYLOR • JIM CALLENDER • JUAN ROMAN CANO
ALEXANDER • PHILIP T. SMAZ • MELODY KRAMER • HOWARD BERGER
PEZ • MARCOS SANTIAGO • MONICA DOYLE • JOSHUA ZAR • MOLLY
ZMAN • TODD HEBRING • LORENZO FARR • SHONDA PERRING • CAM
DAMS • ELIZABETH HOLMES • ROG ____SON • TATE THOMSON • JONN
HARRIS • DANNY GOLDBERG • CH____ • ___ SHIPLEY • PA
JEANINE BRADEN • JA___SON • ____ON STONE •
RVING AZOFF • THO___JOHNS___ • ___
OORE • MATHEW FRE____ • ___O GOMEZ •
TAN • ROBERT PLAN____ • ___OAKENFOLD •
ARLISLE • DONNA D____ • DECLAN CO___
• THERESSA RIPL___ • RICHARD___
RONNIE HARRIS___ • ANIA ROBERT___
OBERT LEE • RI___ • ___FLY • JEFF___
AN FERRY • DAV___ • ___GOSTINO • ___
DEN • EDWARD___

I NEED ANSWERS TO ALL THE STRANGE THINGS THAT HAVE BEEN HAPPENING AND MAYBE DAD HAS THEM.

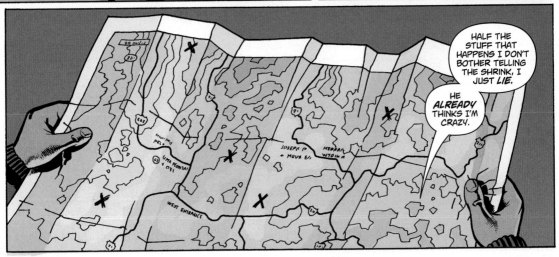

HALF THE STUFF THAT HAPPENS I DON'T BOTHER TELLING THE SHRINK, I JUST *LIE*.

HE *ALREADY* THINKS I'M CRAZY.

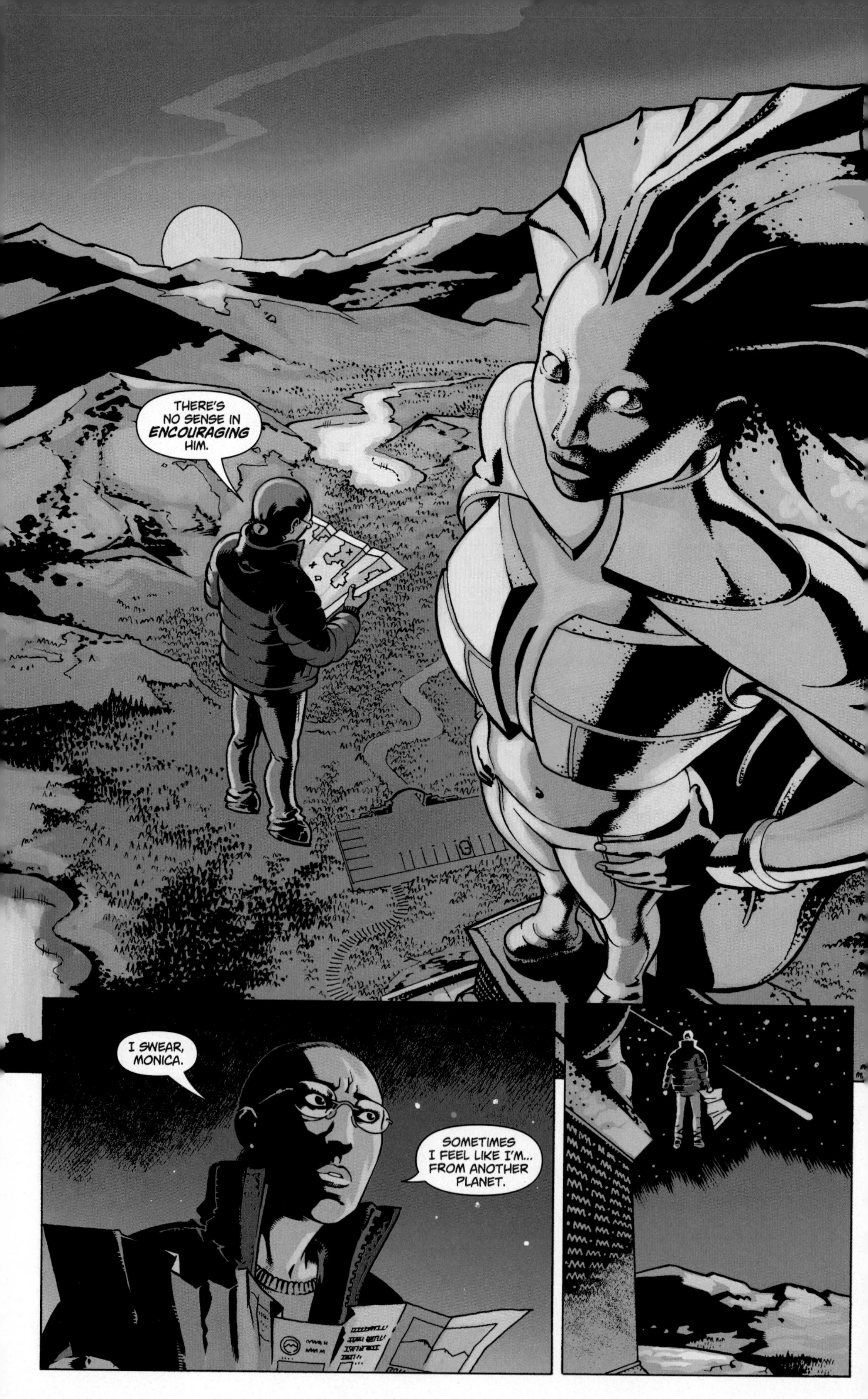
THERE'S NO SENSE IN ENCOURAGING HIM.
I SWEAR, MONICA.
SOMETIMES I FEEL LIKE I'M... FROM ANOTHER PLANET.

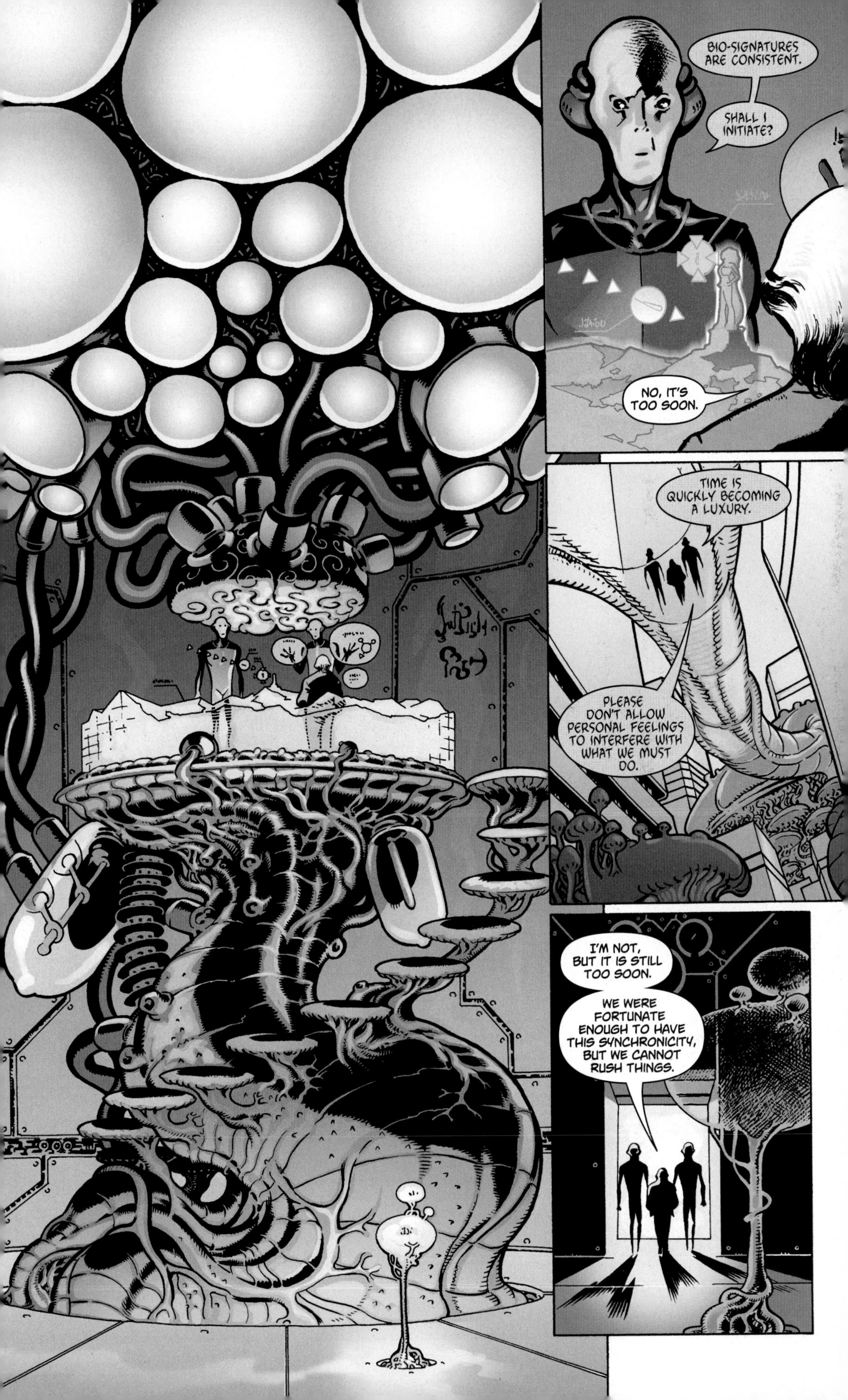
BIO-SIGNATURES ARE CONSISTENT.
SHALL I INITIATE?
NO, IT'S TOO SOON.
TIME IS QUICKLY BECOMING A LUXURY.
PLEASE DON'T ALLOW PERSONAL FEELINGS TO INTERFERE WITH WHAT WE MUST DO.
I'M NOT, BUT IT IS STILL TOO SOON.
WE WERE FORTUNATE ENOUGH TO HAVE THIS SYNCHRONICITY, BUT WE CANNOT RUSH THINGS.

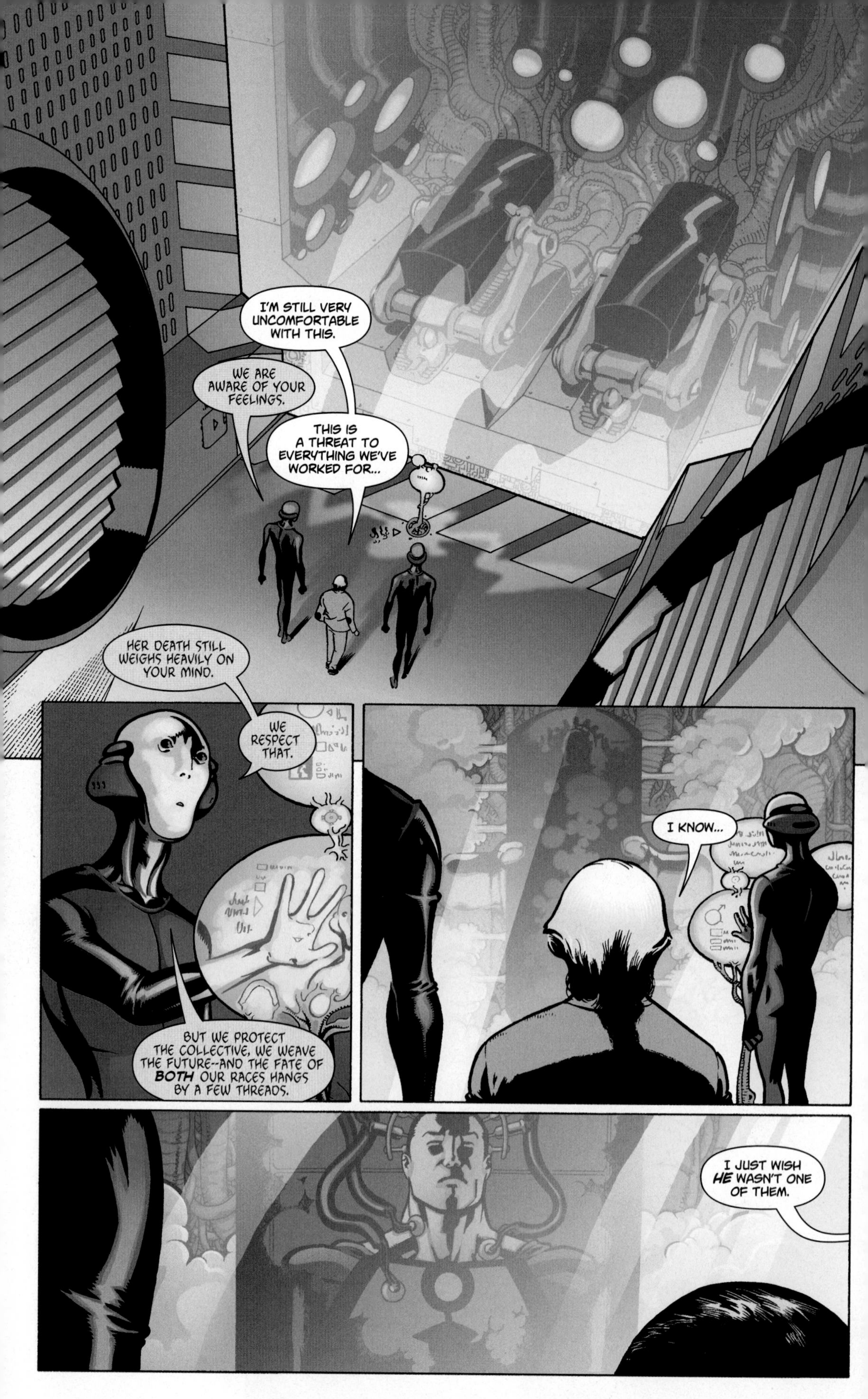
I'M STILL VERY UNCOMFORTABLE WITH THIS.
WE ARE AWARE OF YOUR FEELINGS.
THIS IS A THREAT TO EVERYTHING WE'VE WORKED FOR...
HER DEATH STILL WEIGHS HEAVILY ON YOUR MIND.
WE RESPECT THAT.
BUT WE PROTECT THE COLLECTIVE, WE WEAVE THE FUTURE--AND THE FATE OF BOTH OUR RACES HANGS BY A FEW THREADS.
I KNOW...
I JUST WISH HE WASN'T ONE OF THEM.

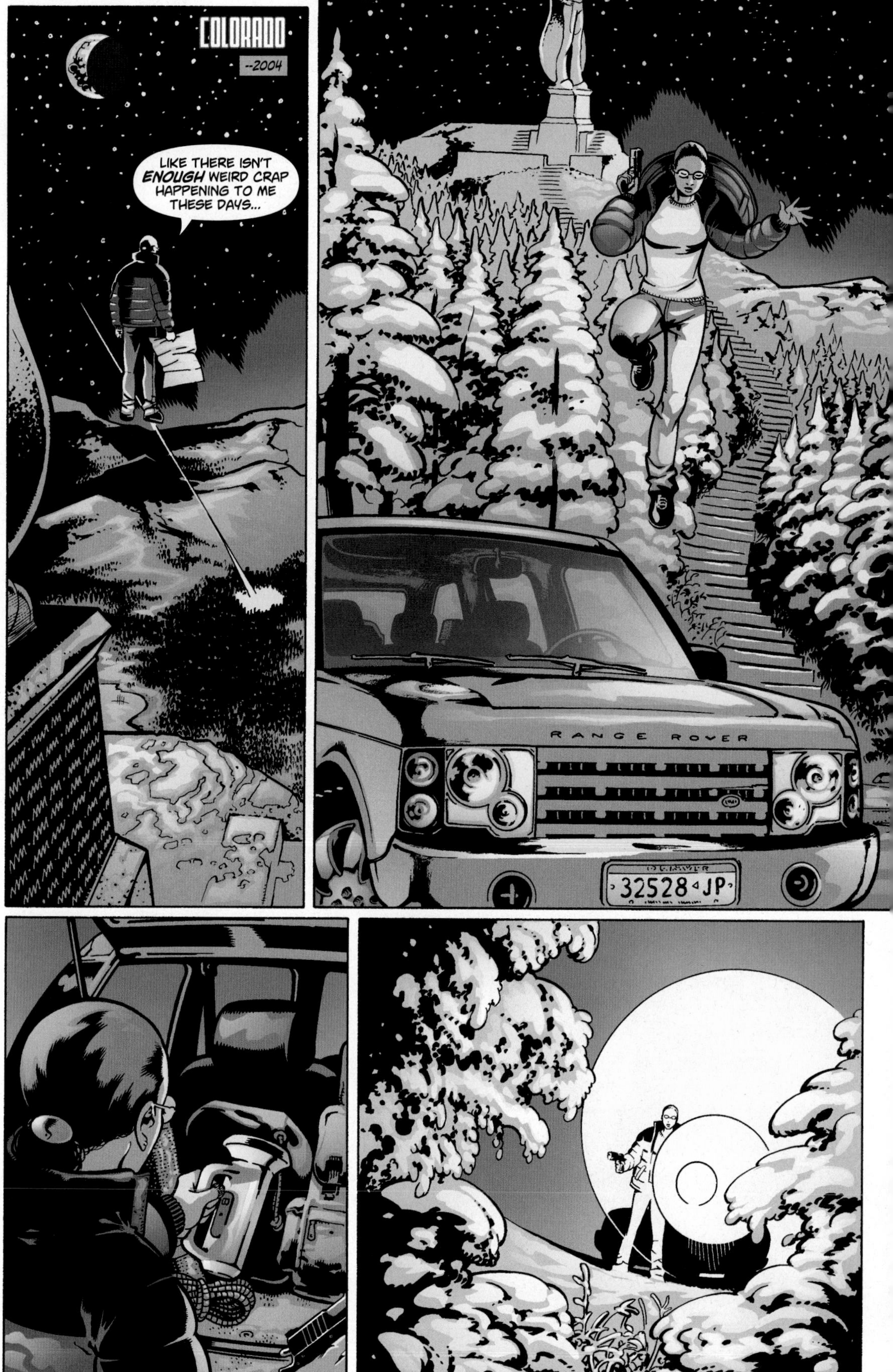
COLORADO
--2004
LIKE THERE ISN'T ENOUGH WEIRD CRAP HAPPENING TO ME THESE DAYS...
RANGE ROVER
32528 JP

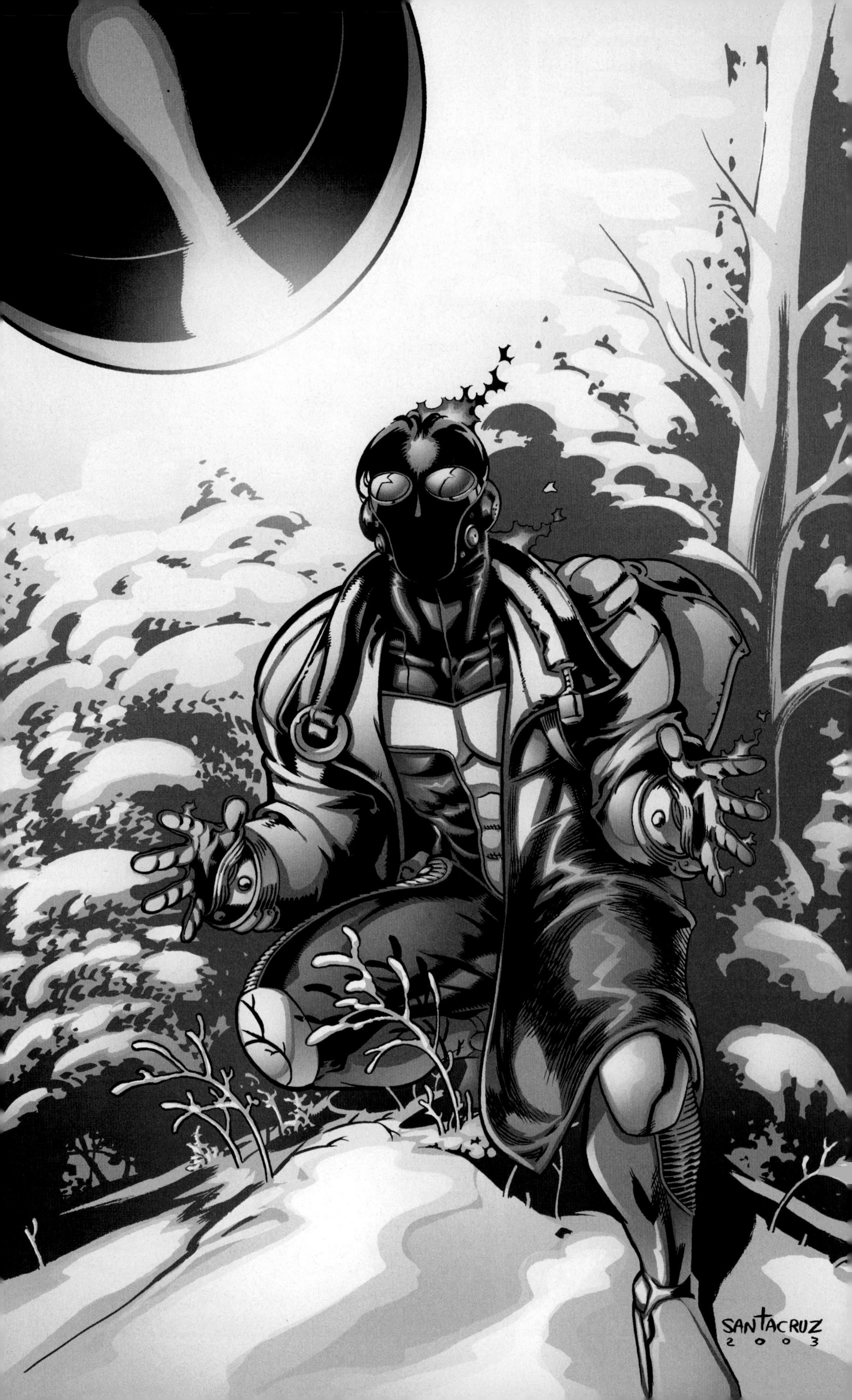
SANTACRUZ
2003

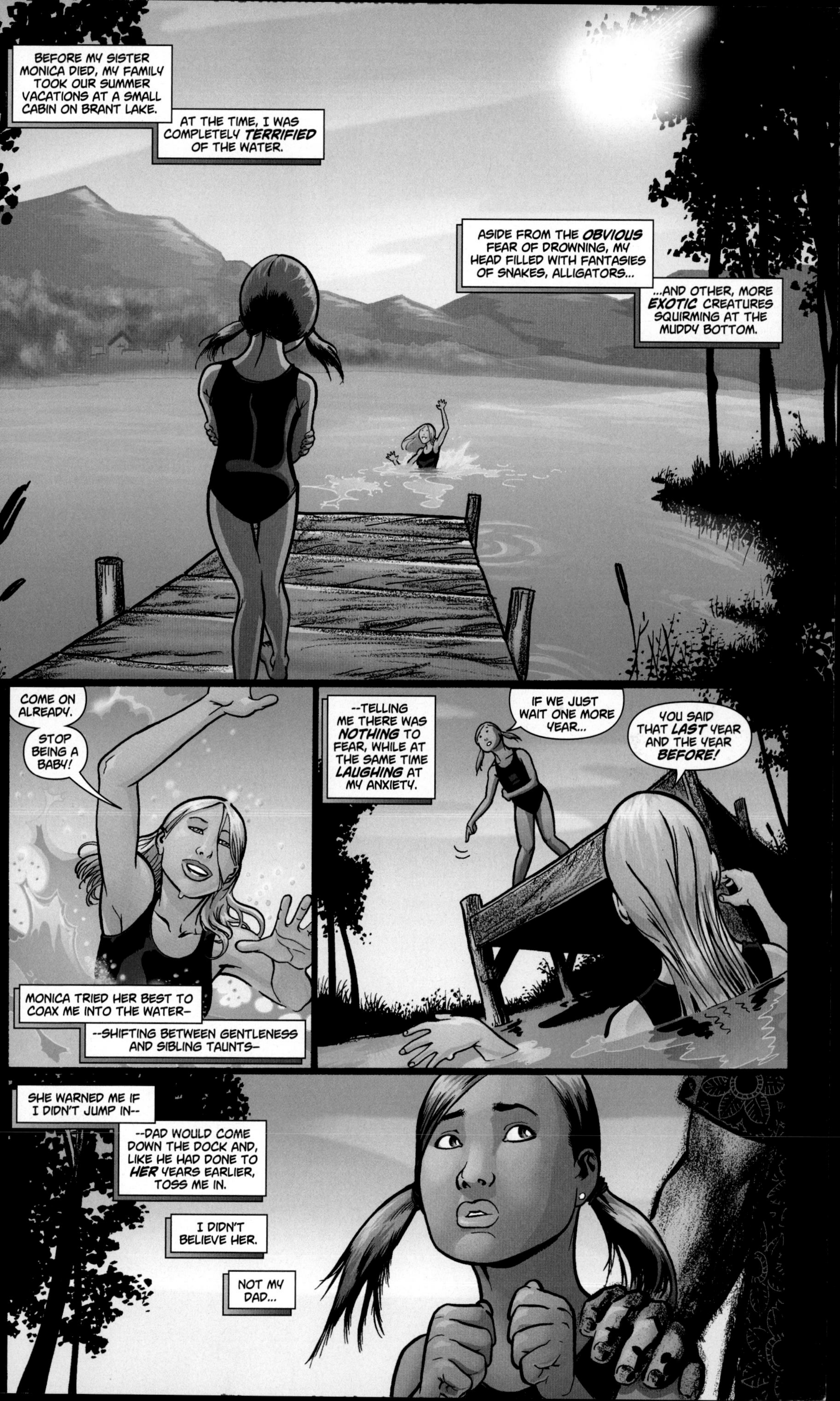

BEFORE MY SISTER MONICA DIED, MY FAMILY TOOK OUR SUMMER VACATIONS AT A SMALL CABIN ON BRANT LAKE.
AT THE TIME, I WAS COMPLETELY *TERRIFIED* OF THE WATER.
ASIDE FROM THE *OBVIOUS* FEAR OF DROWNING, MY HEAD FILLED WITH FANTASIES OF SNAKES, ALLIGATORS...
...AND OTHER, MORE *EXOTIC* CREATURES SQUIRMING AT THE MUDDY BOTTOM.
COME ON ALREADY.
STOP BEING A BABY!
MONICA TRIED HER BEST TO COAX ME INTO THE WATER–
--SHIFTING BETWEEN GENTLENESS AND SIBLING TAUNTS–
--TELLING ME THERE WAS *NOTHING* TO FEAR, WHILE AT THE SAME TIME *LAUGHING* AT MY ANXIETY.
IF WE JUST WAIT ONE MORE YEAR...
YOU SAID THAT *LAST* YEAR AND THE YEAR *BEFORE!*
SHE WARNED ME IF I DIDN'T JUMP IN--
--DAD WOULD COME DOWN THE DOCK AND, LIKE HE HAD DONE TO *HER* YEARS EARLIER, TOSS ME IN.
I DIDN'T BELIEVE HER.
NOT MY DAD...

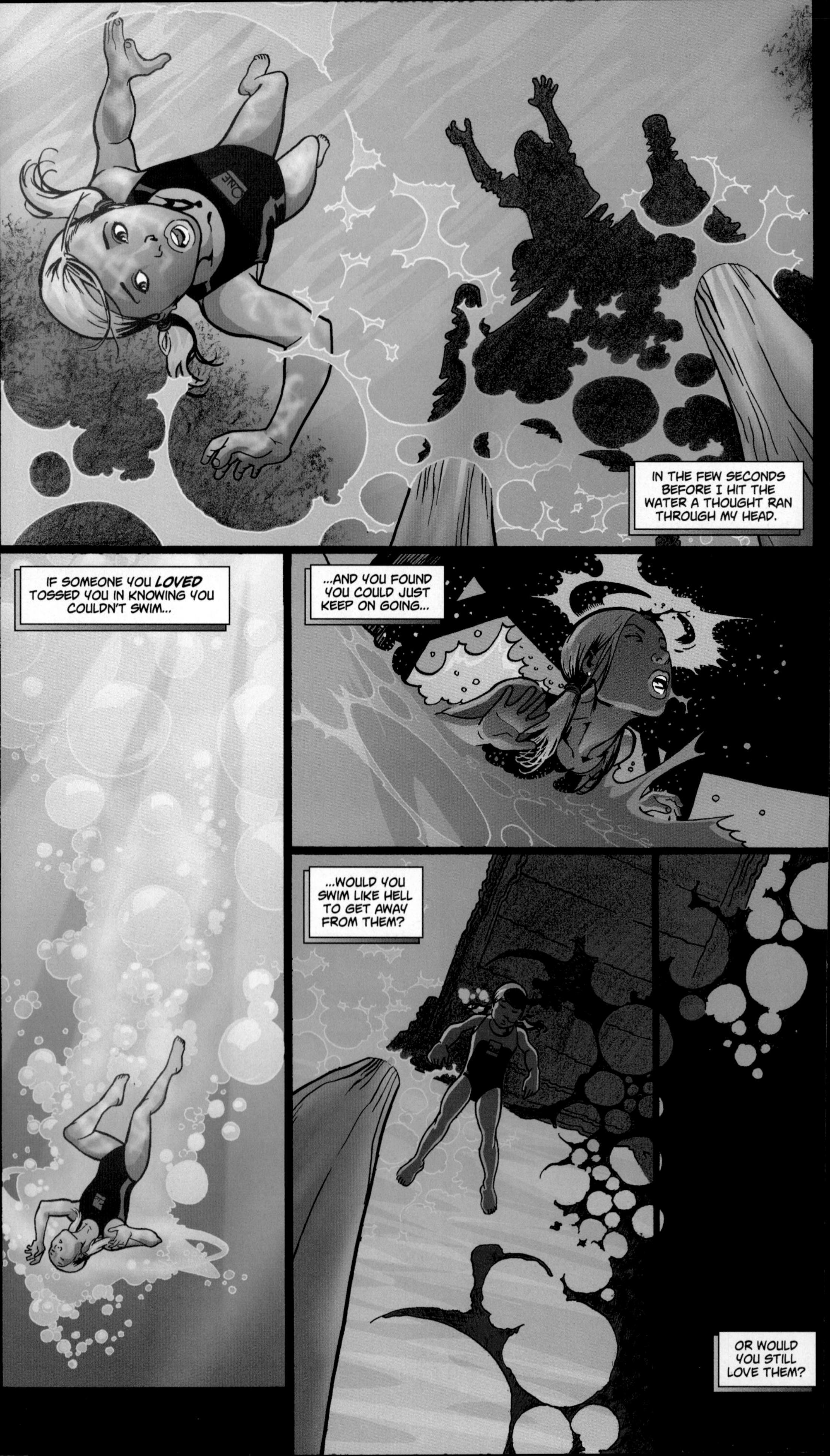
IN THE FEW SECONDS BEFORE I HIT THE WATER A THOUGHT RAN THROUGH MY HEAD.
IF SOMEONE YOU *LOVED* TOSSED YOU IN KNOWING YOU COULDN'T SWIM...
...AND YOU FOUND YOU COULD JUST KEEP ON GOING...
...WOULD YOU SWIM LIKE HELL TO GET AWAY FROM THEM?
OR WOULD YOU STILL LOVE THEM?

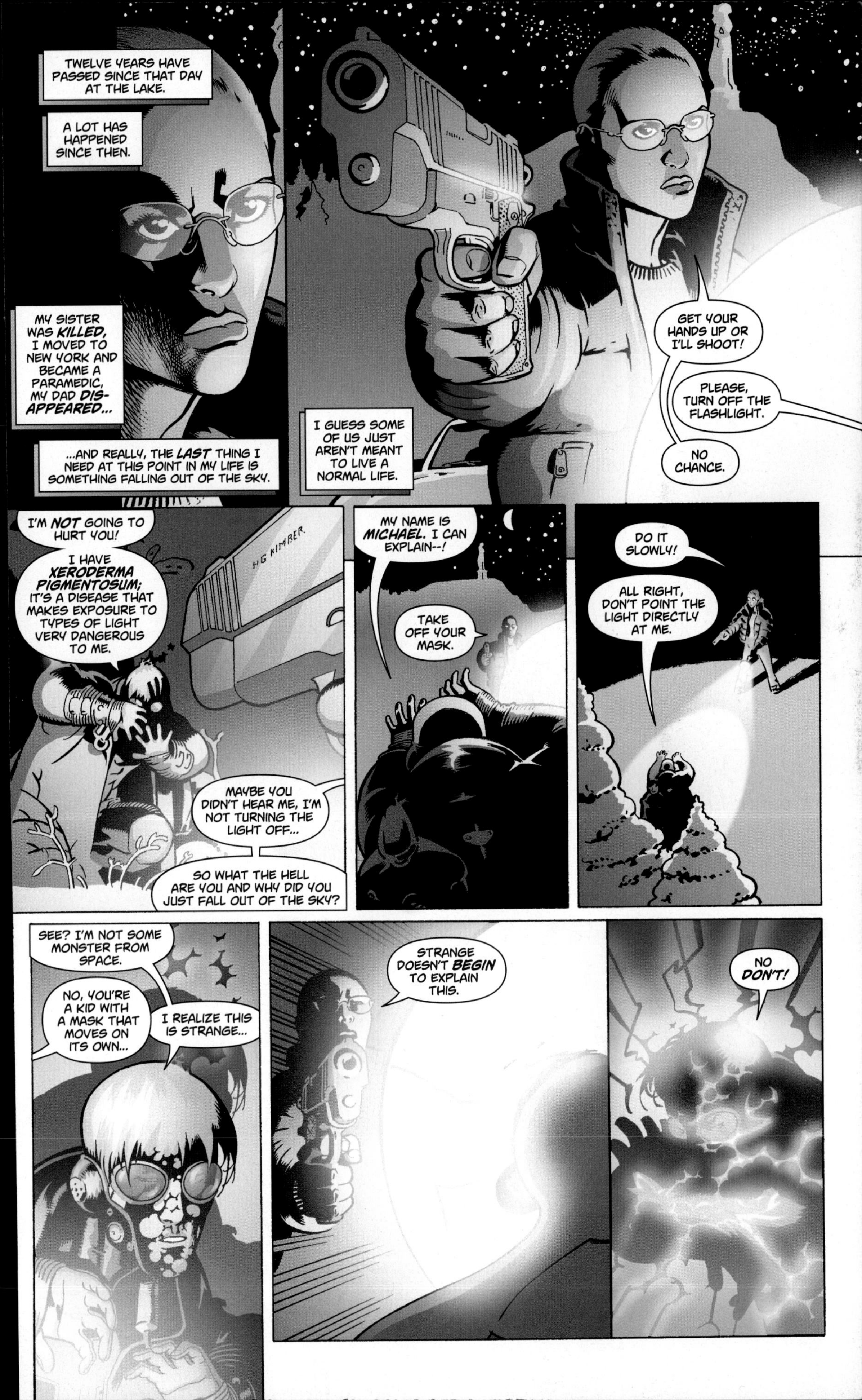
TWELVE YEARS HAVE PASSED SINCE THAT DAY AT THE LAKE.
A LOT HAS HAPPENED SINCE THEN.
MY SISTER WAS **KILLED,** I MOVED TO NEW YORK AND BECAME A PARAMEDIC, MY DAD **DIS-APPEARED...**
...AND REALLY, THE **LAST** THING I NEED AT THIS POINT IN MY LIFE IS SOMETHING FALLING OUT OF THE SKY.
I GUESS SOME OF US JUST AREN'T MEANT TO LIVE A NORMAL LIFE.
GET YOUR HANDS UP OR I'LL SHOOT!
PLEASE, TURN OFF THE FLASHLIGHT.
NO CHANCE.
I'M **NOT** GOING TO HURT YOU!
I HAVE ***XERODERMA PIGMENTOSUM;*** IT'S A DISEASE THAT MAKES EXPOSURE TO TYPES OF LIGHT VERY DANGEROUS TO ME.
H.G KIMBER
MAYBE YOU DIDN'T HEAR ME, I'M NOT TURNING THE LIGHT OFF...
SO WHAT THE HELL ARE YOU AND WHY DID YOU JUST FALL OUT OF THE SKY?
MY NAME IS ***MICHAEL.*** I CAN EXPLAIN--!
TAKE OFF YOUR MASK.
DO IT SLOWLY!
ALL RIGHT, DON'T POINT THE LIGHT DIRECTLY AT ME.
SEE? I'M NOT SOME MONSTER FROM SPACE.
NO, YOU'RE A KID WITH A MASK THAT MOVES ON ITS OWN...
I REALIZE THIS IS STRANGE...
STRANGE DOESN'T ***BEGIN*** TO EXPLAIN THIS.
NO ***DON'T!***

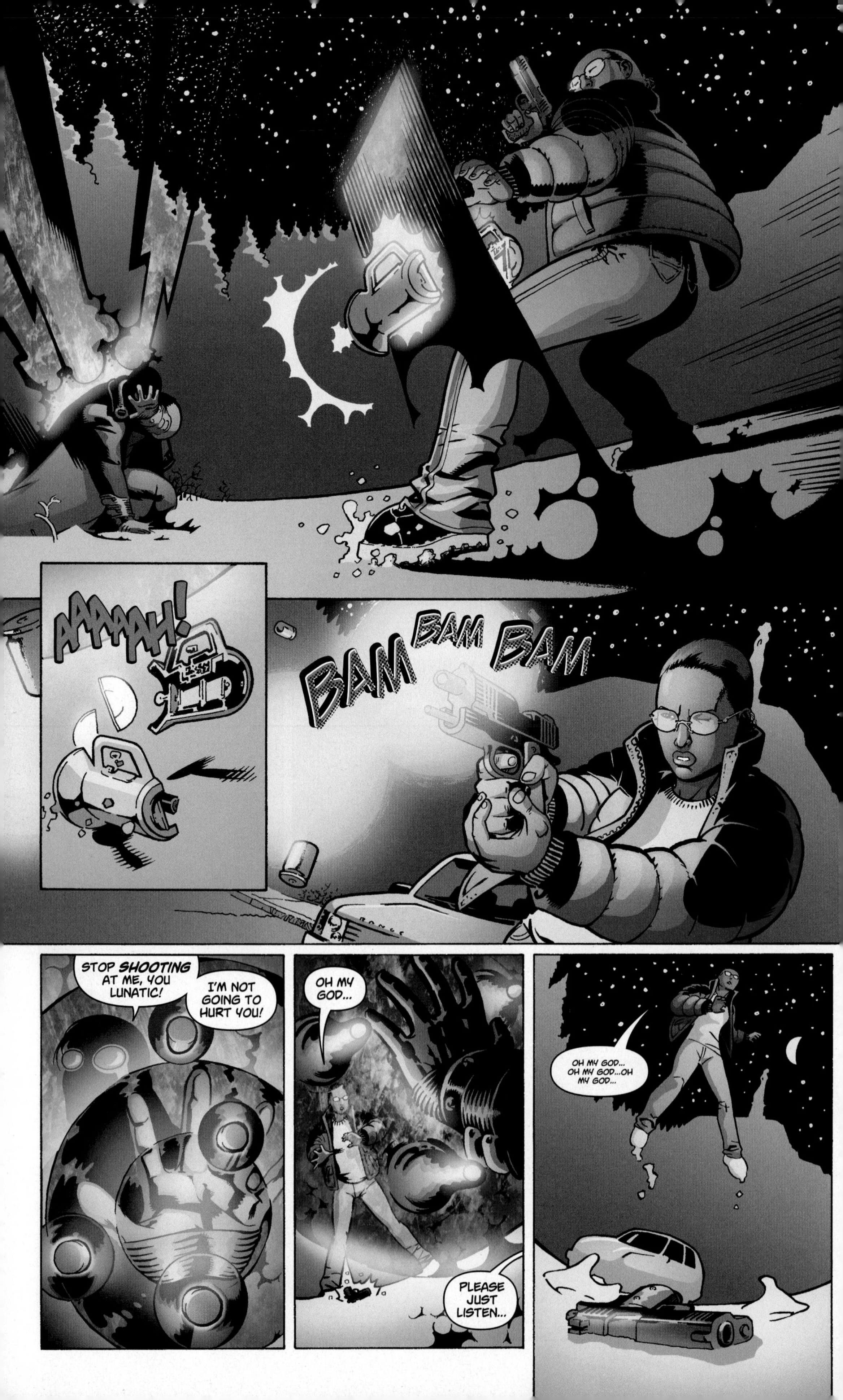
AAAAAH!
BAM BAM BAM
STOP SHOOTING AT ME, YOU LUNATIC!
I'M NOT GOING TO HURT YOU!
OH MY GOD...
PLEASE JUST LISTEN...
OH MY GOD... OH MY GOD...OH MY GOD...

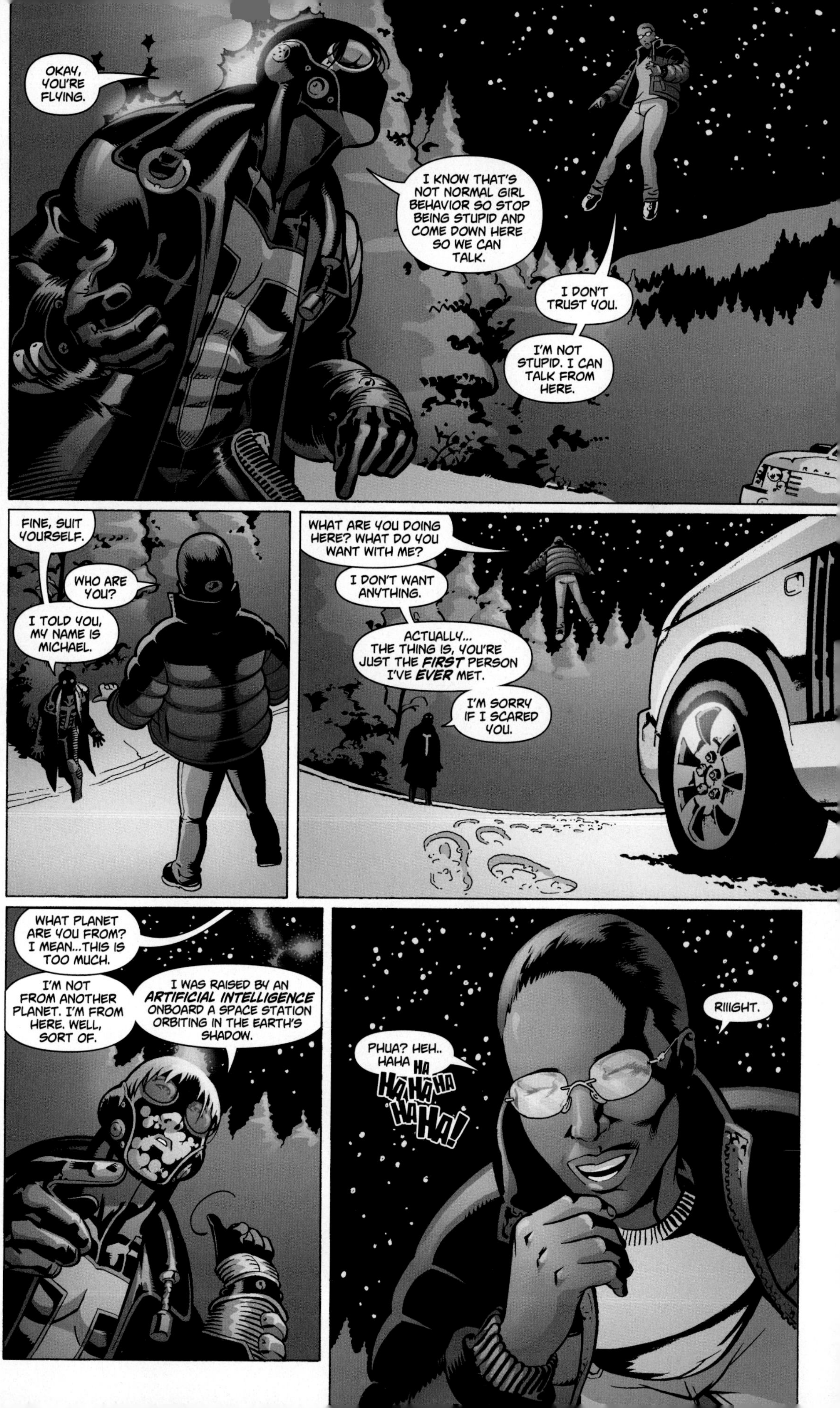
OKAY, YOU'RE FLYING.
I KNOW THAT'S NOT NORMAL GIRL BEHAVIOR SO STOP BEING STUPID AND COME DOWN HERE SO WE CAN TALK.
I DON'T TRUST YOU.
I'M NOT STUPID. I CAN TALK FROM HERE.
FINE, SUIT YOURSELF.
WHO ARE YOU?
I TOLD YOU, MY NAME IS MICHAEL.
WHAT ARE YOU DOING HERE? WHAT DO YOU WANT WITH ME?
I DON'T WANT ANYTHING.
ACTUALLY... THE THING IS, YOU'RE JUST THE FIRST PERSON I'VE EVER MET.
I'M SORRY IF I SCARED YOU.
WHAT PLANET ARE YOU FROM? I MEAN...THIS IS TOO MUCH.
I'M NOT FROM ANOTHER PLANET. I'M FROM HERE. WELL, SORT OF.
I WAS RAISED BY AN ARTIFICIAL INTELLIGENCE ONBOARD A SPACE STATION ORBITING IN THE EARTH'S SHADOW.
RIIIGHT.
PHUA? HEH.. HAHA HA HA HA HA HA HA!

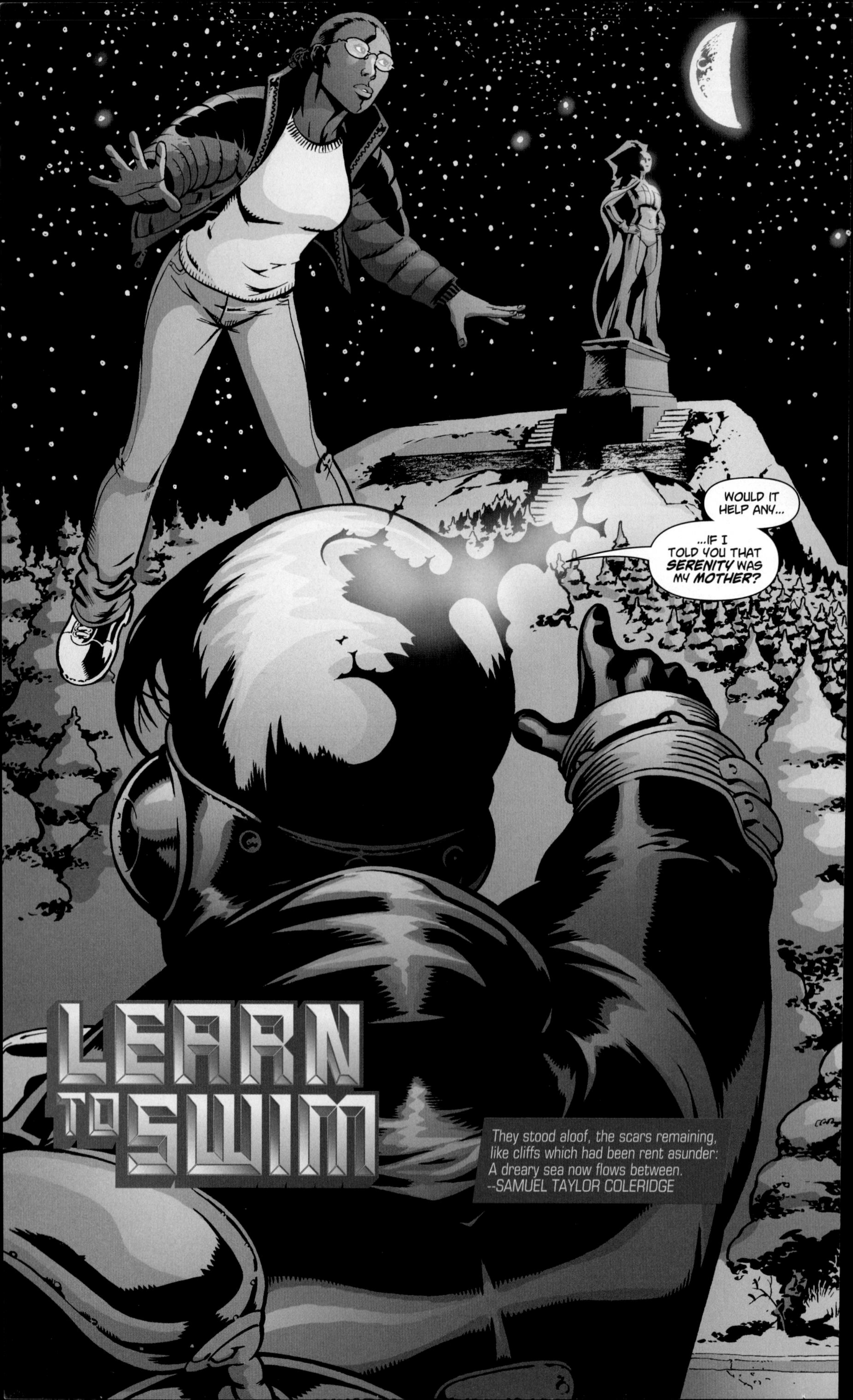
WOULD IT HELP ANY...
...IF I TOLD YOU THAT SERENITY WAS MY MOTHER?
LEARN TO SWIM
They stood aloof, the scars remaining, like cliffs which had been rent asunder: A dreary sea now flows between. --SAMUEL TAYLOR COLERIDGE

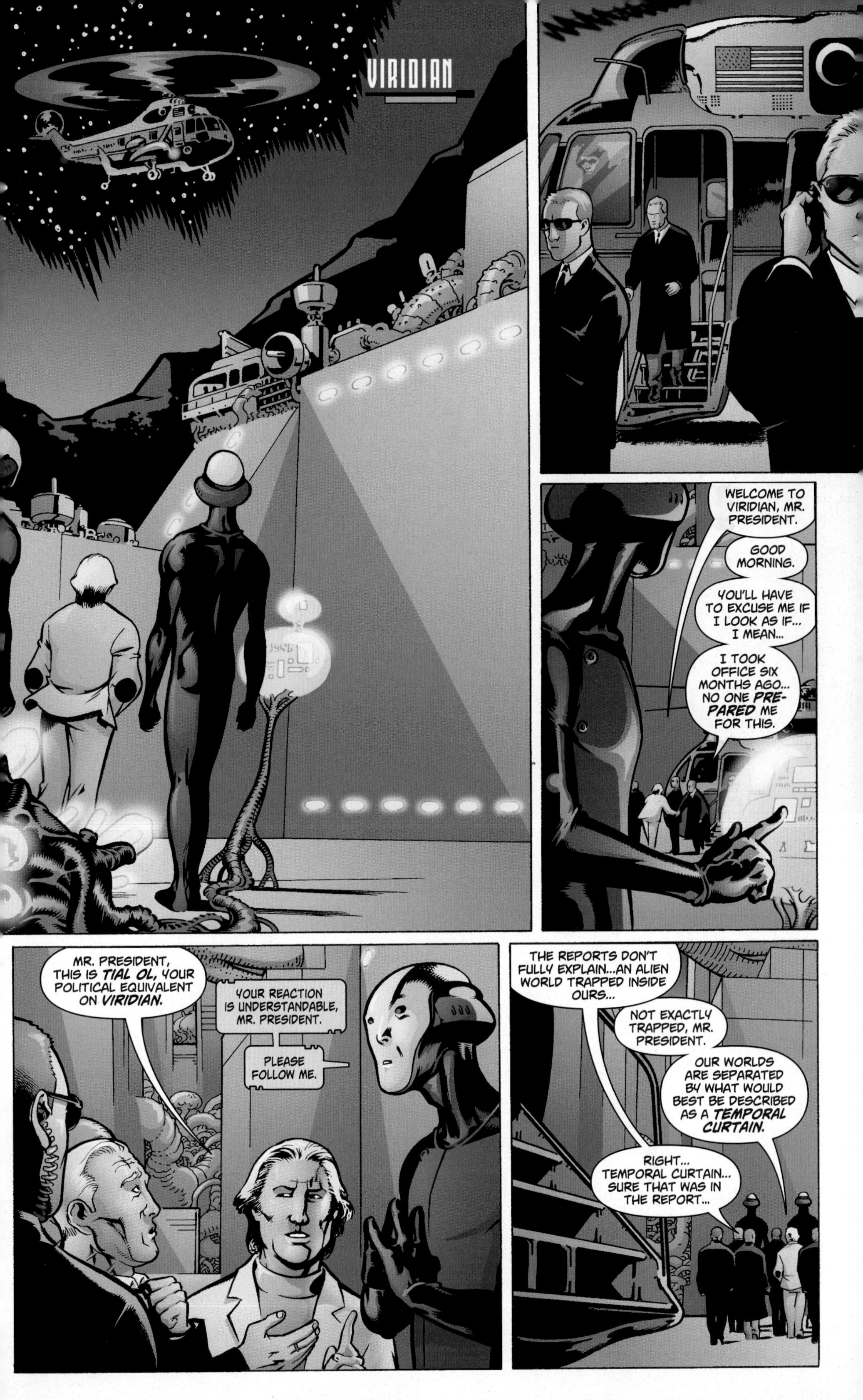
VIRIDIAN
WELCOME TO VIRIDIAN, MR. PRESIDENT.
GOOD MORNING.
YOU'LL HAVE TO EXCUSE ME IF I LOOK AS IF... I MEAN...
I TOOK OFFICE SIX MONTHS AGO... NO ONE PRE-PARED ME FOR THIS.
MR. PRESIDENT, THIS IS TIAL OL, YOUR POLITICAL EQUIVALENT ON VIRIDIAN.
YOUR REACTION IS UNDERSTANDABLE, MR. PRESIDENT.
PLEASE FOLLOW ME.
THE REPORTS DON'T FULLY EXPLAIN...AN ALIEN WORLD TRAPPED INSIDE OURS...
NOT EXACTLY TRAPPED, MR. PRESIDENT.
OUR WORLDS ARE SEPARATED BY WHAT WOULD BEST BE DESCRIBED AS A TEMPORAL CURTAIN.
RIGHT... TEMPORAL CURTAIN... SURE THAT WAS IN THE REPORT...

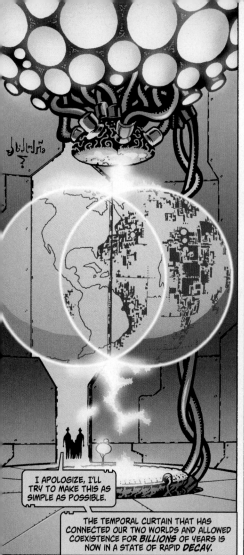

THE DETERIORATION EFFECT WILL BE THE FORMATION OF A BLACK HOLE.

THE END RESULTS WILL BE NATURAL DISASTERS ON A SCALE *NEVER* BEFORE SEEN BY HUMANKIND.

HOW SOON IS THIS SUPPOSED TO HAPPEN?

GIVEN THE CURRENT RATE OF DECAY, I'D ESTIMATE TWO MONTHS, SIR.

I APOLOGIZE, I'LL TRY TO MAKE THIS AS SIMPLE AS POSSIBLE.

THE TEMPORAL CURTAIN THAT HAS CONNECTED OUR TWO WORLDS AND ALLOWED COEXISTENCE FOR *BILLIONS* OF YEARS IS NOW IN A STATE OF RAPID *DECAY*.

MY GOD...

OUR ATTEMPTS TO REPAIR THE DAMAGE MET WITH REPEATED FAILURE.

FURTHER INVESTIGATION OF THE PROBLEM REVEALED THE POSSIBILITY THAT *YOUR* RACE MAY BE PHYSICALLY ABLE TO SEAL THE RIFT.

AS A RESULT, WITH THE HELP OF PROFESSOR DOYLE, WE INITIATED A FAILSAFE CALLED *PROJECT FIRST LIGHT.*

AS YOU KNOW THE PROJECT MET WITH UNFORTUNATE RESULTS.

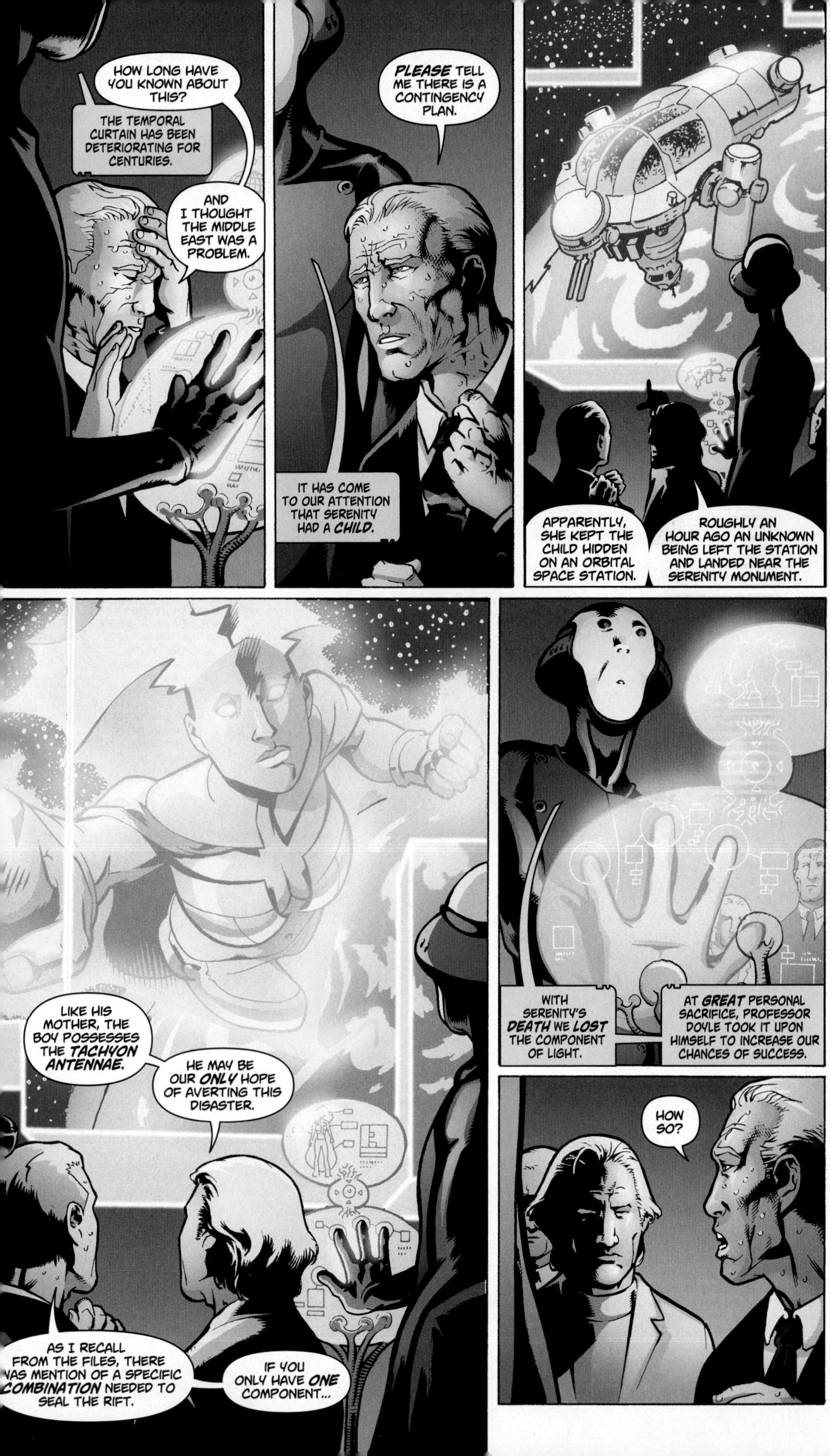
HOW LONG HAVE YOU KNOWN ABOUT THIS?
THE TEMPORAL CURTAIN HAS BEEN DETERIORATING FOR CENTURIES.
AND I THOUGHT THE MIDDLE EAST WAS A PROBLEM.
PLEASE TELL ME THERE IS A CONTINGENCY PLAN.
IT HAS COME TO OUR ATTENTION THAT SERENITY HAD A CHILD.
APPARENTLY, SHE KEPT THE CHILD HIDDEN ON AN ORBITAL SPACE STATION.
ROUGHLY AN HOUR AGO AN UNKNOWN BEING LEFT THE STATION AND LANDED NEAR THE SERENITY MONUMENT.
LIKE HIS MOTHER, THE BOY POSSESSES THE TACHYON ANTENNAE.
HE MAY BE OUR ONLY HOPE OF AVERTING THIS DISASTER.
WITH SERENITY'S DEATH WE LOST THE COMPONENT OF LIGHT.
AT GREAT PERSONAL SACRIFICE, PROFESSOR DOYLE TOOK IT UPON HIMSELF TO INCREASE OUR CHANCES OF SUCCESS.
HOW SO?
AS I RECALL FROM THE FILES, THERE WAS MENTION OF A SPECIFIC COMBINATION NEEDED TO SEAL THE RIFT.
IF YOU ONLY HAVE ONE COMPONENT...

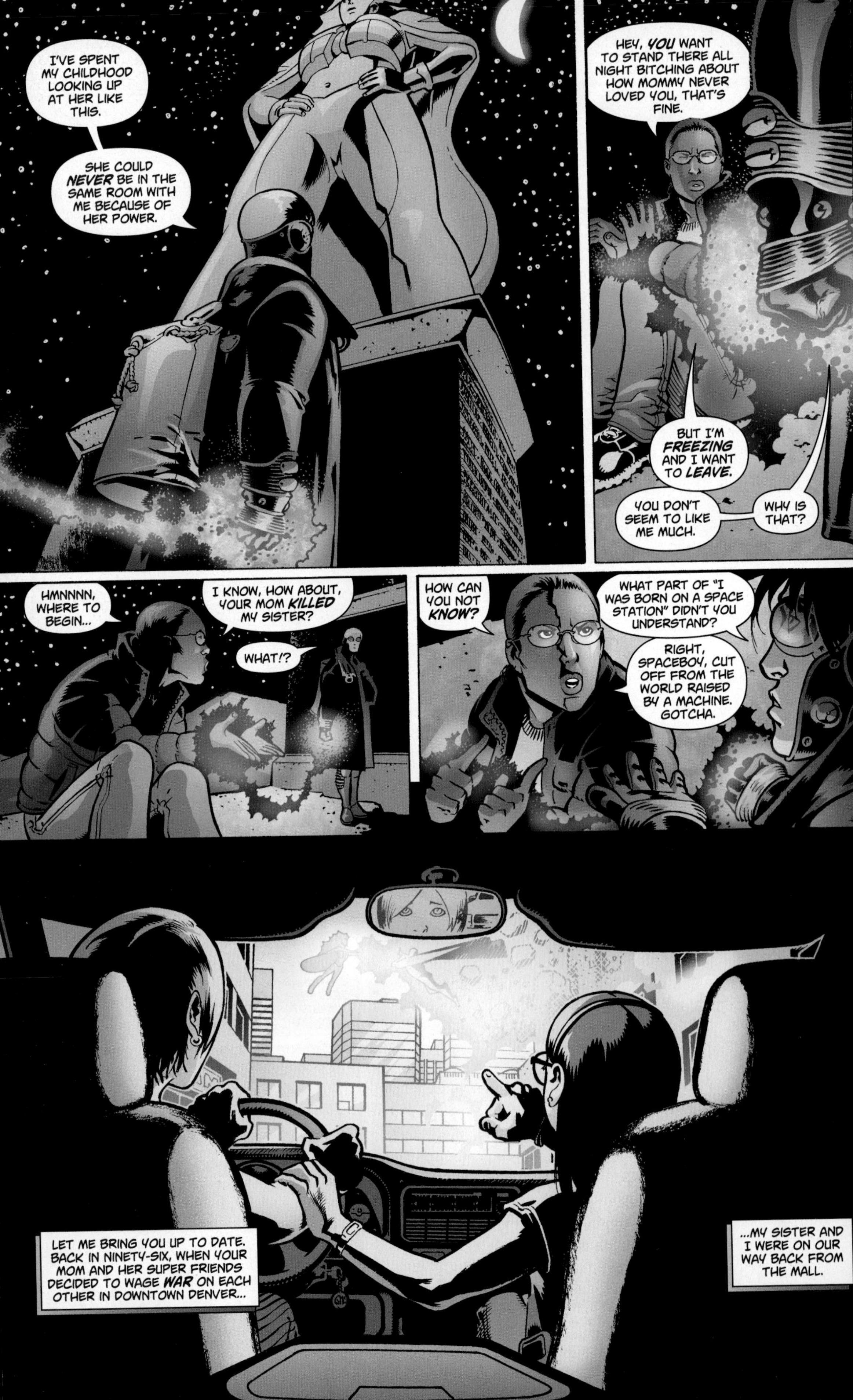

I'VE SPENT MY CHILDHOOD LOOKING UP AT HER LIKE THIS.
SHE COULD NEVER BE IN THE SAME ROOM WITH ME BECAUSE OF HER POWER.
HEY, YOU WANT TO STAND THERE ALL NIGHT BITCHING ABOUT HOW MOMMY NEVER LOVED YOU, THAT'S FINE.
BUT I'M FREEZING AND I WANT TO LEAVE.
YOU DON'T SEEM TO LIKE ME MUCH.
WHY IS THAT?
HMNNNN, WHERE TO BEGIN...
I KNOW, HOW ABOUT, YOUR MOM KILLED MY SISTER?
WHAT!?
HOW CAN YOU NOT KNOW?
WHAT PART OF "I WAS BORN ON A SPACE STATION" DIDN'T YOU UNDERSTAND?
RIGHT, SPACEBOY, CUT OFF FROM THE WORLD RAISED BY A MACHINE. GOTCHA.
LET ME BRING YOU UP TO DATE. BACK IN NINETY-SIX, WHEN YOUR MOM AND HER SUPER FRIENDS DECIDED TO WAGE WAR ON EACH OTHER IN DOWNTOWN DENVER...
...MY SISTER AND I WERE ON OUR WAY BACK FROM THE MALL.

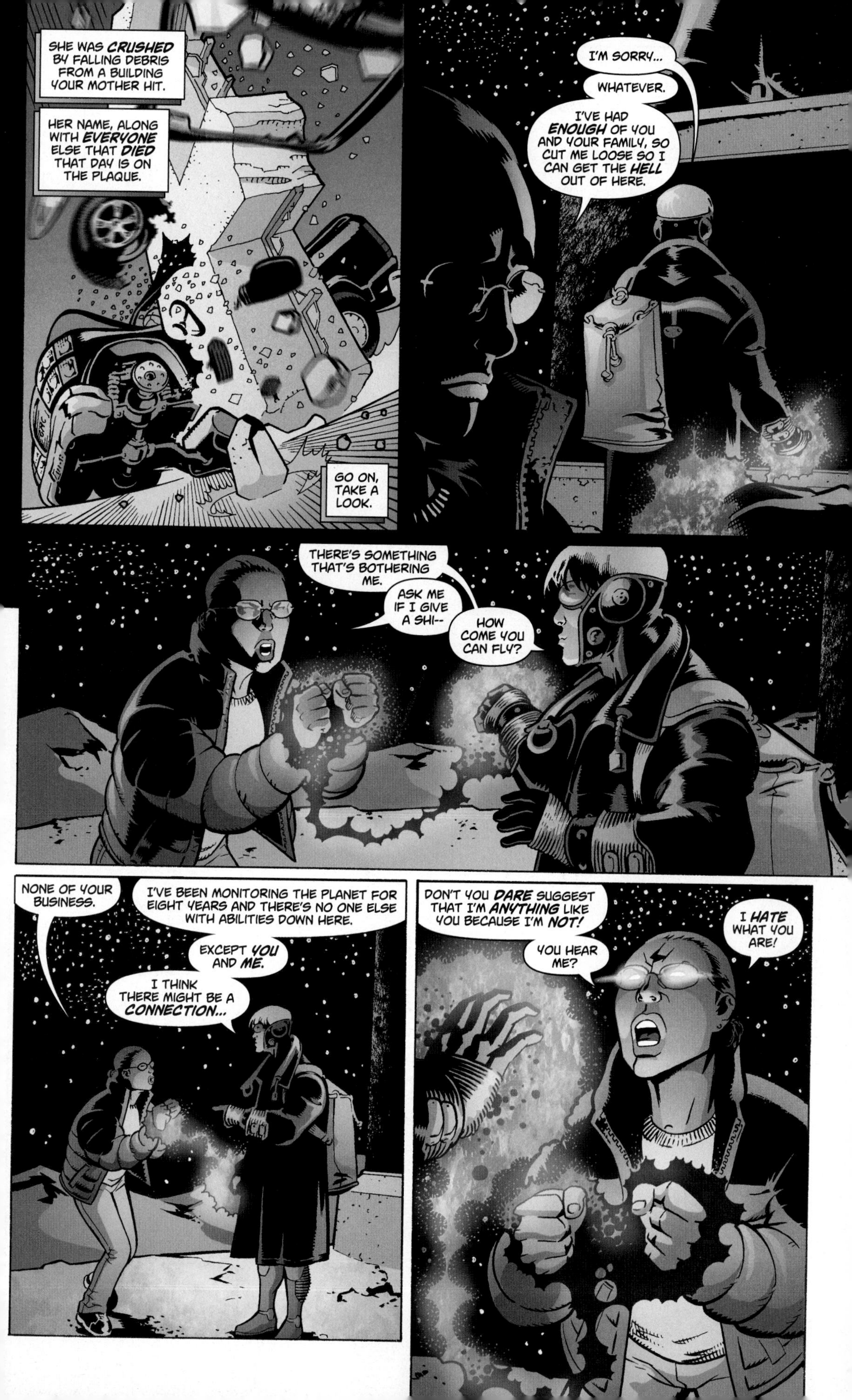
SHE WAS CRUSHED BY FALLING DEBRIS FROM A BUILDING YOUR MOTHER HIT.
HER NAME, ALONG WITH EVERYONE ELSE THAT DIED THAT DAY IS ON THE PLAQUE.
GO ON, TAKE A LOOK.
I'M SORRY...
WHATEVER.
I'VE HAD ENOUGH OF YOU AND YOUR FAMILY, SO CUT ME LOOSE SO I CAN GET THE HELL OUT OF HERE.
THERE'S SOMETHING THAT'S BOTHERING ME.
ASK ME IF I GIVE A SHI--
HOW COME YOU CAN FLY?
NONE OF YOUR BUSINESS.
I'VE BEEN MONITORING THE PLANET FOR EIGHT YEARS AND THERE'S NO ONE ELSE WITH ABILITIES DOWN HERE.
EXCEPT YOU AND ME.
I THINK THERE MIGHT BE A CONNECTION...
DON'T YOU DARE SUGGEST THAT I'M ANYTHING LIKE YOU BECAUSE I'M NOT!
YOU HEAR ME?
I HATE WHAT YOU ARE!

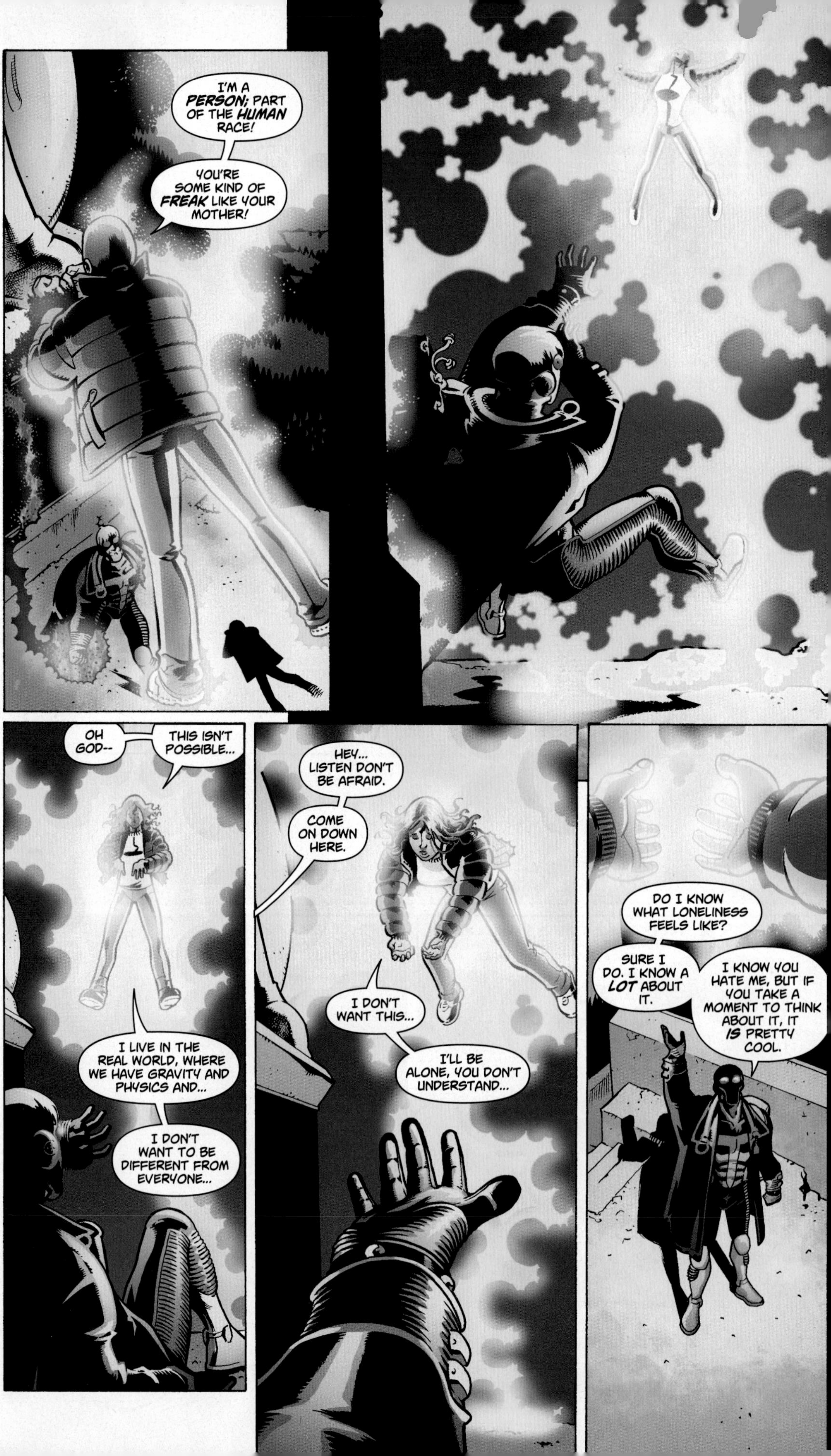
I'M A PERSON; PART OF THE HUMAN RACE!
YOU'RE SOME KIND OF FREAK LIKE YOUR MOTHER!
OH GOD--
THIS ISN'T POSSIBLE...
I LIVE IN THE REAL WORLD, WHERE WE HAVE GRAVITY AND PHYSICS AND...
I DON'T WANT TO BE DIFFERENT FROM EVERYONE...
HEY... LISTEN DON'T BE AFRAID.
COME ON DOWN HERE.
I DON'T WANT THIS...
I'LL BE ALONE, YOU DON'T UNDERSTAND...
DO I KNOW WHAT LONELINESS FEELS LIKE?
SURE I DO. I KNOW A LOT ABOUT IT.
I KNOW YOU HATE ME, BUT IF YOU TAKE A MOMENT TO THINK ABOUT IT, IT IS PRETTY COOL.

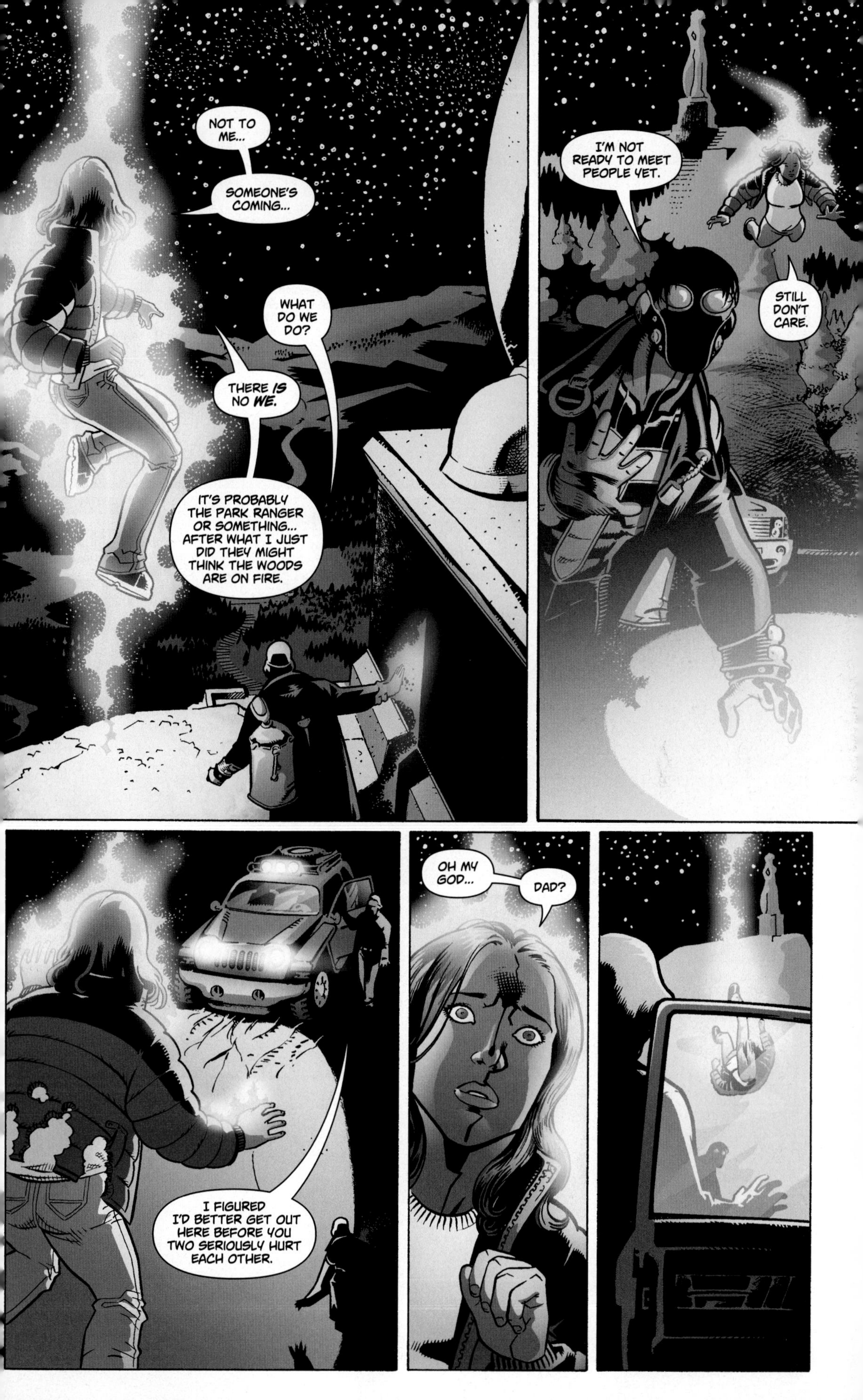

NOT TO ME...
SOMEONE'S COMING...
WHAT DO WE DO?
THERE IS NO WE.
IT'S PROBABLY THE PARK RANGER OR SOMETHING... AFTER WHAT I JUST DID THEY MIGHT THINK THE WOODS ARE ON FIRE.
I'M NOT READY TO MEET PEOPLE YET.
STILL DON'T CARE.
I FIGURED I'D BETTER GET OUT HERE BEFORE YOU TWO SERIOUSLY HURT EACH OTHER.
OH MY GOD...
DAD?

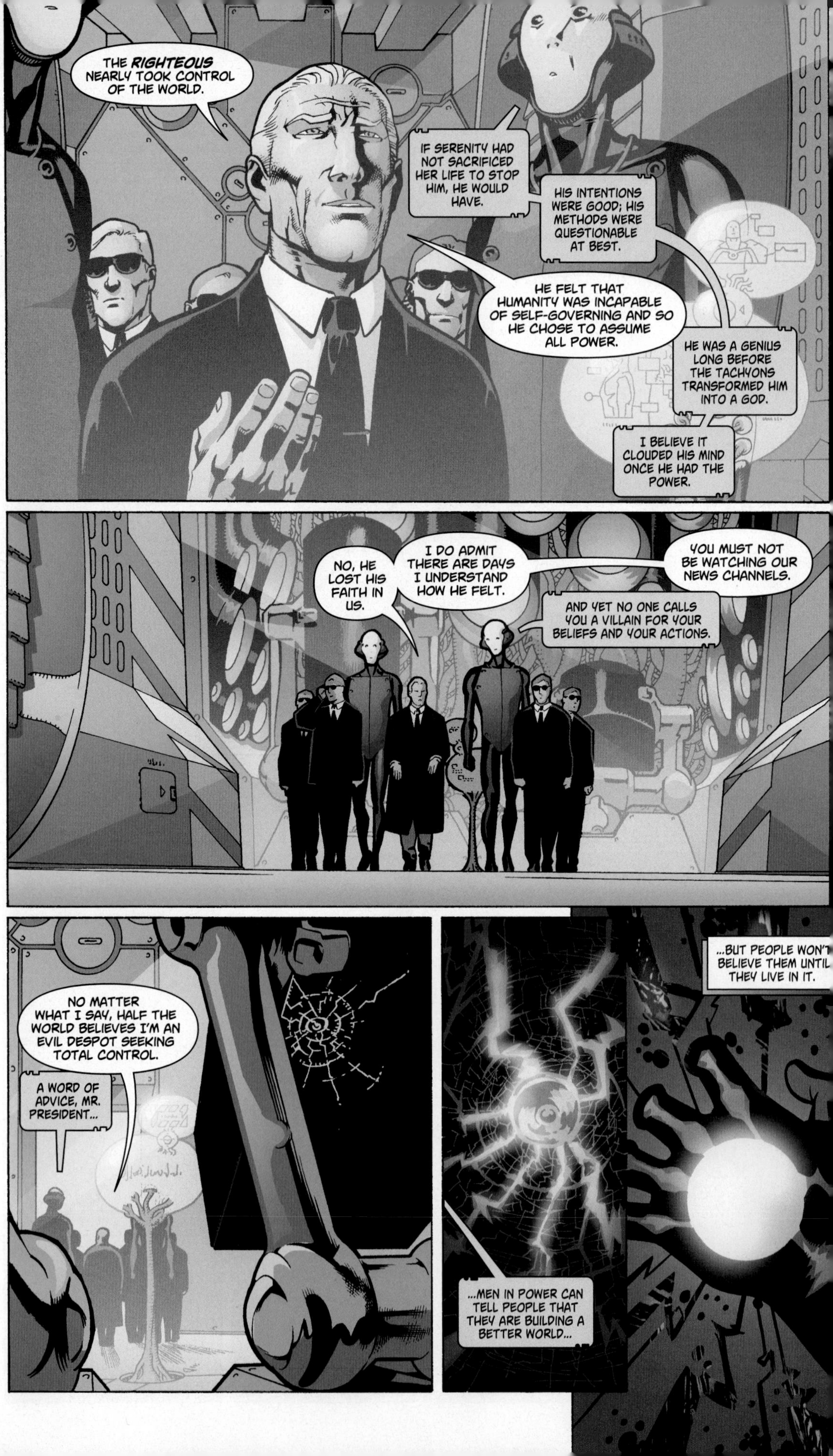
THE RIGHTEOUS NEARLY TOOK CONTROL OF THE WORLD.
IF SERENITY HAD NOT SACRIFICED HER LIFE TO STOP HIM, HE WOULD HAVE.
HIS INTENTIONS WERE GOOD; HIS METHODS WERE QUESTIONABLE AT BEST.
HE FELT THAT HUMANITY WAS INCAPABLE OF SELF-GOVERNING AND SO HE CHOSE TO ASSUME ALL POWER.
HE WAS A GENIUS LONG BEFORE THE TACHYONS TRANSFORMED HIM INTO A GOD.
I BELIEVE IT CLOUDED HIS MIND ONCE HE HAD THE POWER.
NO, HE LOST HIS FAITH IN US.
I DO ADMIT THERE ARE DAYS I UNDERSTAND HOW HE FELT.
YOU MUST NOT BE WATCHING OUR NEWS CHANNELS.
AND YET NO ONE CALLS YOU A VILLAIN FOR YOUR BELIEFS AND YOUR ACTIONS.
NO MATTER WHAT I SAY, HALF THE WORLD BELIEVES I'M AN EVIL DESPOT SEEKING TOTAL CONTROL.
A WORD OF ADVICE, MR. PRESIDENT...
...MEN IN POWER CAN TELL PEOPLE THAT THEY ARE BUILDING A BETTER WORLD...
...BUT PEOPLE WON'T BELIEVE THEM UNTIL THEY LIVE IN IT.

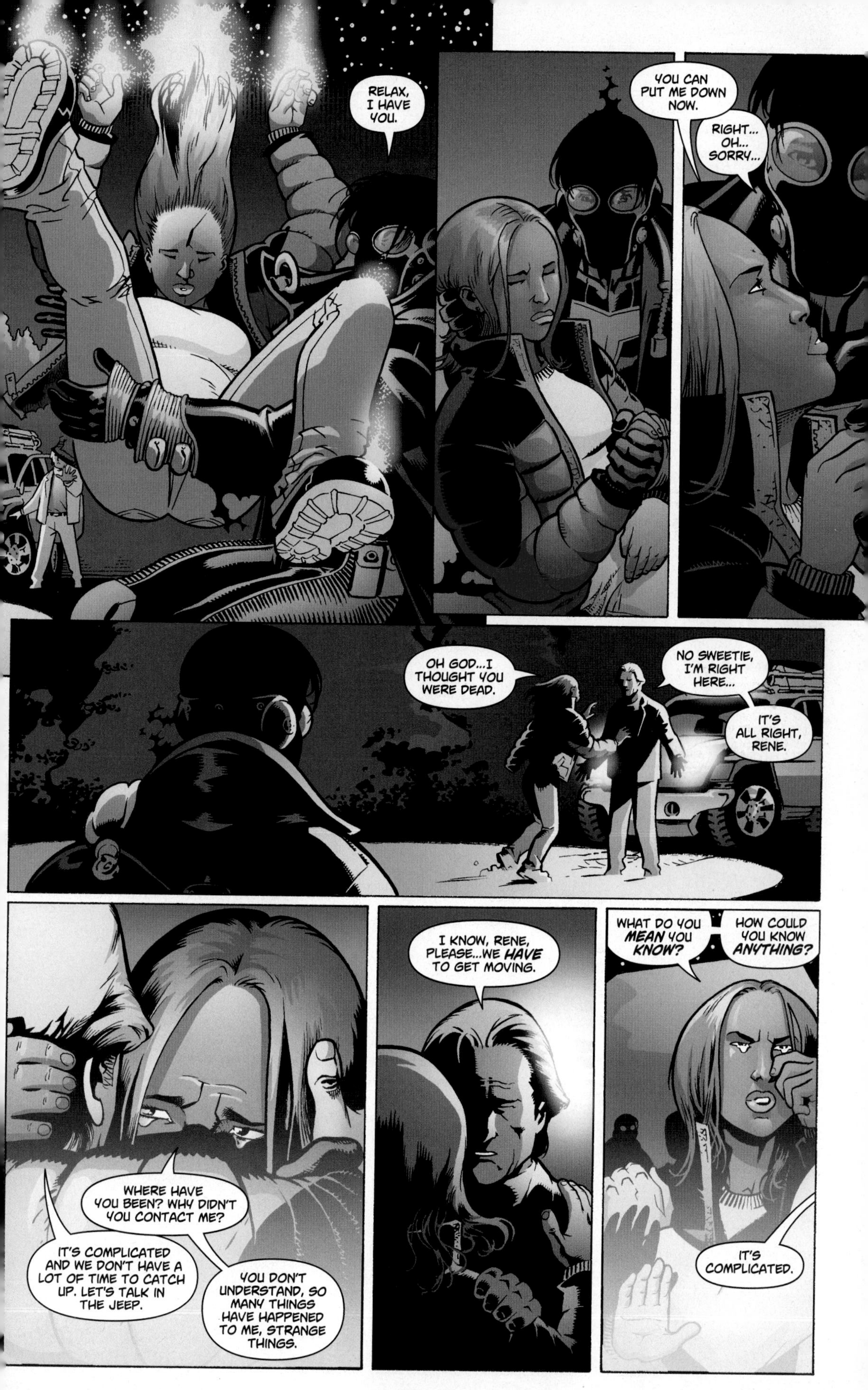
RELAX, I HAVE YOU.
YOU CAN PUT ME DOWN NOW.
RIGHT... OH... SORRY...
OH GOD...I THOUGHT YOU WERE DEAD.
NO SWEETIE, I'M RIGHT HERE...
IT'S ALL RIGHT, RENE.
WHERE HAVE YOU BEEN? WHY DIDN'T YOU CONTACT ME?
IT'S COMPLICATED AND WE DON'T HAVE A LOT OF TIME TO CATCH UP. LET'S TALK IN THE JEEP.
YOU DON'T UNDERSTAND, SO MANY THINGS HAVE HAPPENED TO ME, STRANGE THINGS.
I KNOW, RENE, PLEASE...WE HAVE TO GET MOVING.
WHAT DO YOU MEAN YOU KNOW?
HOW COULD YOU KNOW ANYTHING?
IT'S COMPLICATED.

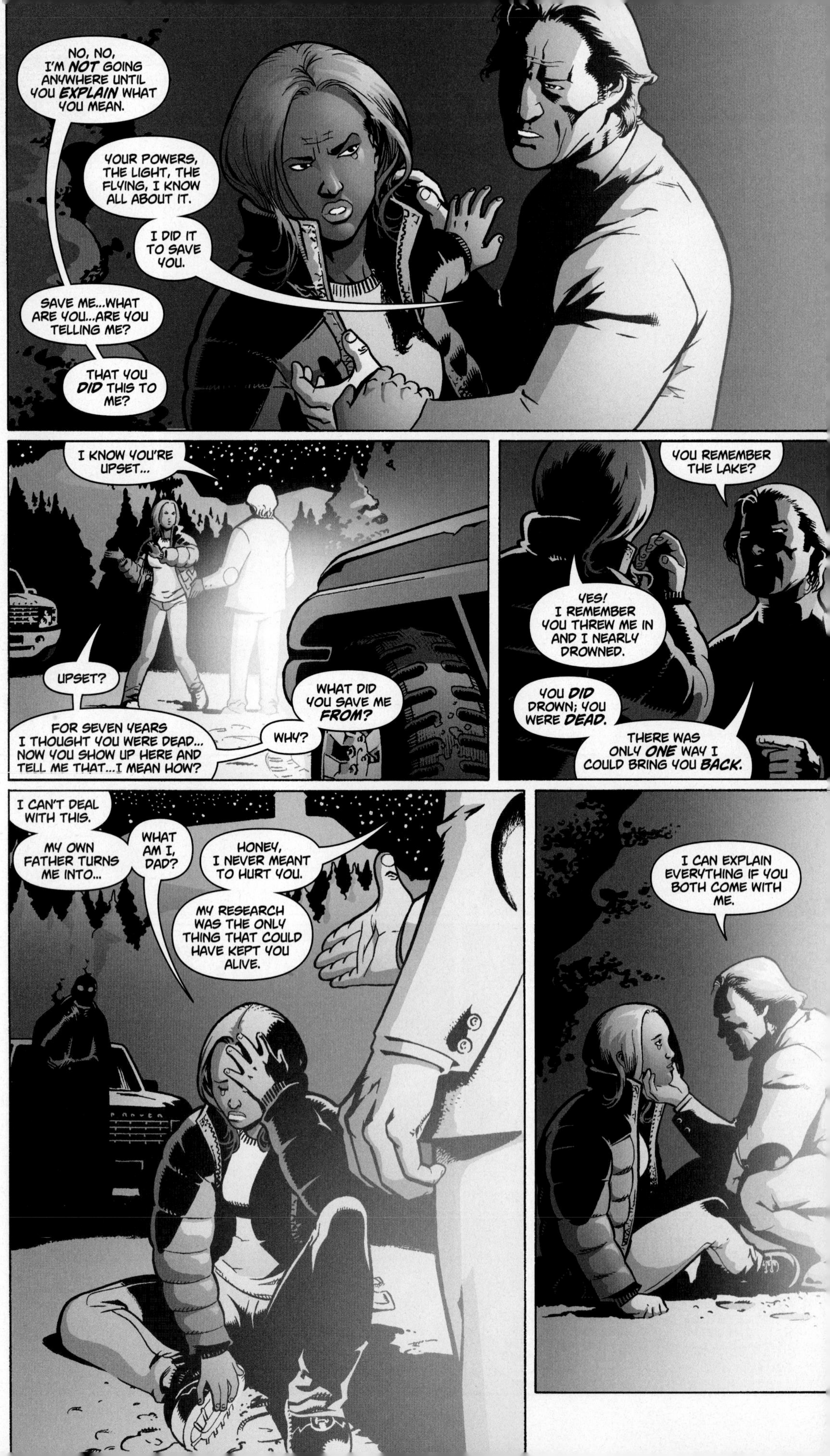
NO, NO, I'M NOT GOING ANYWHERE UNTIL YOU EXPLAIN WHAT YOU MEAN.
YOUR POWERS, THE LIGHT, THE FLYING, I KNOW ALL ABOUT IT.
I DID IT TO SAVE YOU.
SAVE ME...WHAT ARE YOU...ARE YOU TELLING ME?
THAT YOU DID THIS TO ME?
I KNOW YOU'RE UPSET...
UPSET?
FOR SEVEN YEARS I THOUGHT YOU WERE DEAD... NOW YOU SHOW UP HERE AND TELL ME THAT...I MEAN HOW?
WHY?
WHAT DID YOU SAVE ME FROM?
YOU REMEMBER THE LAKE?
YES! I REMEMBER YOU THREW ME IN AND I NEARLY DROWNED.
YOU DID DROWN; YOU WERE DEAD.
THERE WAS ONLY ONE WAY I COULD BRING YOU BACK.
I CAN'T DEAL WITH THIS.
MY OWN FATHER TURNS ME INTO...
WHAT AM I, DAD?
HONEY, I NEVER MEANT TO HURT YOU.
MY RESEARCH WAS THE ONLY THING THAT COULD HAVE KEPT YOU ALIVE.
I CAN EXPLAIN EVERYTHING IF YOU BOTH COME WITH ME.

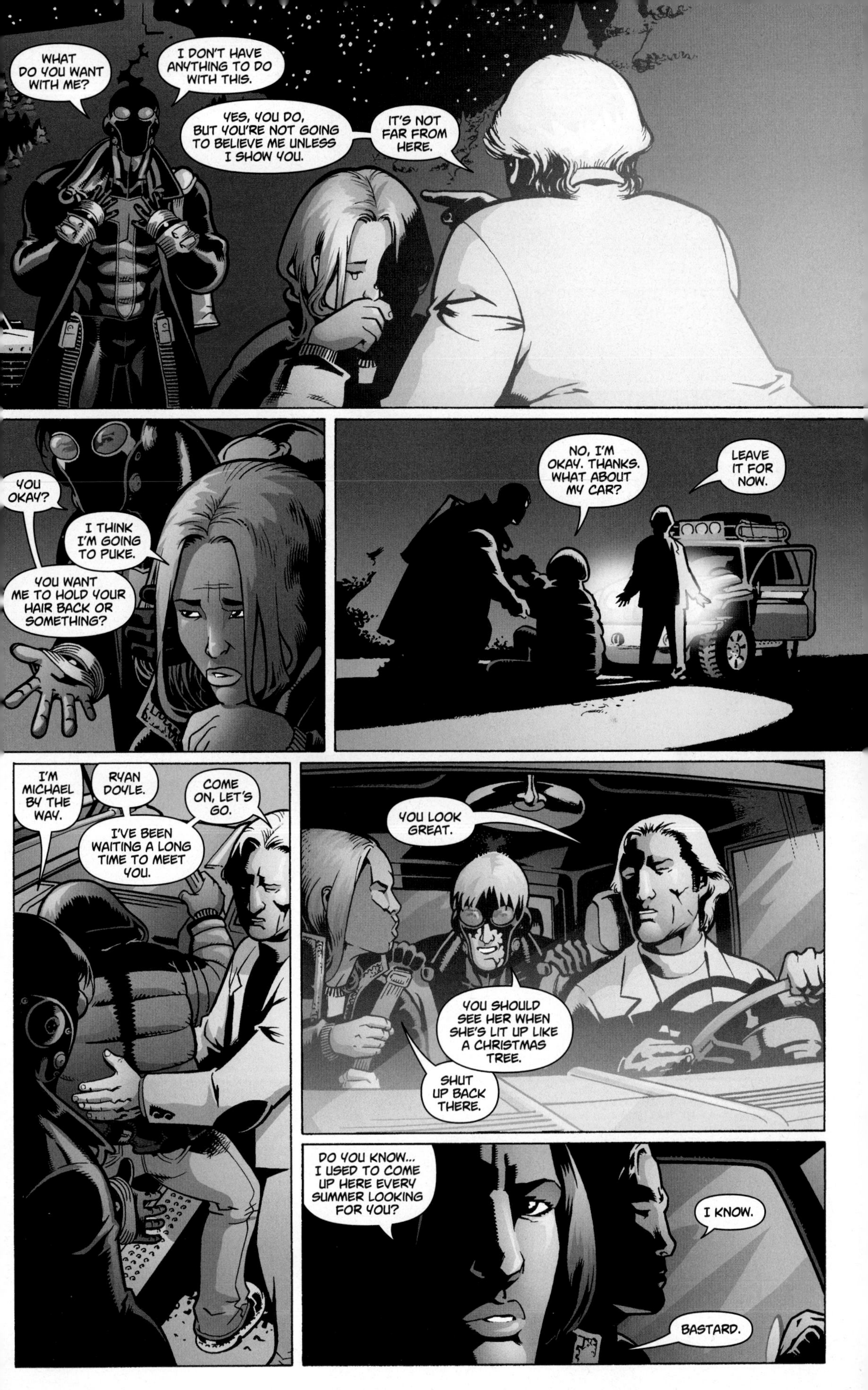
WHAT DO YOU WANT WITH ME?
I DON'T HAVE ANYTHING TO DO WITH THIS.
YES, YOU DO, BUT YOU'RE NOT GOING TO BELIEVE ME UNLESS I SHOW YOU.
IT'S NOT FAR FROM HERE.
YOU OKAY?
I THINK I'M GOING TO PUKE.
YOU WANT ME TO HOLD YOUR HAIR BACK OR SOMETHING?
NO, I'M OKAY. THANKS. WHAT ABOUT MY CAR?
LEAVE IT FOR NOW.
I'M MICHAEL BY THE WAY.
RYAN DOYLE.
I'VE BEEN WAITING A LONG TIME TO MEET YOU.
COME ON, LET'S GO.
YOU LOOK GREAT.
YOU SHOULD SEE HER WHEN SHE'S LIT UP LIKE A CHRISTMAS TREE.
SHUT UP BACK THERE.
DO YOU KNOW... I USED TO COME UP HERE EVERY SUMMER LOOKING FOR YOU?
I KNOW.
BASTARD.

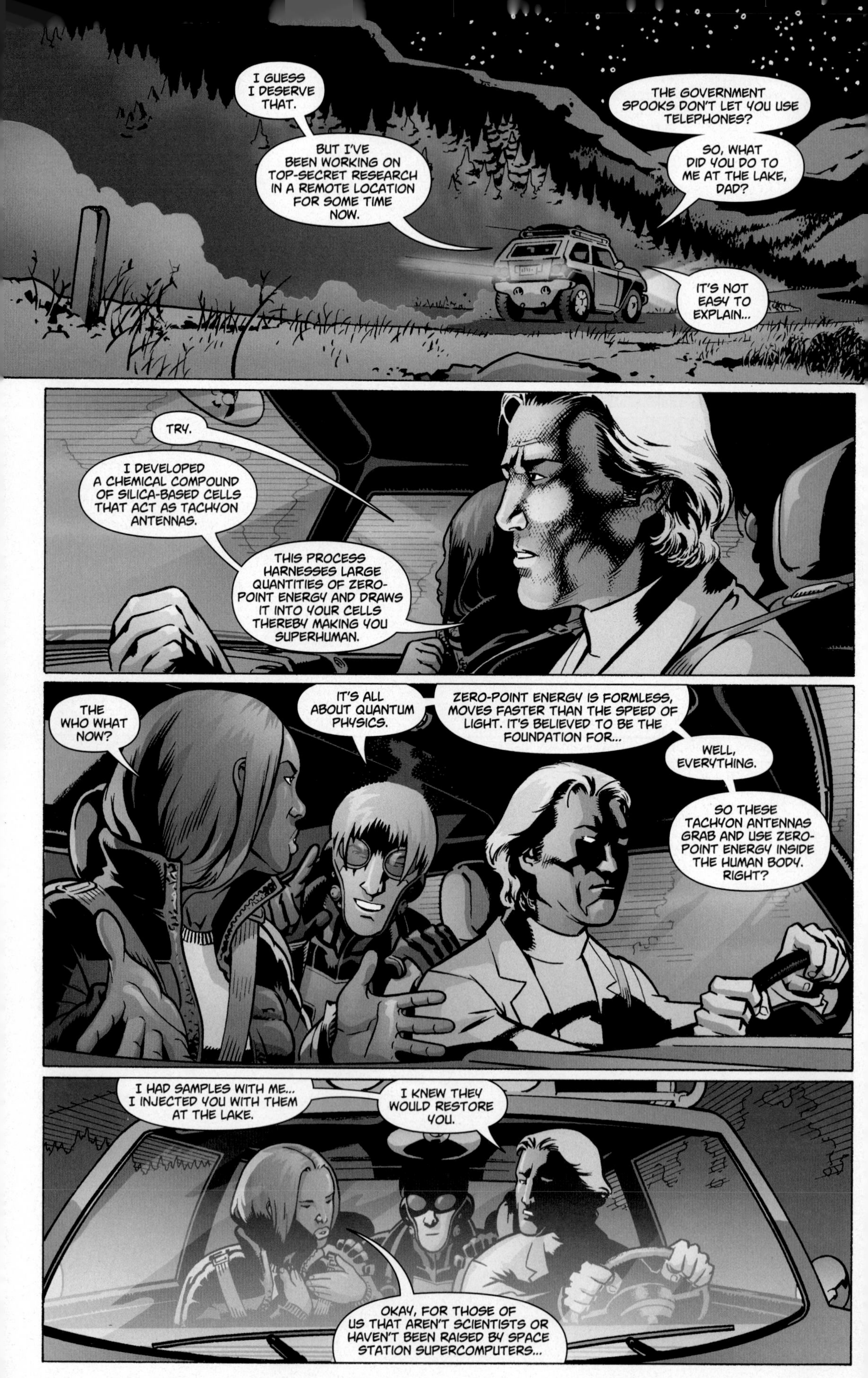
I GUESS I DESERVE THAT.
BUT I'VE BEEN WORKING ON TOP-SECRET RESEARCH IN A REMOTE LOCATION FOR SOME TIME NOW.
THE GOVERNMENT SPOOKS DON'T LET YOU USE TELEPHONES?
SO, WHAT DID YOU DO TO ME AT THE LAKE, DAD?
IT'S NOT EASY TO EXPLAIN...
TRY.
I DEVELOPED A CHEMICAL COMPOUND OF SILICA-BASED CELLS THAT ACT AS TACHYON ANTENNAS.
THIS PROCESS HARNESSES LARGE QUANTITIES OF ZERO-POINT ENERGY AND DRAWS IT INTO YOUR CELLS THEREBY MAKING YOU SUPERHUMAN.
THE WHO WHAT NOW?
IT'S ALL ABOUT QUANTUM PHYSICS.
ZERO-POINT ENERGY IS FORMLESS, MOVES FASTER THAN THE SPEED OF LIGHT. IT'S BELIEVED TO BE THE FOUNDATION FOR...
WELL, EVERYTHING.
SO THESE TACHYON ANTENNAS GRAB AND USE ZERO-POINT ENERGY INSIDE THE HUMAN BODY. RIGHT?
I HAD SAMPLES WITH ME... I INJECTED YOU WITH THEM AT THE LAKE.
I KNEW THEY WOULD RESTORE YOU.
OKAY, FOR THOSE OF US THAT AREN'T SCIENTISTS OR HAVEN'T BEEN RAISED BY SPACE STATION SUPERCOMPUTERS...

THINK OF IT LIKE THIS RADIO PICKING UP A BROADCAST FROM DOWNTOWN DENVER.

ONLY THIS BROADCAST IS *UNIVERSAL QUANTUM ENERGY* IN ITS SIMPLEST FORM AND YOU'RE THE *RECEIVER*.

THE BROADCAST IS *CONSTANT* AND *EVERYWHERE*.

THE ENERGY WORKS THROUGH YOU.

SO YOU'RE SAYING YOU TURNED ME INTO A *RADIO?*

IN A MANNER OF SPEAKING-- YES.

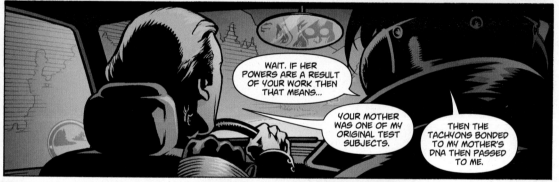

WAIT. IF HER POWERS ARE A RESULT OF YOUR WORK THEN THAT MEANS...

YOUR MOTHER WAS ONE OF MY ORIGINAL TEST SUBJECTS.

THEN THE TACHYONS BONDED TO MY MOTHER'S DNA THEN PASSED TO ME.

TRUE, BUT THEY WOULD HAVE MINGLED WITH YOUR FATHER'S DNA, POSSIBLY CAUSING A MUTATION.

I NEVER KNEW MY FATHER...

WAIT A SECOND, ARE YOU SAYING THAT THIS STUFF YOU PUT INSIDE ME IS THE SAME THING THAT CREATED THE PEOPLE THAT KILLED MONICA?

HOW COULD YOU DO THIS? HOW COULD YOU MAKE ME INTO ONE OF THEM?

AND MY KIDS WILL HAVE THIS CRAP INSIDE THEM TOO?

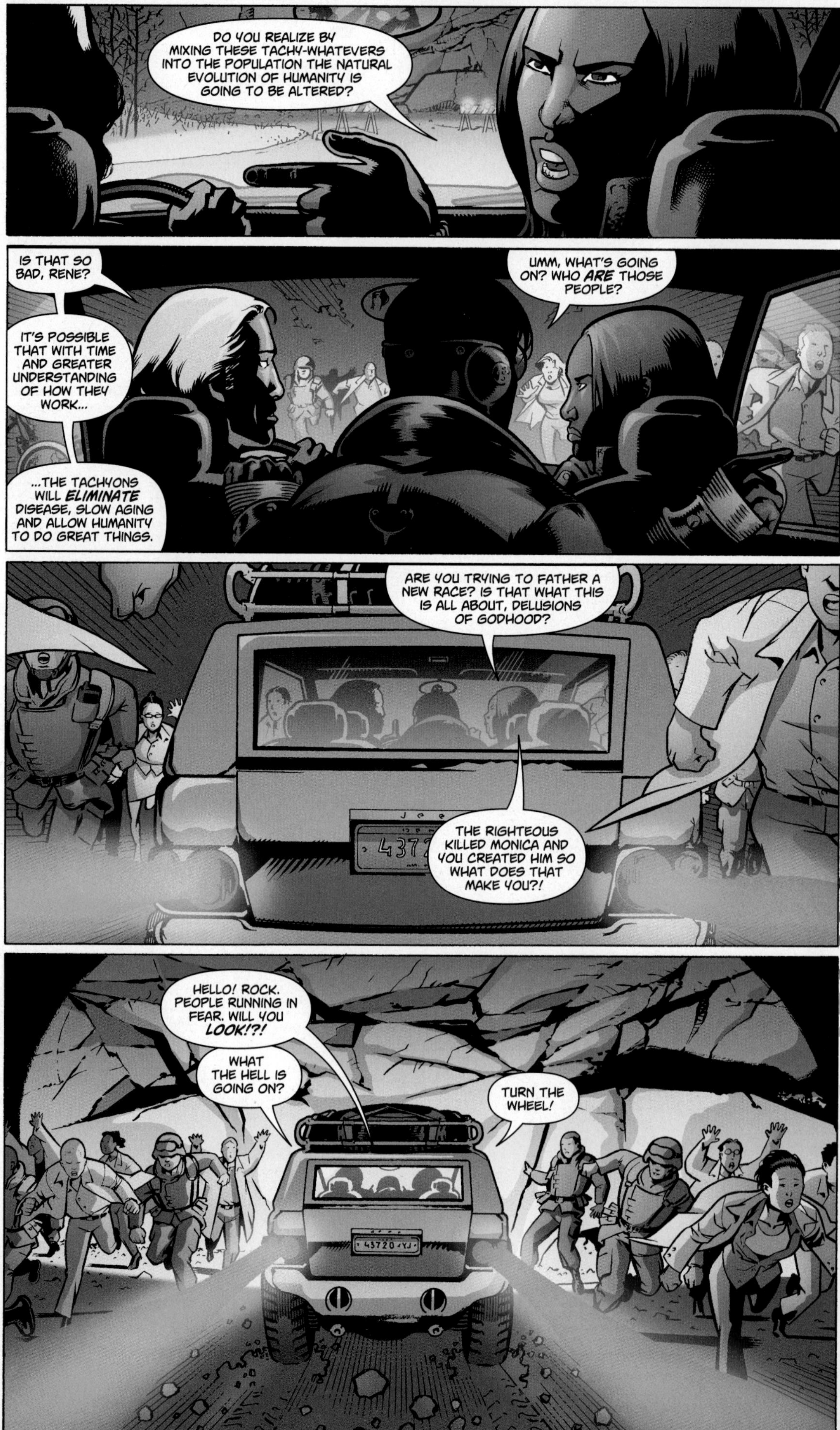
DO YOU REALIZE BY MIXING THESE TACHY-WHATEVERS INTO THE POPULATION THE NATURAL EVOLUTION OF HUMANITY IS GOING TO BE ALTERED?
IS THAT SO BAD, RENE?
IT'S POSSIBLE THAT WITH TIME AND GREATER UNDERSTANDING OF HOW THEY WORK...
...THE TACHYONS WILL **ELIMINATE** DISEASE, SLOW AGING AND ALLOW HUMANITY TO DO GREAT THINGS.
UMM, WHAT'S GOING ON? WHO **ARE** THOSE PEOPLE?
ARE YOU TRYING TO FATHER A NEW RACE? IS THAT WHAT THIS IS ALL ABOUT, DELUSIONS OF GODHOOD?
THE RIGHTEOUS KILLED MONICA AND YOU CREATED HIM SO WHAT DOES THAT MAKE YOU?!
HELLO! ROCK. PEOPLE RUNNING IN FEAR. WILL YOU **LOOK!?!**
WHAT THE HELL IS GOING ON?
TURN THE WHEEL!

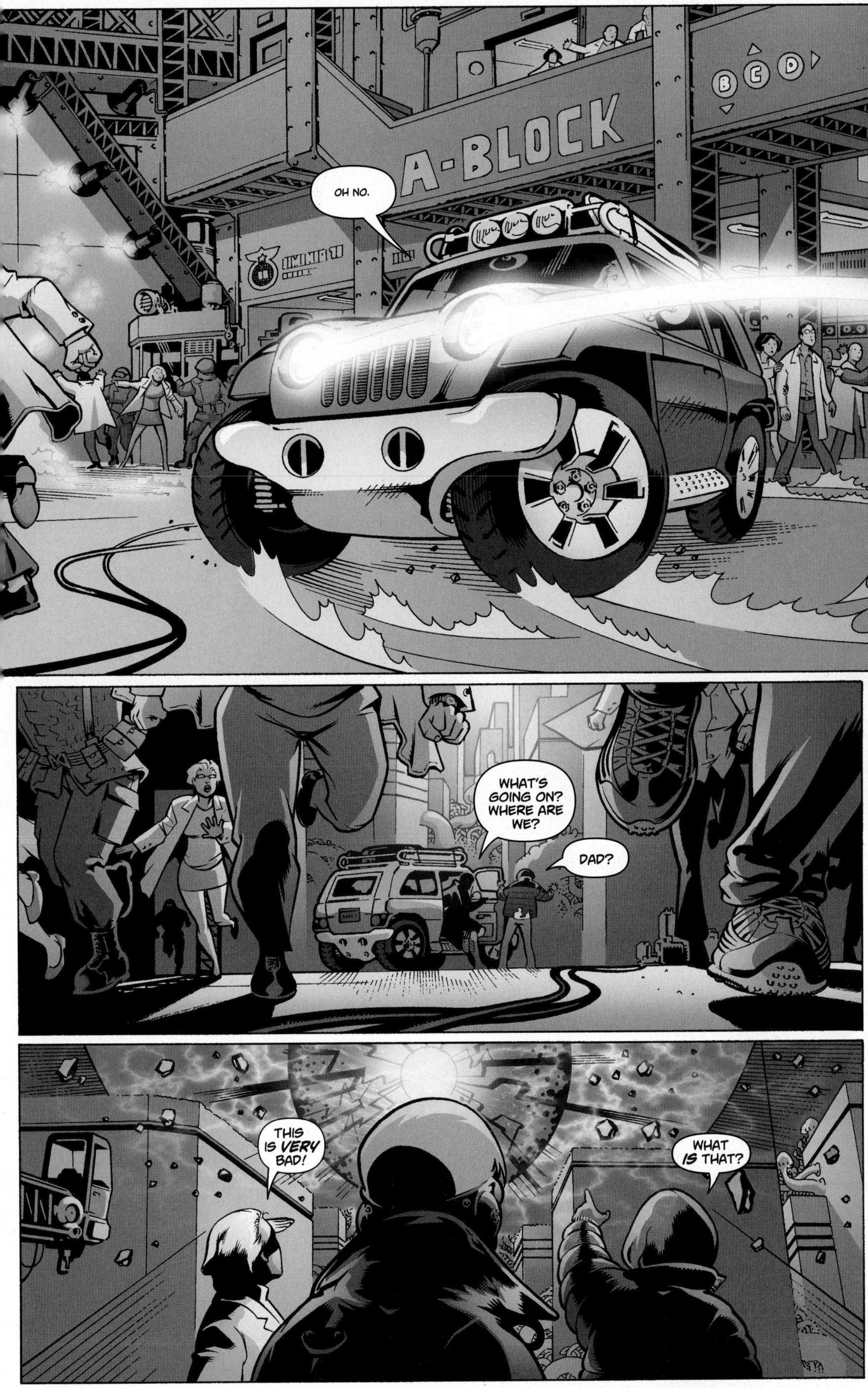
A-BLOCK
B C D
OH NO.
WHAT'S GOING ON? WHERE ARE WE?
DAD?
THIS IS *VERY* BAD!
WHAT *IS* THAT?

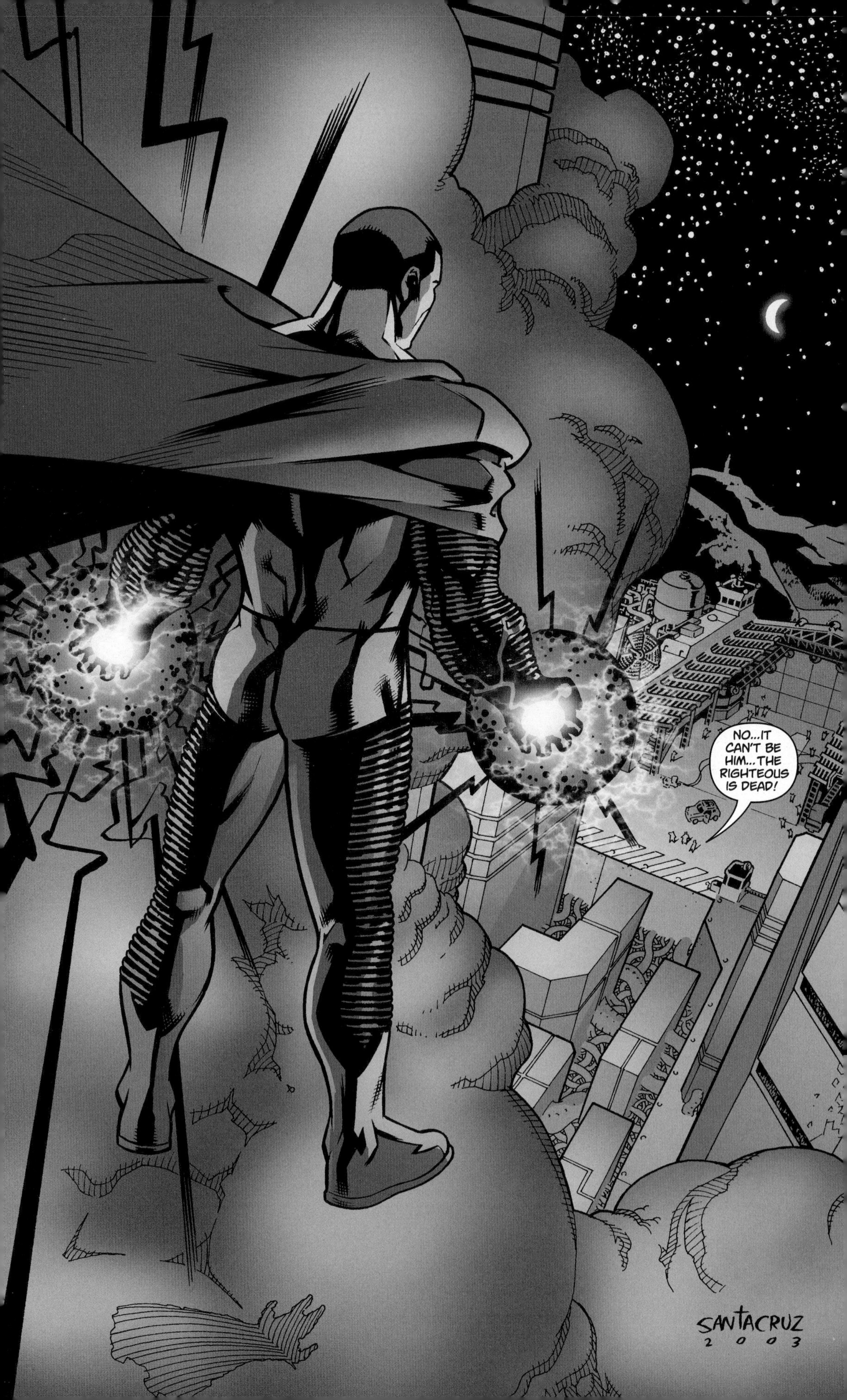
NO...IT CAN'T BE HIM...THE RIGHTEOUS IS DEAD!
SANTACRUZ 2003

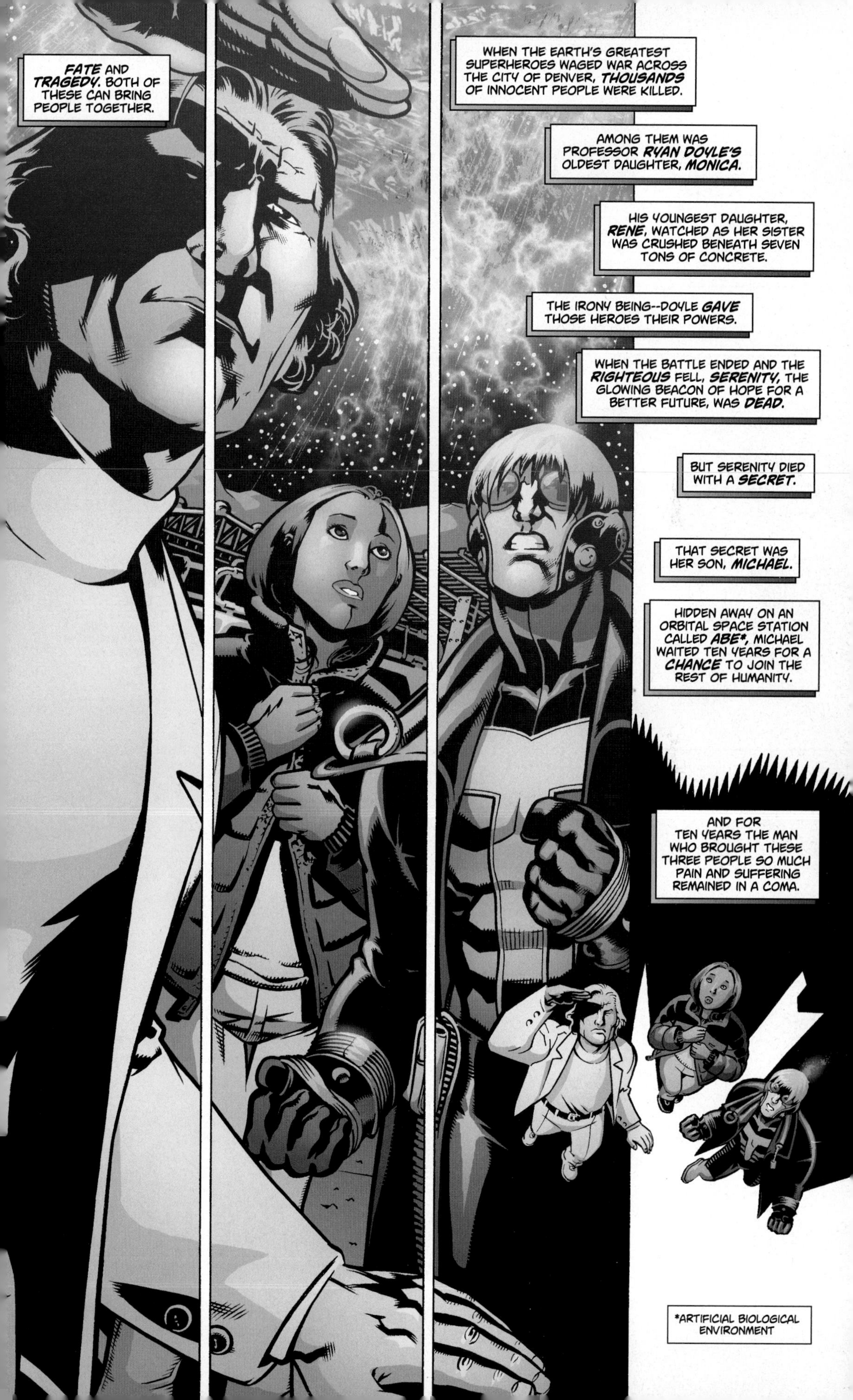
FATE AND TRAGEDY. BOTH OF THESE CAN BRING PEOPLE TOGETHER.
WHEN THE EARTH'S GREATEST SUPERHEROES WAGED WAR ACROSS THE CITY OF DENVER, THOUSANDS OF INNOCENT PEOPLE WERE KILLED.
AMONG THEM WAS PROFESSOR RYAN DOYLE'S OLDEST DAUGHTER, MONICA.
HIS YOUNGEST DAUGHTER, RENE, WATCHED AS HER SISTER WAS CRUSHED BENEATH SEVEN TONS OF CONCRETE.
THE IRONY BEING--DOYLE GAVE THOSE HEROES THEIR POWERS.
WHEN THE BATTLE ENDED AND THE RIGHTEOUS FELL, SERENITY, THE GLOWING BEACON OF HOPE FOR A BETTER FUTURE, WAS DEAD.
BUT SERENITY DIED WITH A SECRET.
THAT SECRET WAS HER SON, MICHAEL.
HIDDEN AWAY ON AN ORBITAL SPACE STATION CALLED ABE*, MICHAEL WAITED TEN YEARS FOR A CHANCE TO JOIN THE REST OF HUMANITY.
AND FOR TEN YEARS THE MAN WHO BROUGHT THESE THREE PEOPLE SO MUCH PAIN AND SUFFERING REMAINED IN A COMA.
*ARTIFICIAL BIOLOGICAL ENVIRONMENT

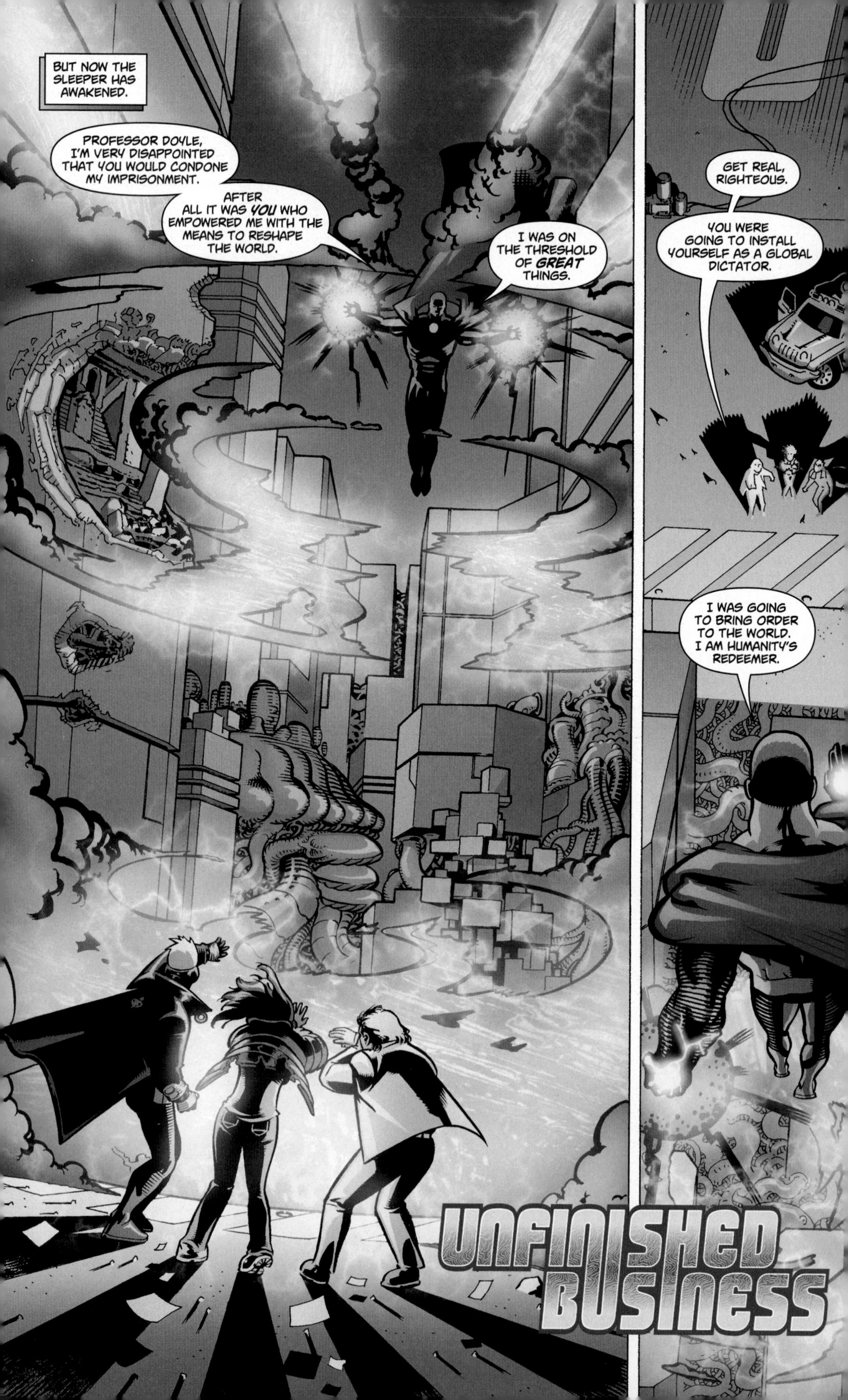
BUT NOW THE SLEEPER HAS AWAKENED.
PROFESSOR DOYLE, I'M VERY DISAPPOINTED THAT YOU WOULD CONDONE MY IMPRISONMENT.
AFTER ALL IT WAS YOU WHO EMPOWERED ME WITH THE MEANS TO RESHAPE THE WORLD.
I WAS ON THE THRESHOLD OF GREAT THINGS.
GET REAL, RIGHTEOUS.
YOU WERE GOING TO INSTALL YOURSELF AS A GLOBAL DICTATOR.
I WAS GOING TO BRING ORDER TO THE WORLD. I AM HUMANITY'S REDEEMER.
UNFINISHED BUSINESS

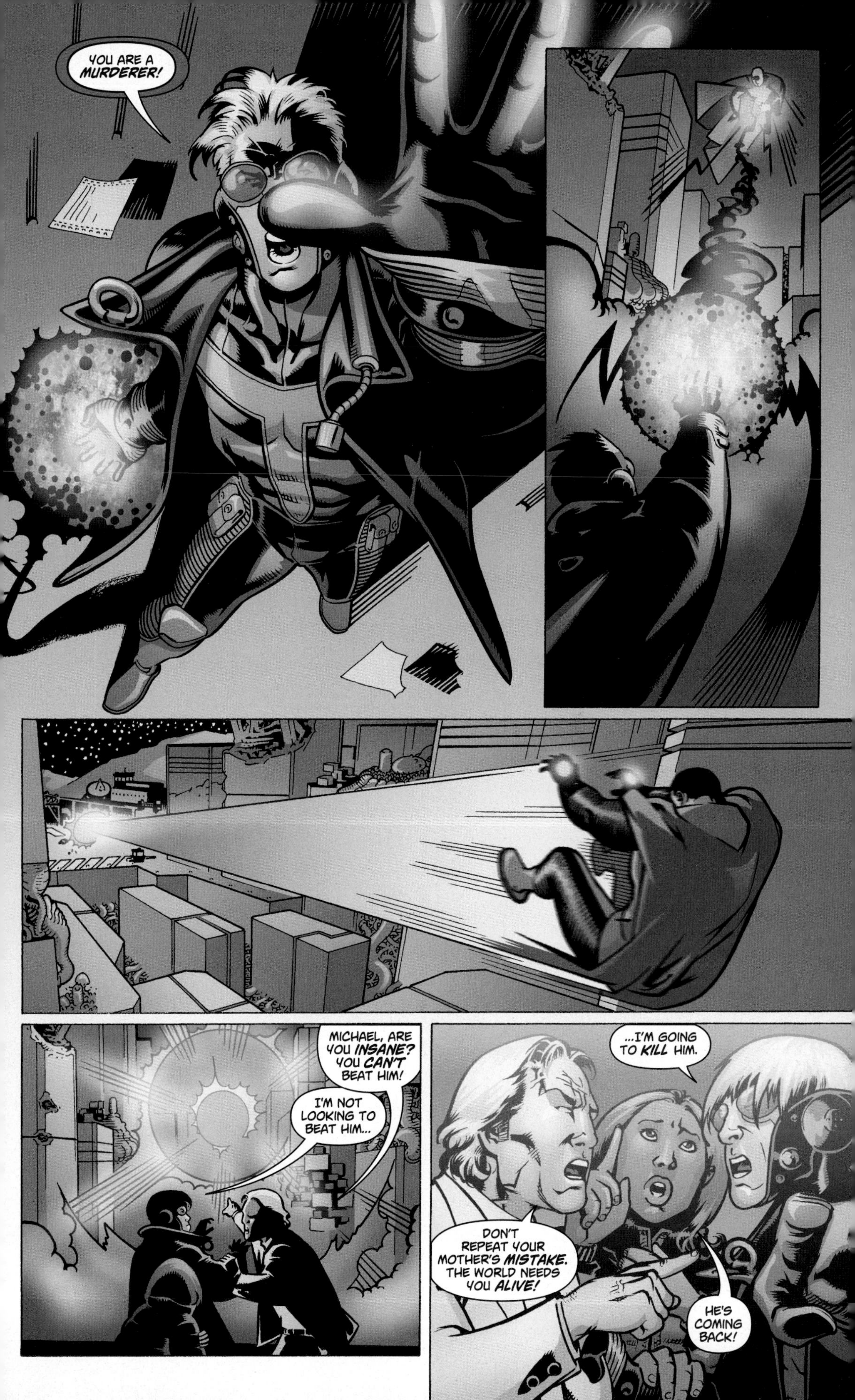
YOU ARE A MURDERER!
MICHAEL, ARE YOU INSANE? YOU CAN'T BEAT HIM!
I'M NOT LOOKING TO BEAT HIM...
...I'M GOING TO KILL HIM.
DON'T REPEAT YOUR MOTHER'S MISTAKE. THE WORLD NEEDS YOU ALIVE!
HE'S COMING BACK!

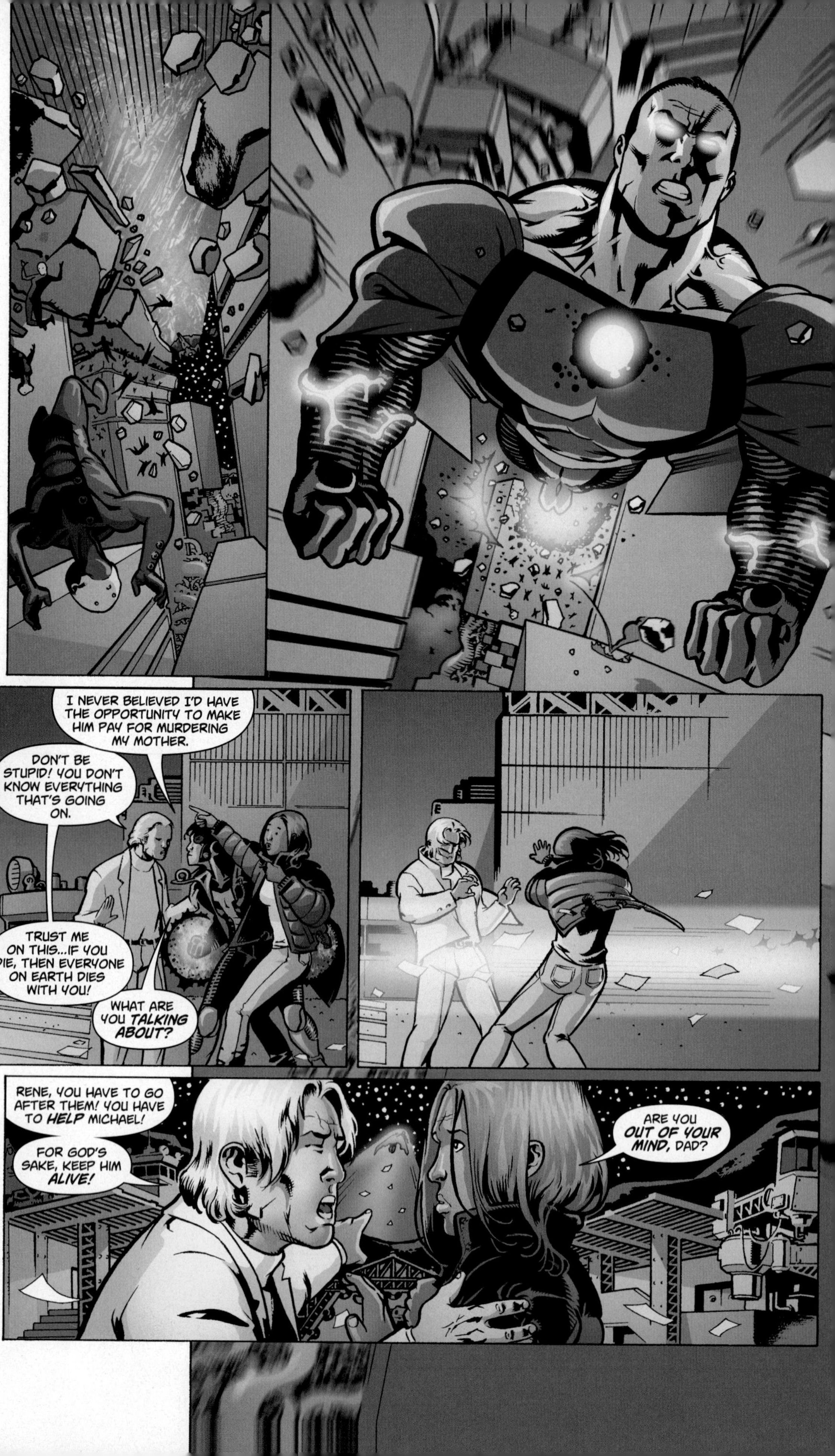

I NEVER BELIEVED I'D HAVE THE OPPORTUNITY TO MAKE HIM PAY FOR MURDERING MY MOTHER.
DON'T BE STUPID! YOU DON'T KNOW EVERYTHING THAT'S GOING ON.
TRUST ME ON THIS...IF YOU DIE, THEN EVERYONE ON EARTH DIES WITH YOU!
WHAT ARE YOU TALKING ABOUT?
RENE, YOU HAVE TO GO AFTER THEM! YOU HAVE TO HELP MICHAEL!
FOR GOD'S SAKE, KEEP HIM ALIVE!
ARE YOU OUT OF YOUR MIND, DAD?

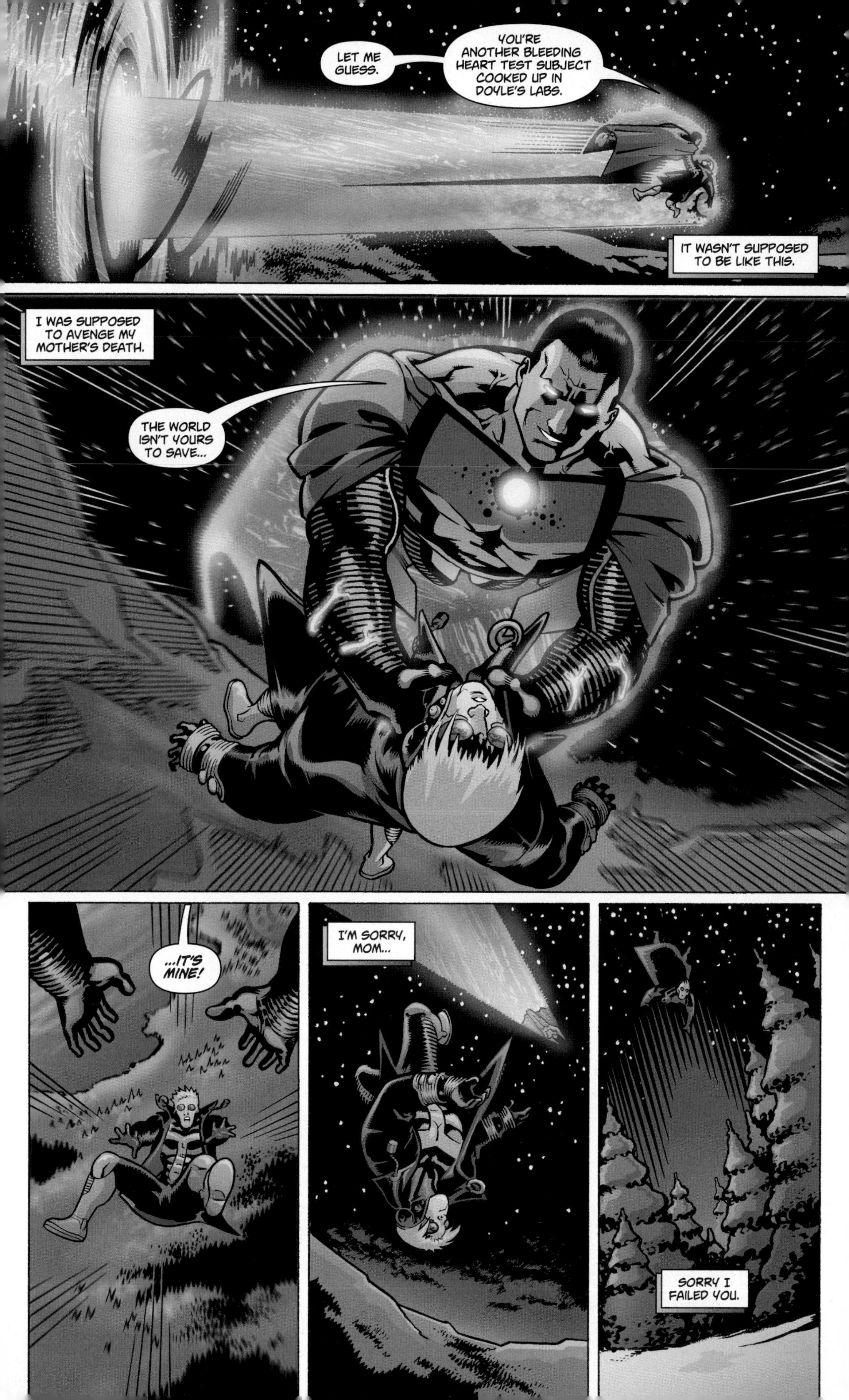
LET ME GUESS.
YOU'RE ANOTHER BLEEDING HEART TEST SUBJECT COOKED UP IN DOYLE'S LABS.
IT WASN'T SUPPOSED TO BE LIKE THIS.
I WAS SUPPOSED TO AVENGE MY MOTHER'S DEATH.
THE WORLD ISN'T YOURS TO SAVE...
...IT'S MINE!
I'M SORRY, MOM...
SORRY I FAILED YOU.

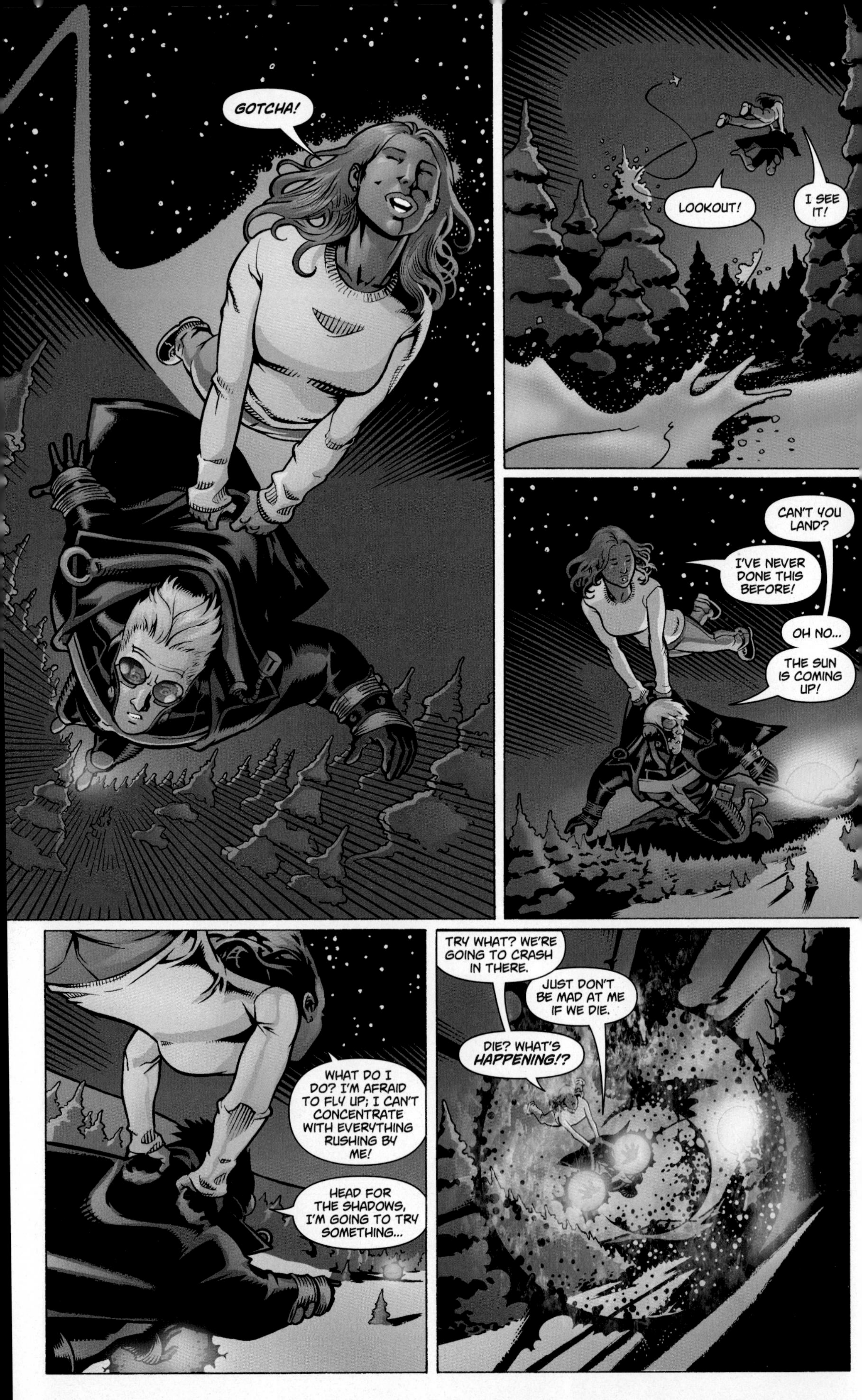
GOTCHA!
LOOKOUT!
I SEE IT!
CAN'T YOU LAND?
I'VE NEVER DONE THIS BEFORE!
OH NO...
THE SUN IS COMING UP!
WHAT DO I DO? I'M AFRAID TO FLY UP; I CAN'T CONCENTRATE WITH EVERYTHING RUSHING BY ME!
HEAD FOR THE SHADOWS, I'M GOING TO TRY SOMETHING...
TRY WHAT? WE'RE GOING TO CRASH IN THERE.
JUST DON'T BE MAD AT ME IF WE DIE.
DIE? WHAT'S HAPPENING!?

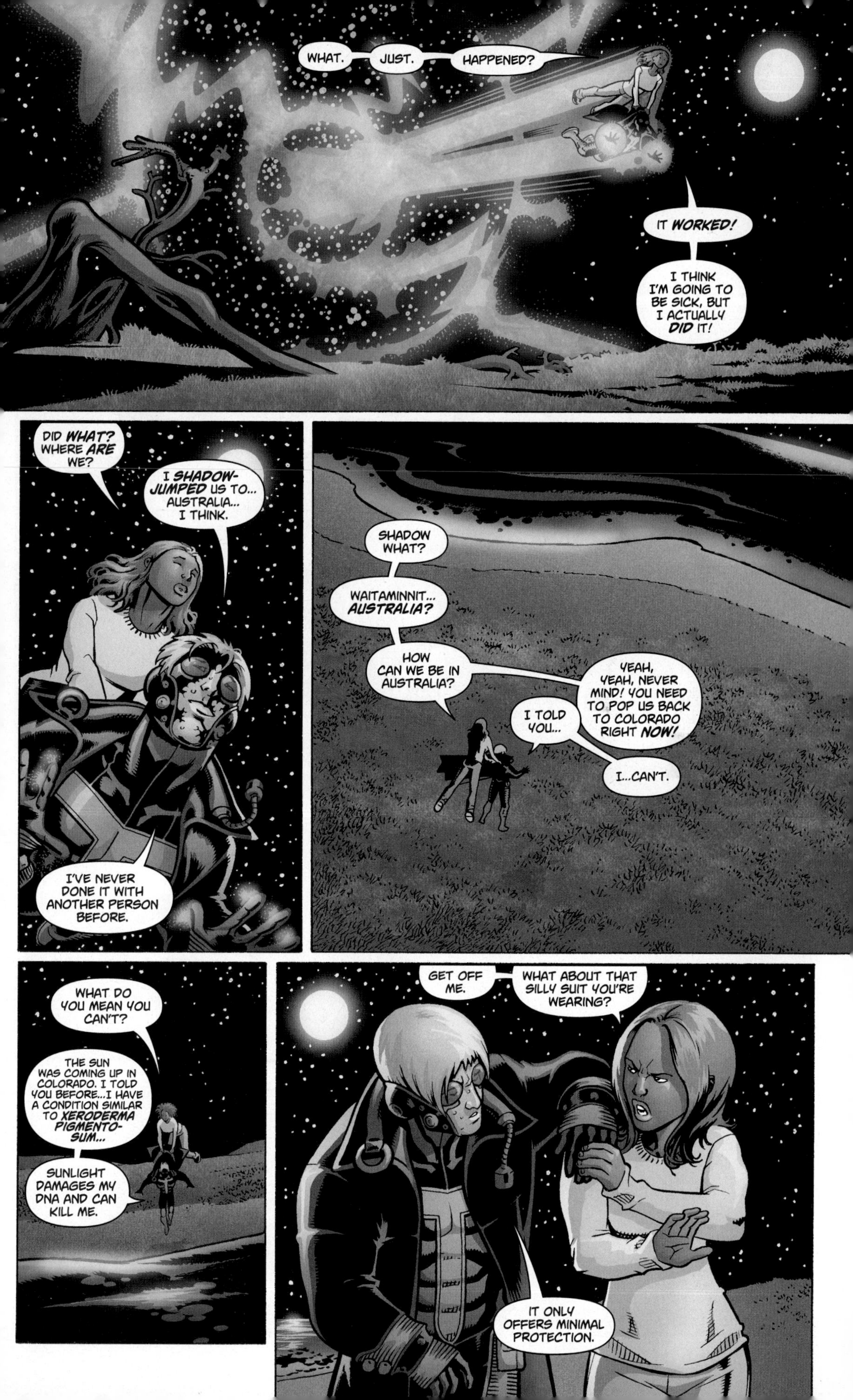
WHAT. JUST. HAPPENED?
IT WORKED!
I THINK I'M GOING TO BE SICK, BUT I ACTUALLY DID IT!
DID WHAT? WHERE ARE WE?
I SHADOW-JUMPED US TO... AUSTRALIA... I THINK.
I'VE NEVER DONE IT WITH ANOTHER PERSON BEFORE.
SHADOW WHAT?
WAITAMINNIT... AUSTRALIA?
HOW CAN WE BE IN AUSTRALIA?
I TOLD YOU...
YEAH, YEAH, NEVER MIND! YOU NEED TO POP US BACK TO COLORADO RIGHT NOW!
I...CAN'T.
WHAT DO YOU MEAN YOU CAN'T?
THE SUN WAS COMING UP IN COLORADO. I TOLD YOU BEFORE...I HAVE A CONDITION SIMILAR TO XERODERMA PIGMENTOSUM...
SUNLIGHT DAMAGES MY DNA AND CAN KILL ME.
GET OFF ME.
WHAT ABOUT THAT SILLY SUIT YOU'RE WEARING?
IT ONLY OFFERS MINIMAL PROTECTION.

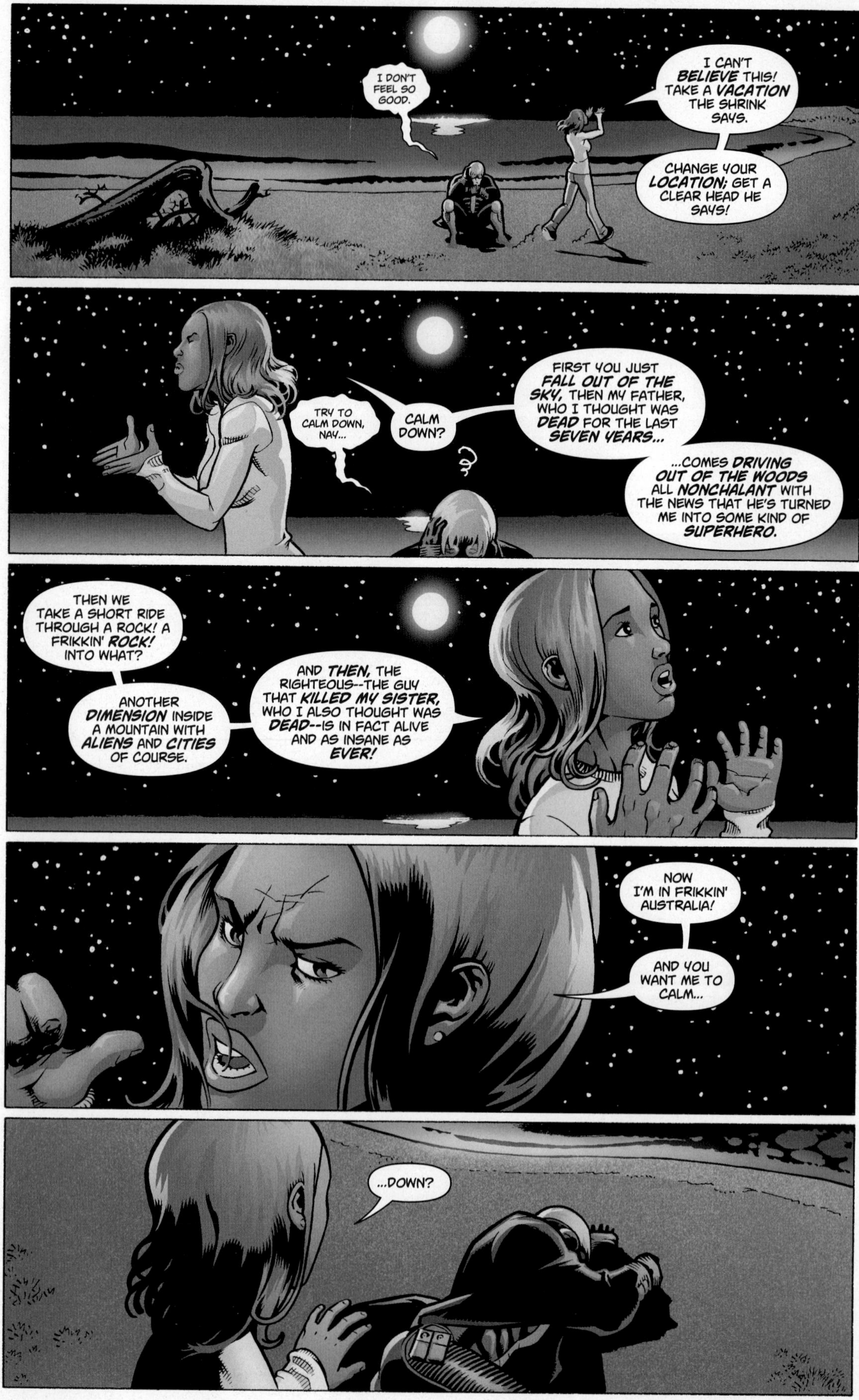
I DON'T FEEL SO GOOD.
I CAN'T BELIEVE THIS! TAKE A VACATION THE SHRINK SAYS.
CHANGE YOUR LOCATION; GET A CLEAR HEAD HE SAYS!
TRY TO CALM DOWN, NAY...
CALM DOWN?
FIRST YOU JUST FALL OUT OF THE SKY, THEN MY FATHER, WHO I THOUGHT WAS DEAD FOR THE LAST SEVEN YEARS...
...COMES DRIVING OUT OF THE WOODS ALL NONCHALANT WITH THE NEWS THAT HE'S TURNED ME INTO SOME KIND OF SUPERHERO.
THEN WE TAKE A SHORT RIDE THROUGH A ROCK! A FRIKKIN' ROCK! INTO WHAT?
ANOTHER DIMENSION INSIDE A MOUNTAIN WITH ALIENS AND CITIES OF COURSE.
AND THEN, THE RIGHTEOUS--THE GUY THAT KILLED MY SISTER, WHO I ALSO THOUGHT WAS DEAD--IS IN FACT ALIVE AND AS INSANE AS EVER!
NOW I'M IN FRIKKIN' AUSTRALIA!
AND YOU WANT ME TO CALM...
...DOWN?

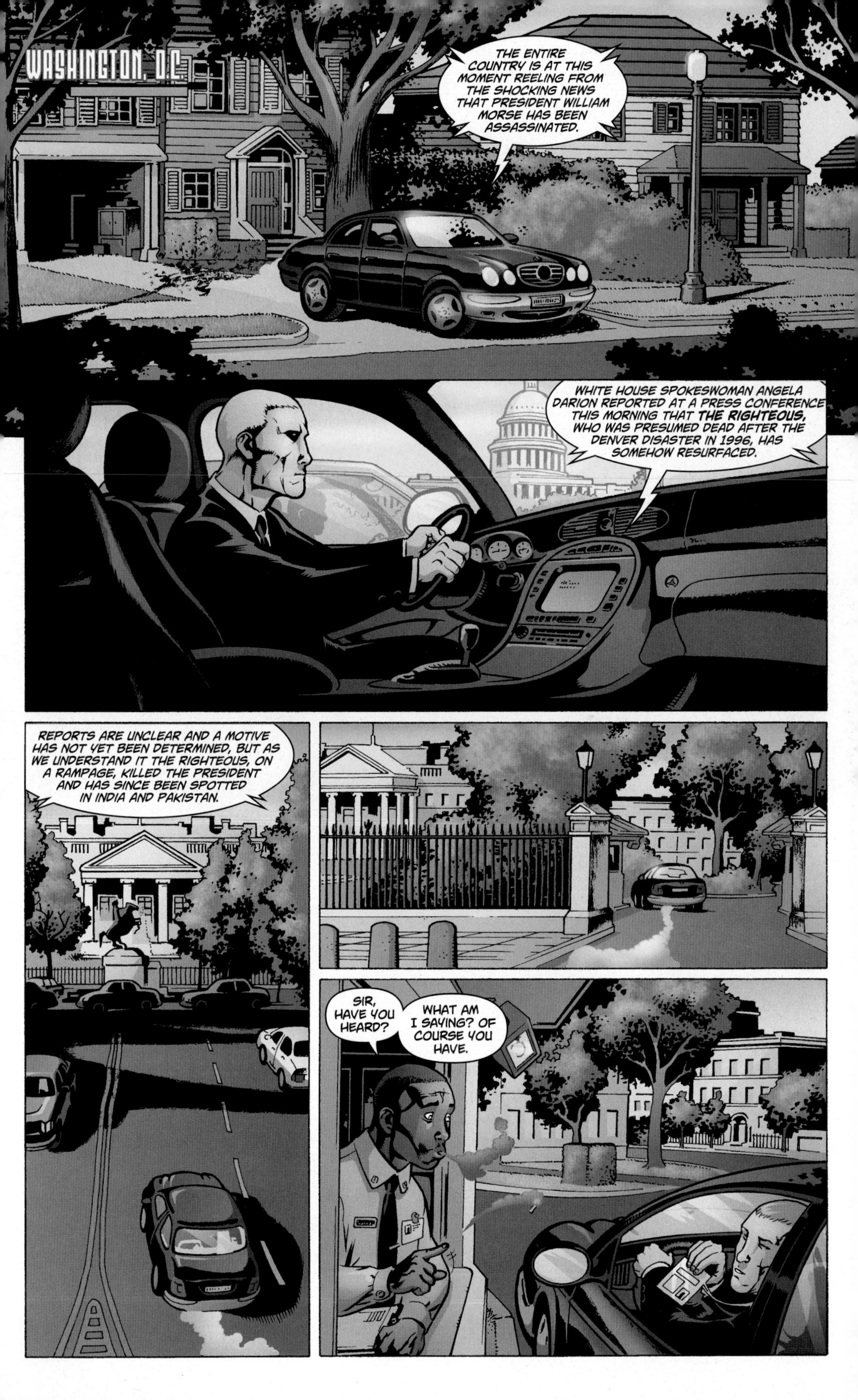
WASHINGTON, D.C.
THE ENTIRE COUNTRY IS AT THIS MOMENT REELING FROM THE SHOCKING NEWS THAT PRESIDENT WILLIAM MORSE HAS BEEN ASSASSINATED.
WHITE HOUSE SPOKESWOMAN ANGELA DARION REPORTED AT A PRESS CONFERENCE THIS MORNING THAT THE RIGHTEOUS, WHO WAS PRESUMED DEAD AFTER THE DENVER DISASTER IN 1996, HAS SOMEHOW RESURFACED.
REPORTS ARE UNCLEAR AND A MOTIVE HAS NOT YET BEEN DETERMINED, BUT AS WE UNDERSTAND IT THE RIGHTEOUS, ON A RAMPAGE, KILLED THE PRESIDENT AND HAS SINCE BEEN SPOTTED IN INDIA AND PAKISTAN.
SIR, HAVE YOU HEARD?
WHAT AM I SAYING? OF COURSE YOU HAVE.

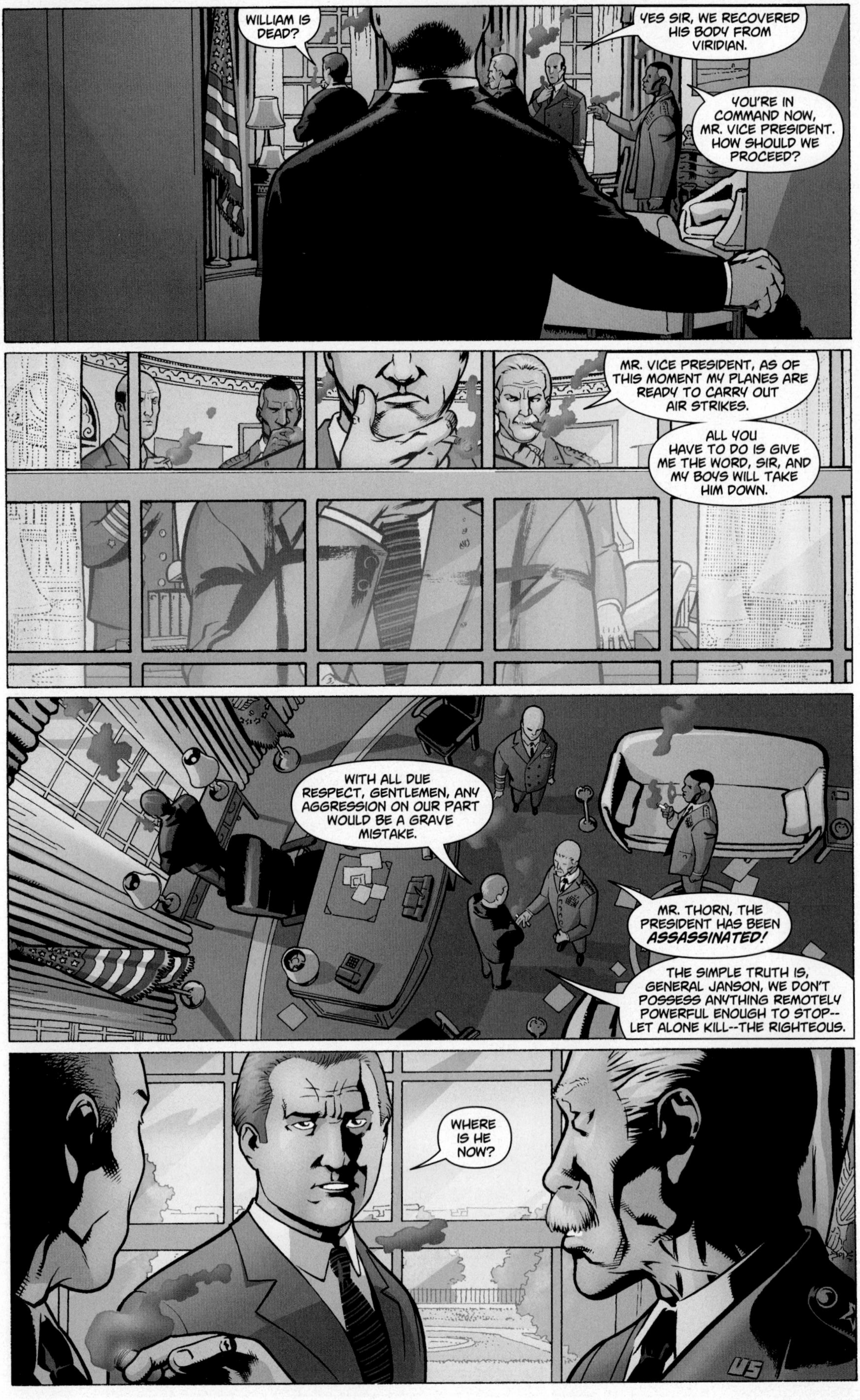
WILLIAM IS DEAD?
YES SIR, WE RECOVERED HIS BODY FROM VIRIDIAN.
YOU'RE IN COMMAND NOW, MR. VICE PRESIDENT. HOW SHOULD WE PROCEED?
MR. VICE PRESIDENT, AS OF THIS MOMENT MY PLANES ARE READY TO CARRY OUT AIR STRIKES.
ALL YOU HAVE TO DO IS GIVE ME THE WORD, SIR, AND MY BOYS WILL TAKE HIM DOWN.
WITH ALL DUE RESPECT, GENTLEMEN, ANY AGGRESSION ON OUR PART WOULD BE A GRAVE MISTAKE.
MR. THORN, THE PRESIDENT HAS BEEN ASSASSINATED!
THE SIMPLE TRUTH IS, GENERAL JANSON, WE DON'T POSSESS ANYTHING REMOTELY POWERFUL ENOUGH TO STOP-- LET ALONE KILL--THE RIGHTEOUS.
WHERE IS HE NOW?

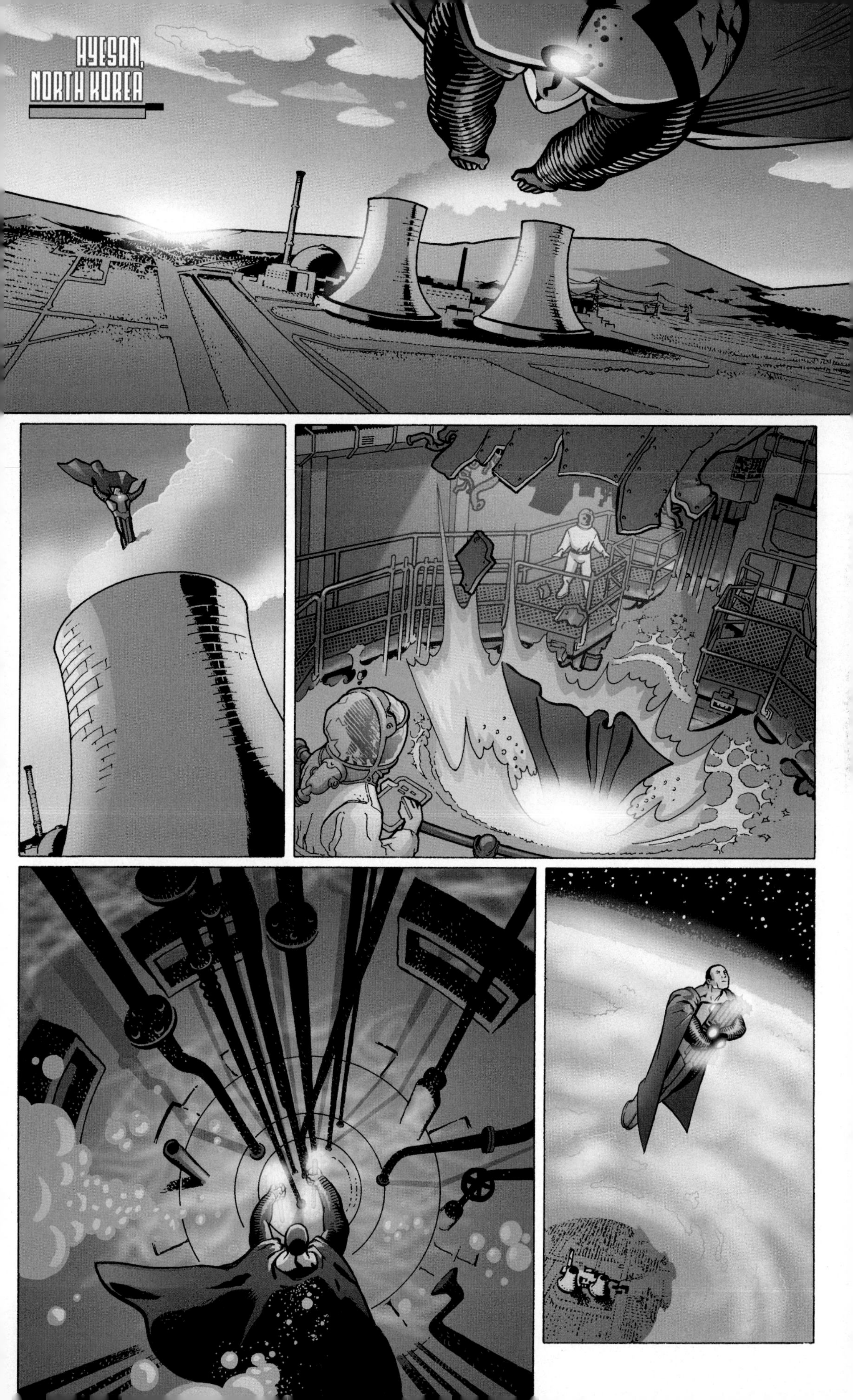
HYESAN, NORTH KOREA

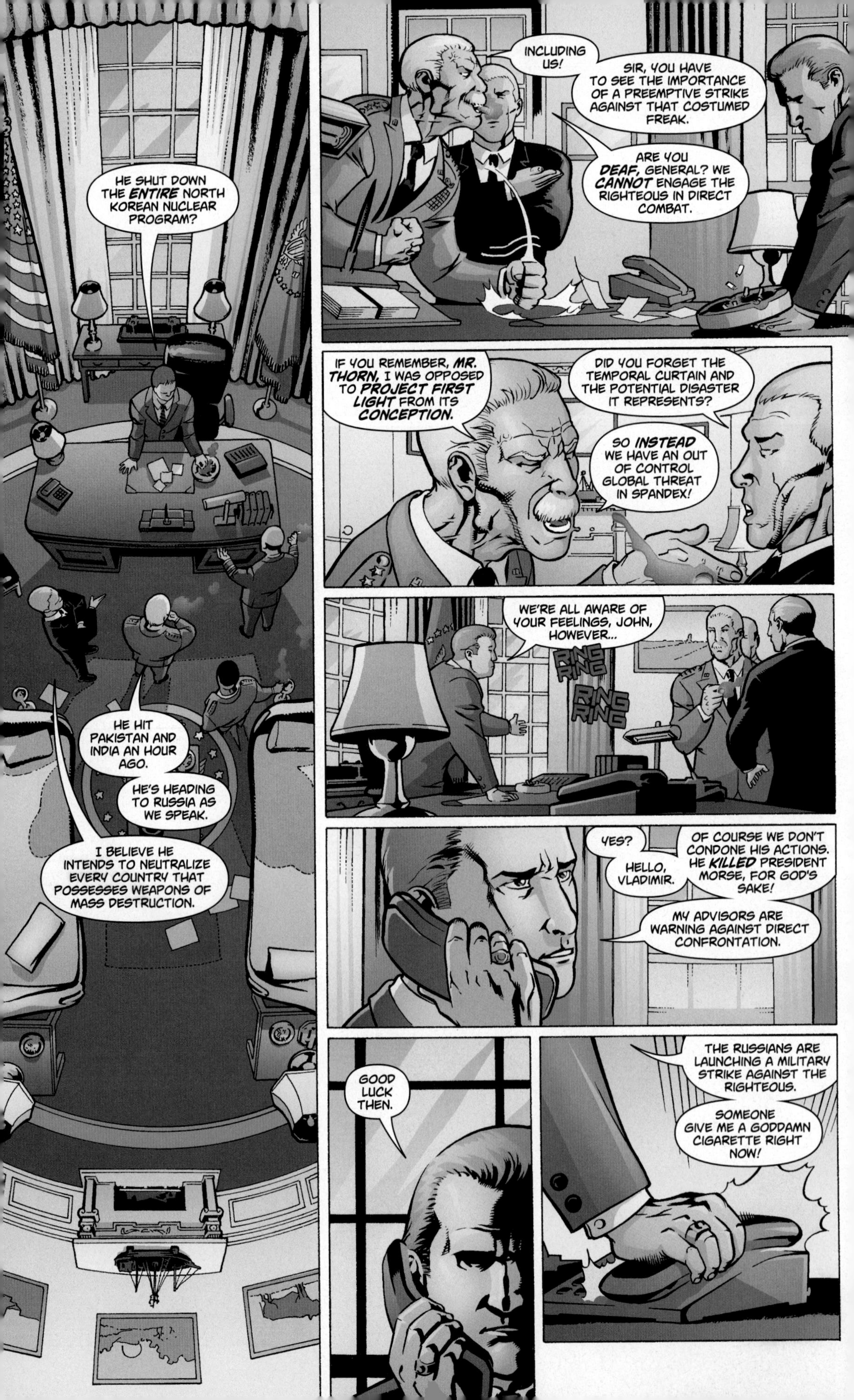
HE SHUT DOWN THE ENTIRE NORTH KOREAN NUCLEAR PROGRAM?
HE HIT PAKISTAN AND INDIA AN HOUR AGO.
HE'S HEADING TO RUSSIA AS WE SPEAK.
I BELIEVE HE INTENDS TO NEUTRALIZE EVERY COUNTRY THAT POSSESSES WEAPONS OF MASS DESTRUCTION.
INCLUDING US!
SIR, YOU HAVE TO SEE THE IMPORTANCE OF A PREEMPTIVE STRIKE AGAINST THAT COSTUMED FREAK.
ARE YOU DEAF, GENERAL? WE CANNOT ENGAGE THE RIGHTEOUS IN DIRECT COMBAT.
IF YOU REMEMBER, MR. THORN, I WAS OPPOSED TO PROJECT FIRST LIGHT FROM ITS CONCEPTION.
DID YOU FORGET THE TEMPORAL CURTAIN AND THE POTENTIAL DISASTER IT REPRESENTS?
SO INSTEAD WE HAVE AN OUT OF CONTROL GLOBAL THREAT IN SPANDEX!
WE'RE ALL AWARE OF YOUR FEELINGS, JOHN, HOWEVER...
RING RING
RING RING
YES?
HELLO, VLADIMIR.
OF COURSE WE DON'T CONDONE HIS ACTIONS. HE KILLED PRESIDENT MORSE, FOR GOD'S SAKE!
MY ADVISORS ARE WARNING AGAINST DIRECT CONFRONTATION.
GOOD LUCK THEN.
THE RUSSIANS ARE LAUNCHING A MILITARY STRIKE AGAINST THE RIGHTEOUS.
SOMEONE GIVE ME A GODDAMN CIGARETTE RIGHT NOW!

〈TARGET IN SIGHT. ENGAGING MISSILE STRIKE.〉

〈OH NO. GOODBYE MY SWEET POKINSKI.〉

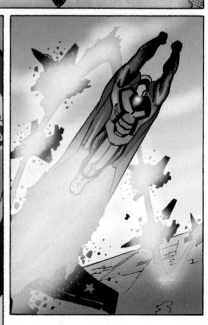

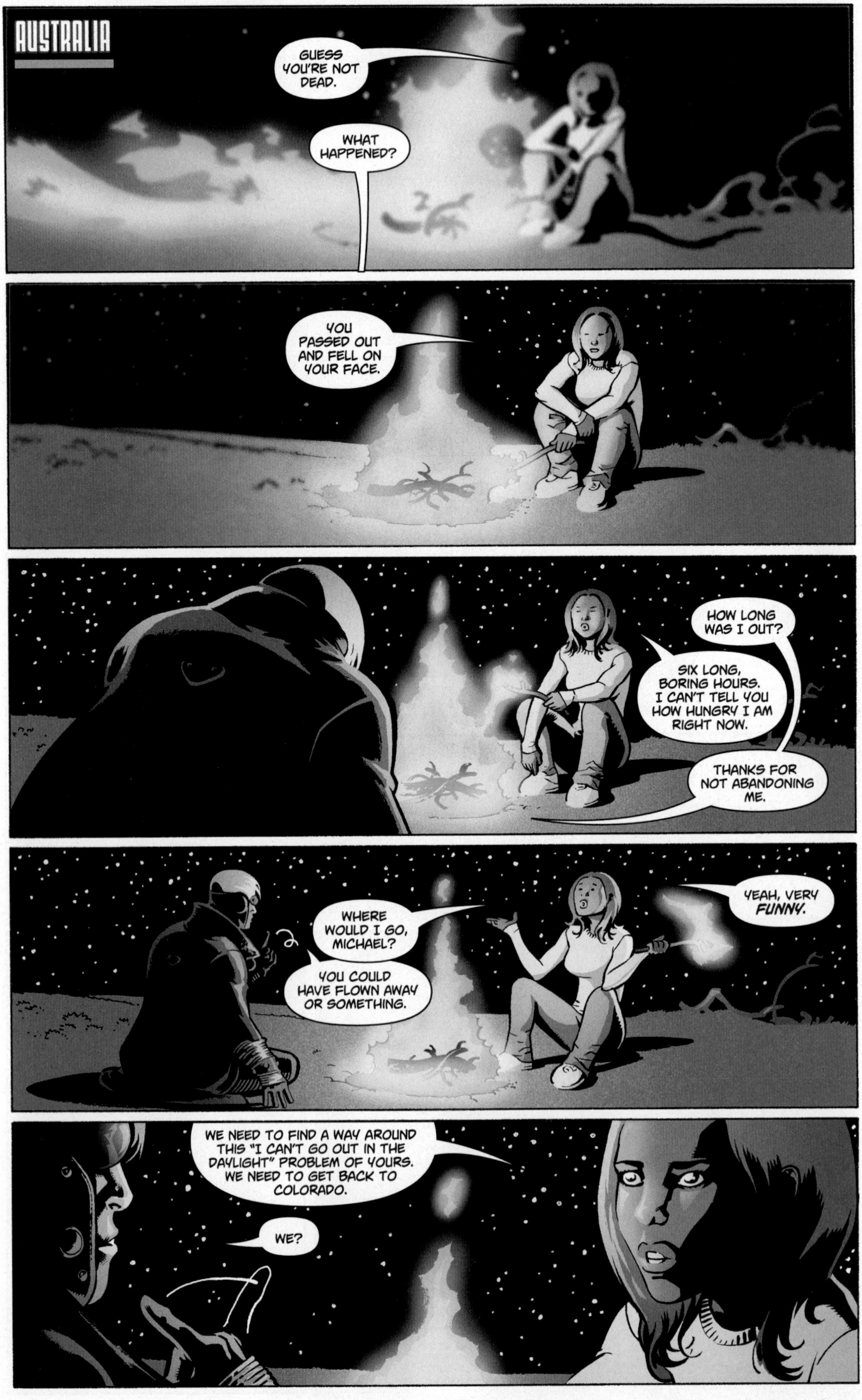
AUSTRALIA
GUESS YOU'RE NOT DEAD.
WHAT HAPPENED?
YOU PASSED OUT AND FELL ON YOUR FACE.
HOW LONG WAS I OUT?
SIX LONG, BORING HOURS. I CAN'T TELL YOU HOW HUNGRY I AM RIGHT NOW.
THANKS FOR NOT ABANDONING ME.
WHERE WOULD I GO, MICHAEL?
YOU COULD HAVE FLOWN AWAY OR SOMETHING.
YEAH, VERY FUNNY.
WE NEED TO FIND A WAY AROUND THIS "I CAN'T GO OUT IN THE DAYLIGHT" PROBLEM OF YOURS. WE NEED TO GET BACK TO COLORADO.
WE?

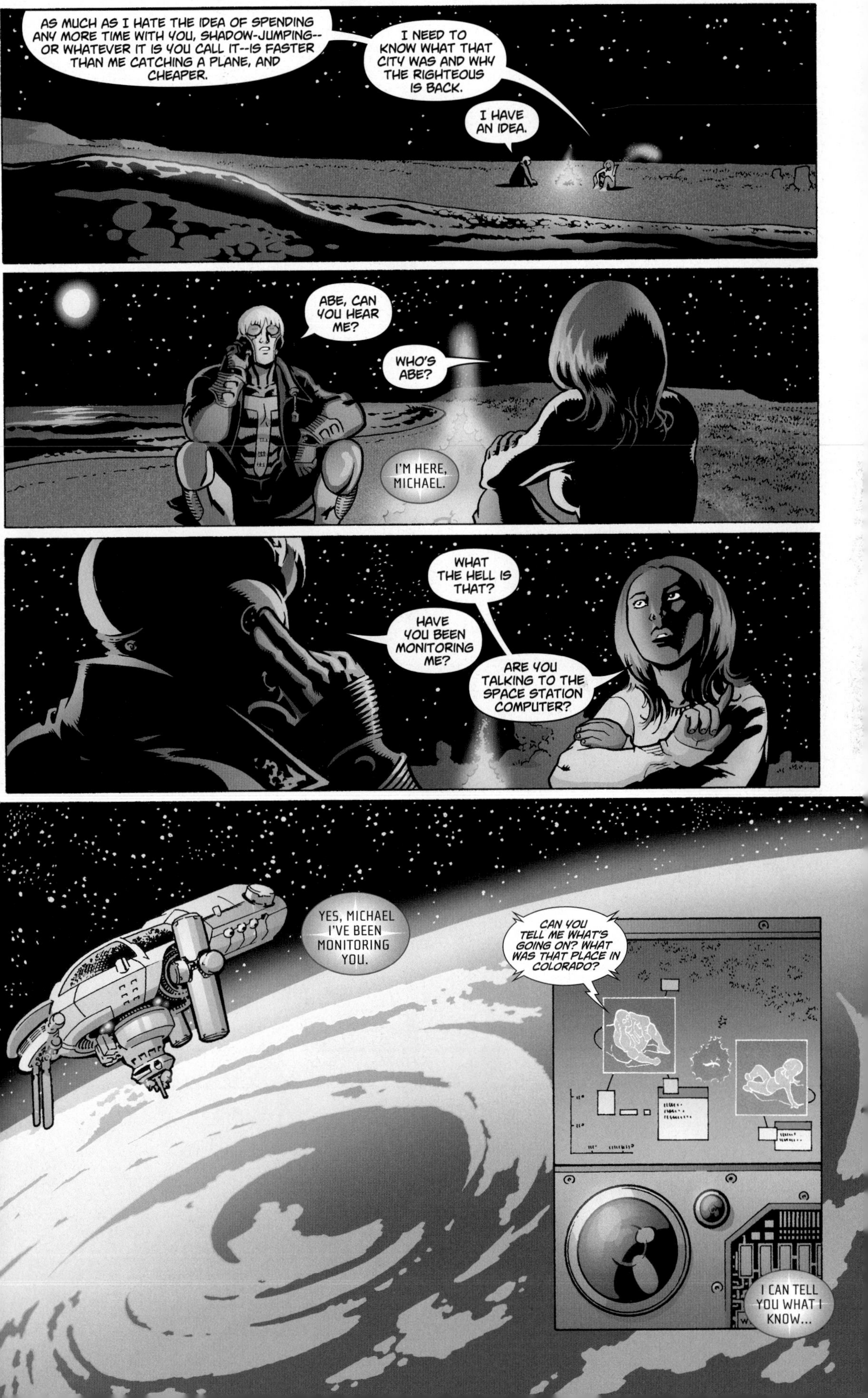
AS MUCH AS I HATE THE IDEA OF SPENDING ANY MORE TIME WITH YOU, SHADOW-JUMPING--OR WHATEVER IT IS YOU CALL IT--IS FASTER THAN ME CATCHING A PLANE, AND CHEAPER.
I NEED TO KNOW WHAT THAT CITY WAS AND WHY THE RIGHTEOUS IS BACK.
I HAVE AN IDEA.
ABE, CAN YOU HEAR ME?
WHO'S ABE?
I'M HERE, MICHAEL.
WHAT THE HELL IS THAT?
HAVE YOU BEEN MONITORING ME?
ARE YOU TALKING TO THE SPACE STATION COMPUTER?
YES, MICHAEL I'VE BEEN MONITORING YOU.
CAN YOU TELL ME WHAT'S GOING ON? WHAT WAS THAT PLACE IN COLORADO?
I CAN TELL YOU WHAT I KNOW...

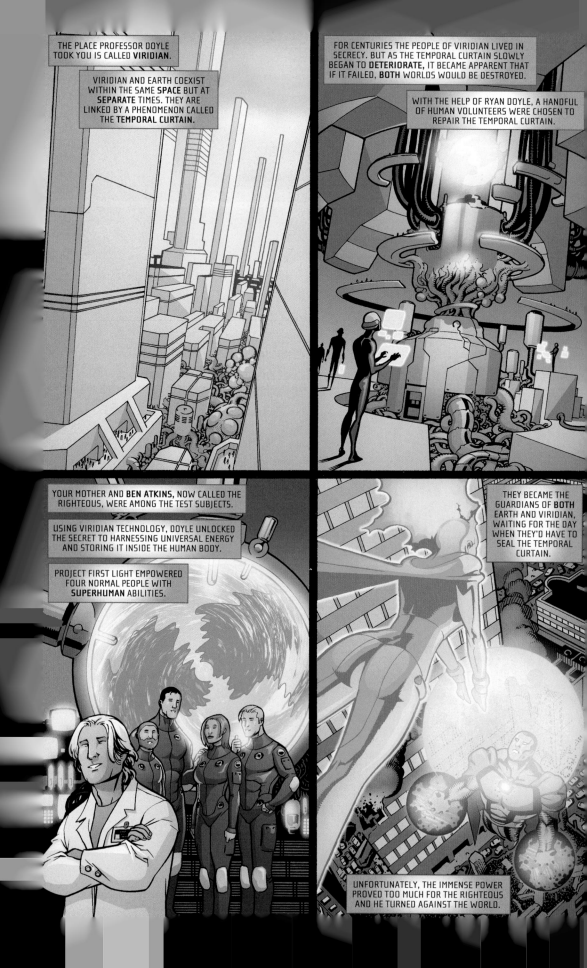

THE PLACE PROFESSOR DOYLE TOOK YOU IS CALLED **VIRIDIAN**.

VIRIDIAN AND EARTH COEXIST WITHIN THE SAME **SPACE** BUT AT **SEPARATE** TIMES. THEY ARE LINKED BY A PHENOMENON CALLED THE **TEMPORAL CURTAIN**.

FOR CENTURIES THE PEOPLE OF VIRIDIAN LIVED IN SECRECY. BUT AS THE TEMPORAL CURTAIN SLOWLY BEGAN TO **DETERIORATE**, IT BECAME APPARENT THAT IF IT FAILED, **BOTH** WORLDS WOULD BE DESTROYED.

WITH THE HELP OF RYAN DOYLE, A HANDFUL OF HUMAN VOLUNTEERS WERE CHOSEN TO REPAIR THE TEMPORAL CURTAIN.

YOUR MOTHER AND **BEN ATKINS**, NOW CALLED THE RIGHTEOUS, WERE AMONG THE TEST SUBJECTS.

USING VIRIDIAN TECHNOLOGY, DOYLE UNLOCKED THE SECRET TO HARNESSING UNIVERSAL ENERGY AND STORING IT INSIDE THE HUMAN BODY.

PROJECT FIRST LIGHT EMPOWERED FOUR NORMAL PEOPLE WITH **SUPERHUMAN** ABILITIES.

THEY BECAME THE GUARDIANS OF **BOTH** EARTH AND VIRIDIAN, WAITING FOR THE DAY WHEN THEY'D HAVE TO SEAL THE TEMPORAL CURTAIN.

UNFORTUNATELY, THE IMMENSE POWER PROVED TOO MUCH FOR THE RIGHTEOUS AND HE TURNED AGAINST THE WORLD.

DEFEATED, **BARELY** ALIVE, HIS COMATOSE BODY WAS RETURNED TO VIRIDIAN IN A STASIS CHAMBER DESIGNED TO IMPRISON HIM.

BUT HE'S ESCAPED.

HE'S DONE MORE THAN THAT, I'M AFRAID.

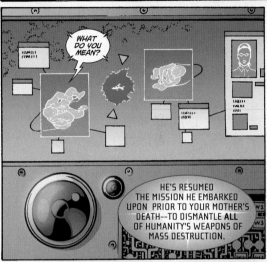

WHAT DO YOU MEAN?

HE'S RESUMED THE MISSION HE EMBARKED UPON PRIOR TO YOUR MOTHER'S DEATH--TO DISMANTLE **ALL** OF HUMANITY'S WEAPONS OF MASS DESTRUCTION.

WHAT'S SO TERRIBLE ABOUT THAT?

NOTHING.

BUT HIS NEXT PRIORITY WILL BE TO SEIZE CONTROL OF THE GLOBAL POWER STRUCTURE AND DISSOLVE **ALL** EXISTING GOVERNMENTS.

ANY FORCE HE DEEMS **NECESSARY** WILL BE USED TO ACHIEVE THAT CONTROL.

THAT'S AN *INSANE* UNDERTAKING. NOT EVEN THE RIGHTEOUS COULD CONTROL AN ENTIRE PLANET BY HIMSELF.

HE CAN'T BE EVERYWHERE AT ONCE. THERE ARE WAY TOO MANY PEOPLE.

BY ORDER OF THE COMMUNIST PARTY, YOU ARE TO LEAVE CHINESE TERRITORY IMMEDIATELY.

SURRENDER YOUR NUCLEAR ARMAMENTS AND CHEMICAL WEAPONS FOR DISPOSAL AND I WILL LEAVE YOU IN PEACE.

IMPOSSIBLE! YOU HAVE NO RIGHT WITH WHICH TO MAKE SUCH DEMANDS.

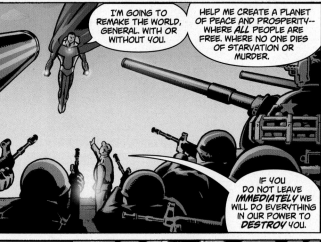

I'M GOING TO REMAKE THE WORLD, GENERAL. WITH OR WITHOUT YOU.

HELP ME CREATE A PLANET OF PEACE AND PROSPERITY-- WHERE *ALL* PEOPLE ARE FREE. WHERE NO ONE DIES OF STARVATION OR MURDER.

IF YOU DO NOT LEAVE *IMMEDIATELY* WE WILL DO EVERYTHING IN OUR POWER TO *DESTROY* YOU.

IS THAT ALL YOU UNDERSTAND?

DESTRUCTION?

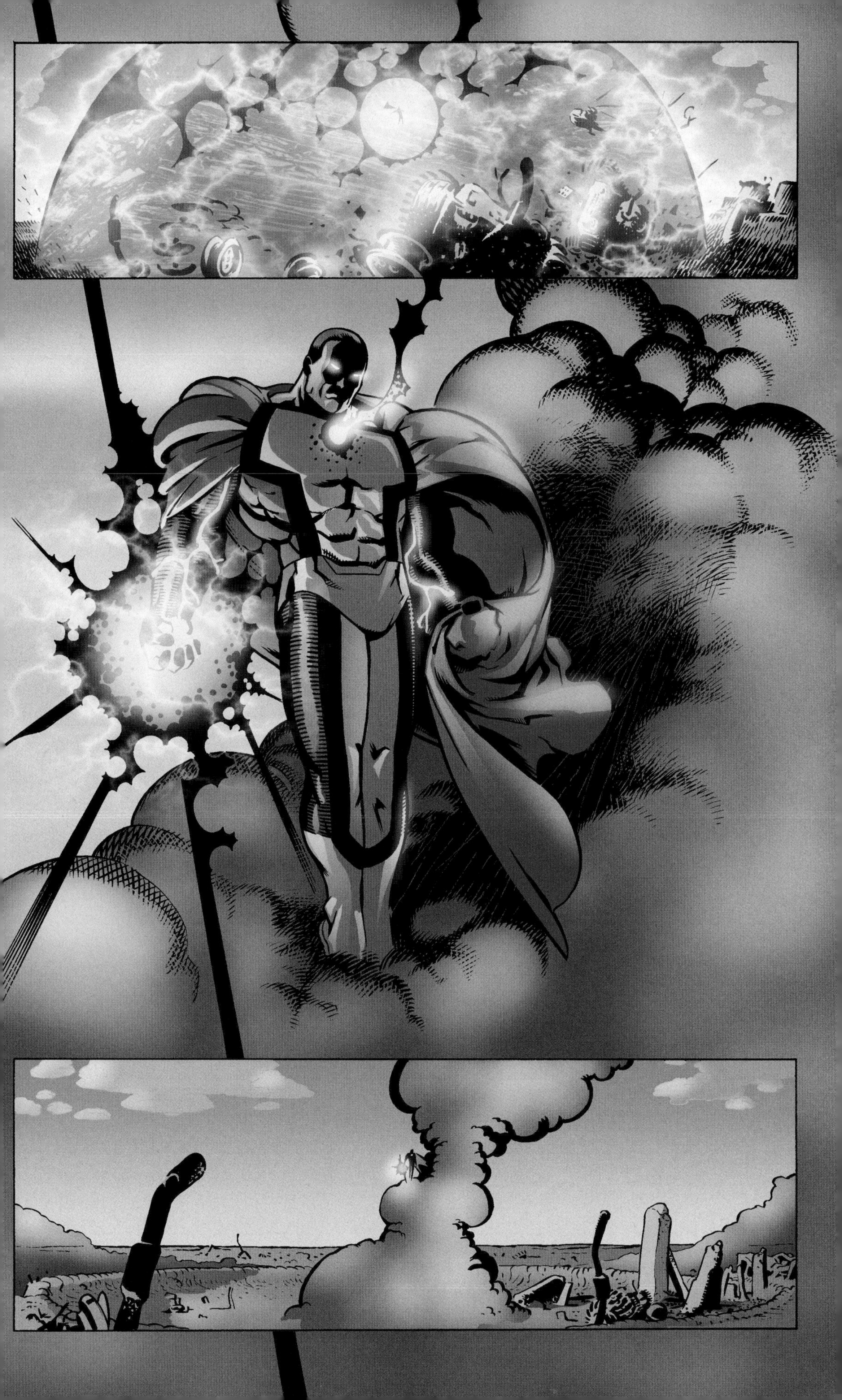

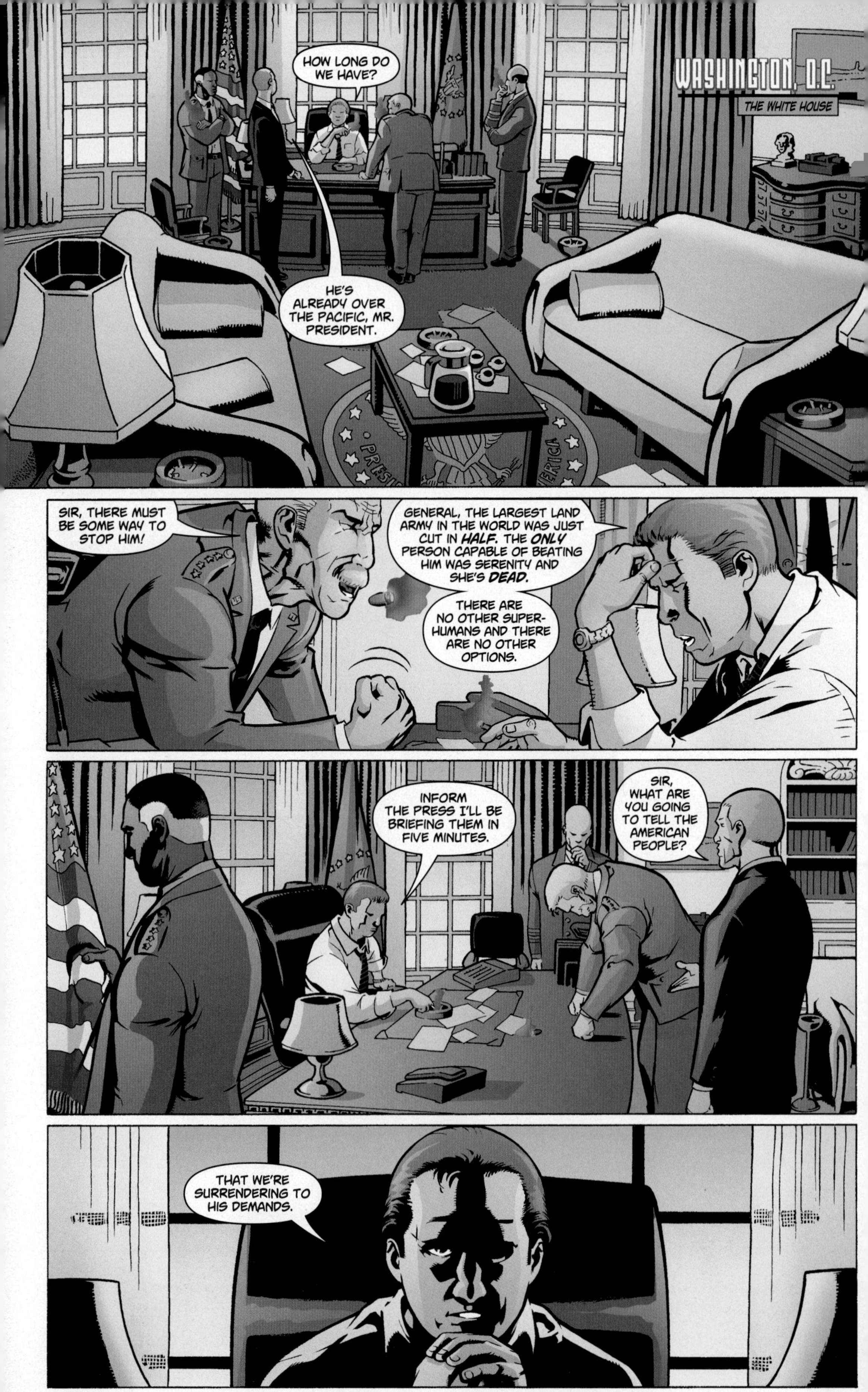
WASHINGTON, D.C.
THE WHITE HOUSE
HOW LONG DO WE HAVE?
HE'S ALREADY OVER THE PACIFIC, MR. PRESIDENT.
SIR, THERE MUST BE SOME WAY TO STOP HIM!
GENERAL, THE LARGEST LAND ARMY IN THE WORLD WAS JUST CUT IN HALF. THE ONLY PERSON CAPABLE OF BEATING HIM WAS SERENITY AND SHE'S DEAD.
THERE ARE NO OTHER SUPER-HUMANS AND THERE ARE NO OTHER OPTIONS.
INFORM THE PRESS I'LL BE BRIEFING THEM IN FIVE MINUTES.
SIR, WHAT ARE YOU GOING TO TELL THE AMERICAN PEOPLE?
THAT WE'RE SURRENDERING TO HIS DEMANDS.

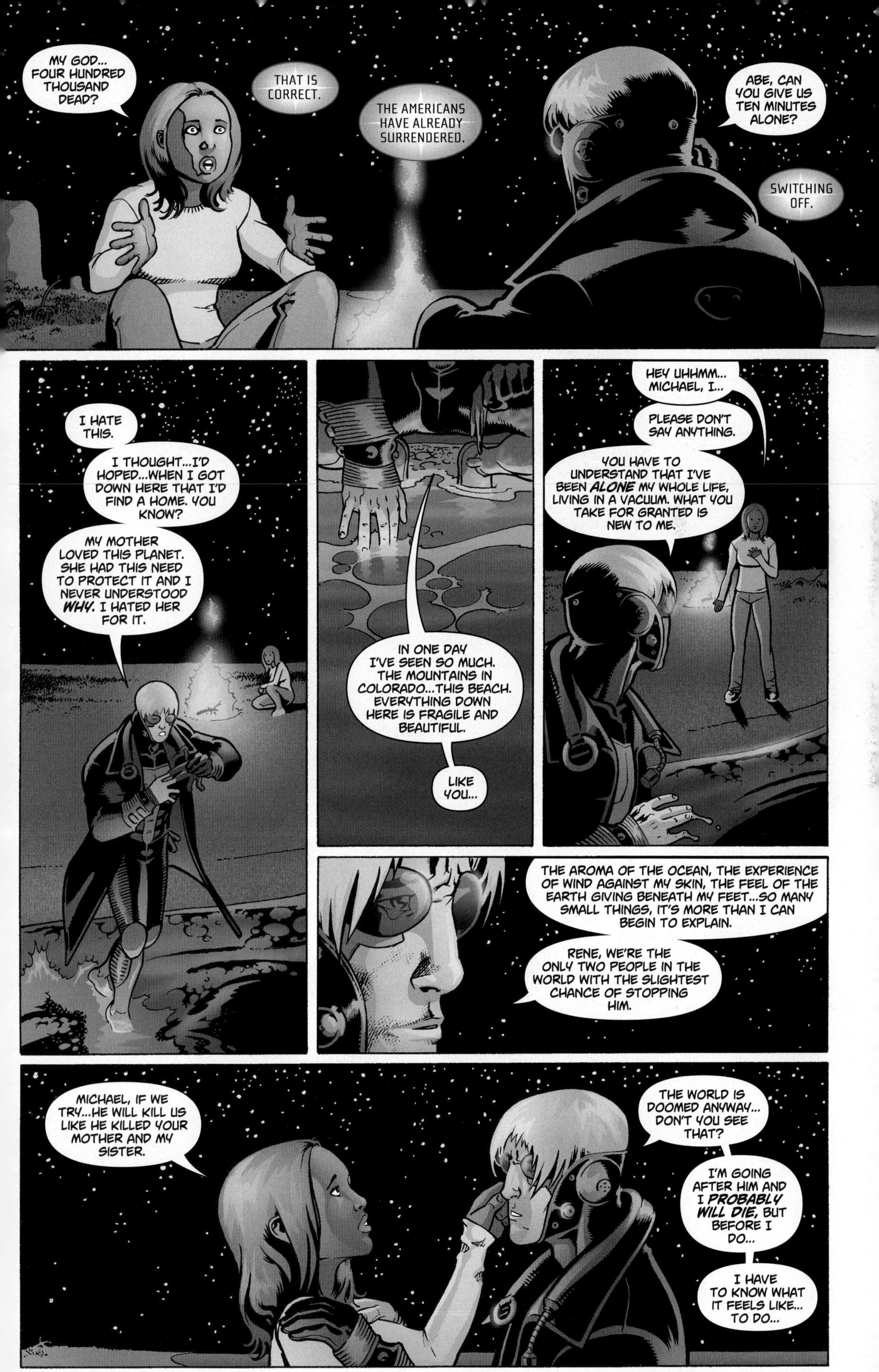
MY GOD... FOUR HUNDRED THOUSAND DEAD?
THAT IS CORRECT.
THE AMERICANS HAVE ALREADY SURRENDERED.
ABE, CAN YOU GIVE US TEN MINUTES ALONE?
SWITCHING OFF.
I HATE THIS.
I THOUGHT...I'D HOPED...WHEN I GOT DOWN HERE THAT I'D FIND A HOME. YOU KNOW?
MY MOTHER LOVED THIS PLANET. SHE HAD THIS NEED TO PROTECT IT AND I NEVER UNDERSTOOD WHY. I HATED HER FOR IT.
IN ONE DAY I'VE SEEN SO MUCH. THE MOUNTAINS IN COLORADO...THIS BEACH. EVERYTHING DOWN HERE IS FRAGILE AND BEAUTIFUL.
LIKE YOU...
HEY UHHMM... MICHAEL, I...
PLEASE DON'T SAY ANYTHING.
YOU HAVE TO UNDERSTAND THAT I'VE BEEN ALONE MY WHOLE LIFE, LIVING IN A VACUUM. WHAT YOU TAKE FOR GRANTED IS NEW TO ME.
THE AROMA OF THE OCEAN, THE EXPERIENCE OF WIND AGAINST MY SKIN, THE FEEL OF THE EARTH GIVING BENEATH MY FEET...SO MANY SMALL THINGS, IT'S MORE THAN I CAN BEGIN TO EXPLAIN.
RENE, WE'RE THE ONLY TWO PEOPLE IN THE WORLD WITH THE SLIGHTEST CHANCE OF STOPPING HIM.
MICHAEL, IF WE TRY...HE WILL KILL US LIKE HE KILLED YOUR MOTHER AND MY SISTER.
THE WORLD IS DOOMED ANYWAY... DON'T YOU SEE THAT?
I'M GOING AFTER HIM AND I PROBABLY WILL DIE, BUT BEFORE I DO...
I HAVE TO KNOW WHAT IT FEELS LIKE... TO DO...

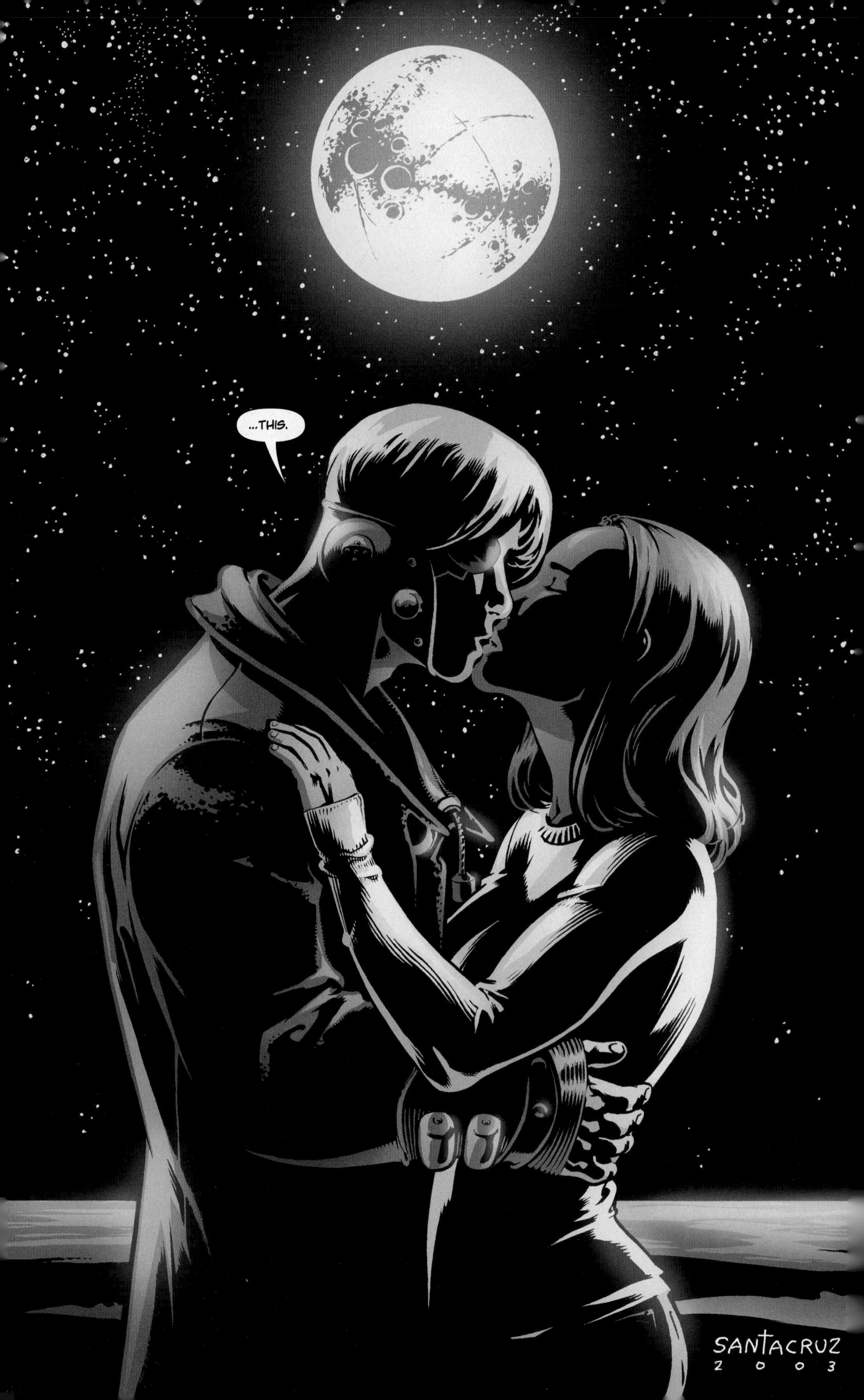
...THIS.
SANTACRUZ 2003

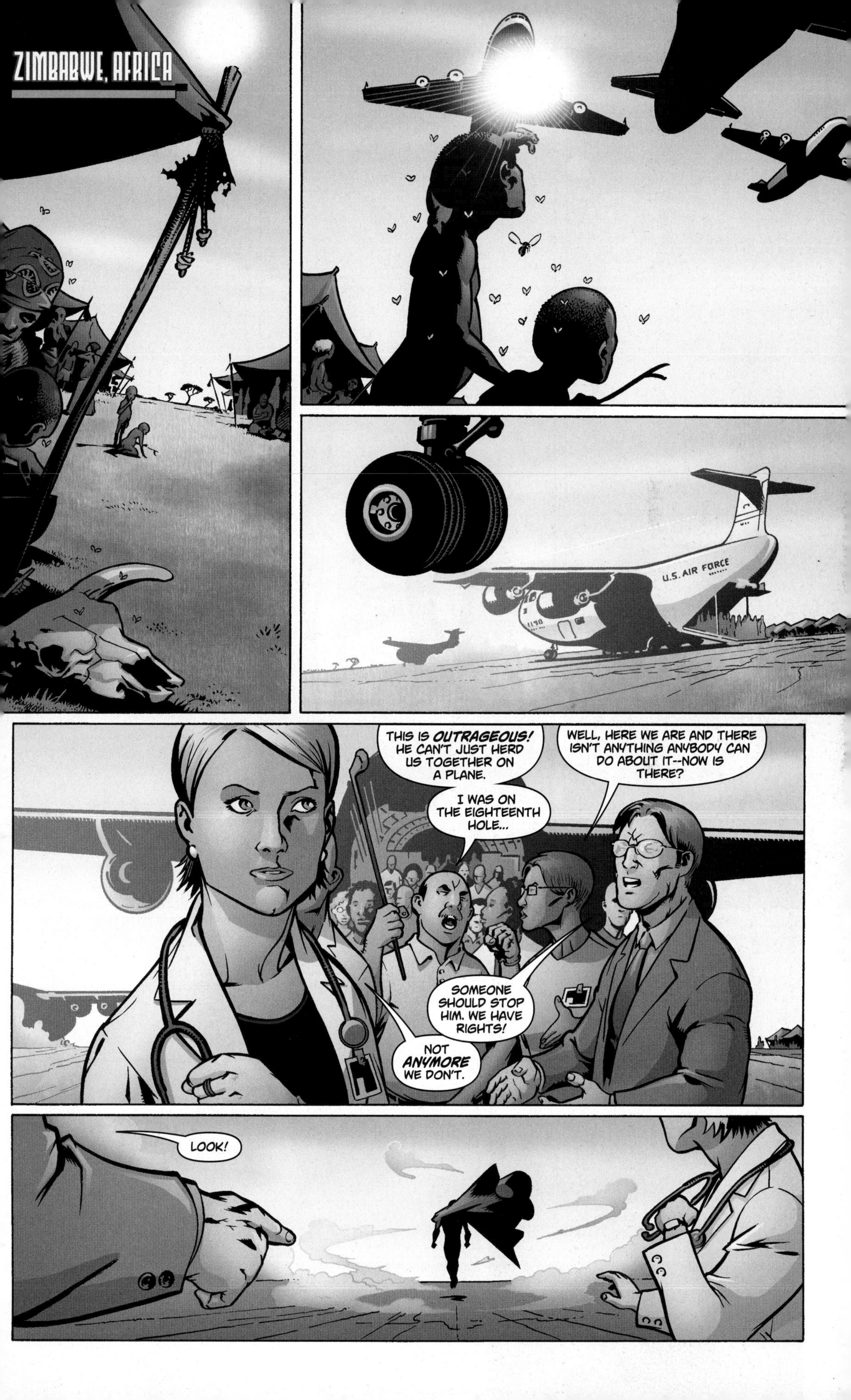
ZIMBABWE, AFRICA
U.S. AIR FORCE
THIS IS OUTRAGEOUS! HE CAN'T JUST HERD US TOGETHER ON A PLANE.
I WAS ON THE EIGHTEENTH HOLE...
WELL, HERE WE ARE AND THERE ISN'T ANYTHING ANYBODY CAN DO ABOUT IT--NOW IS THERE?
SOMEONE SHOULD STOP HIM. WE HAVE RIGHTS!
NOT ANYMORE WE DON'T.
LOOK!

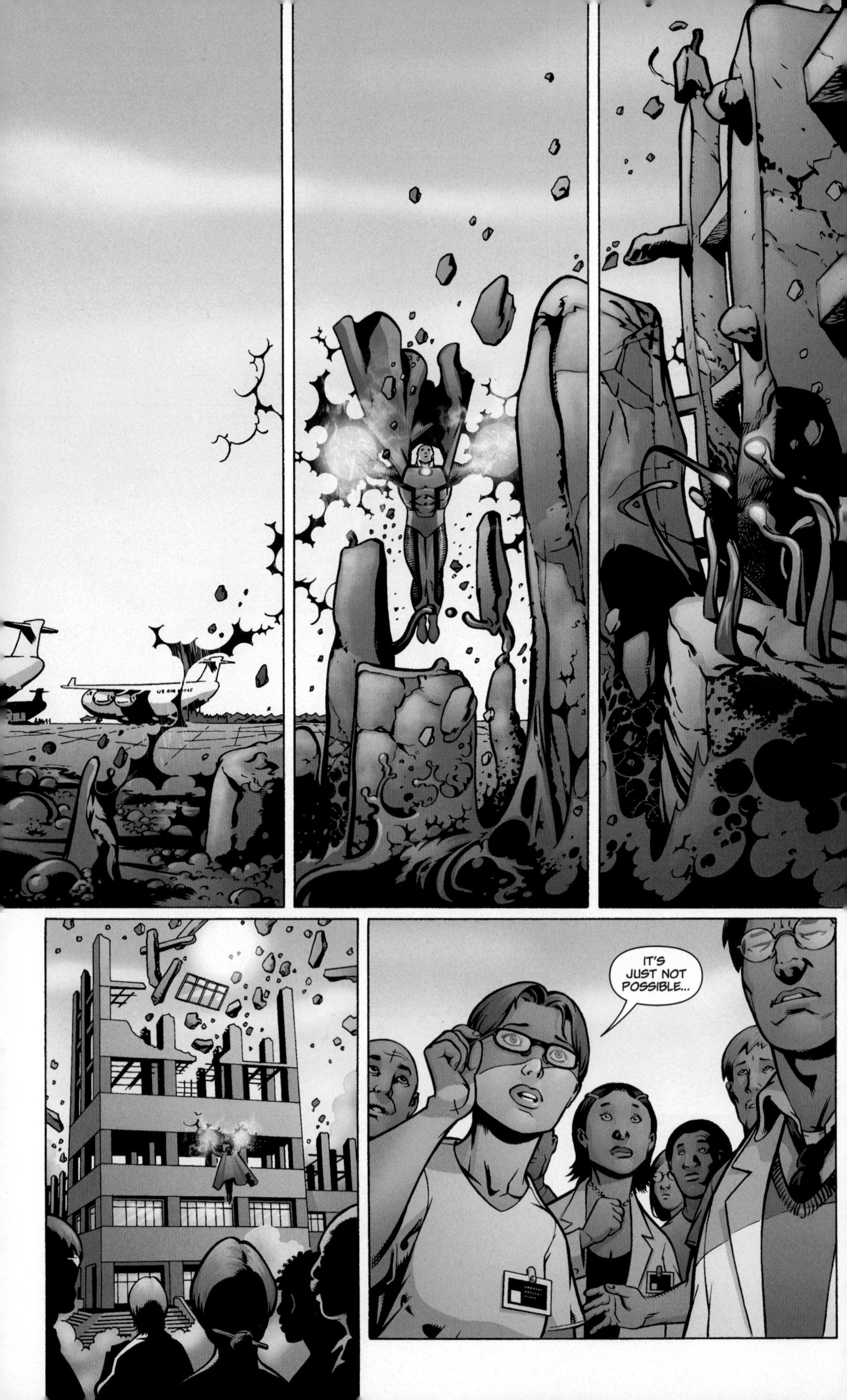
IT'S JUST NOT POSSIBLE...

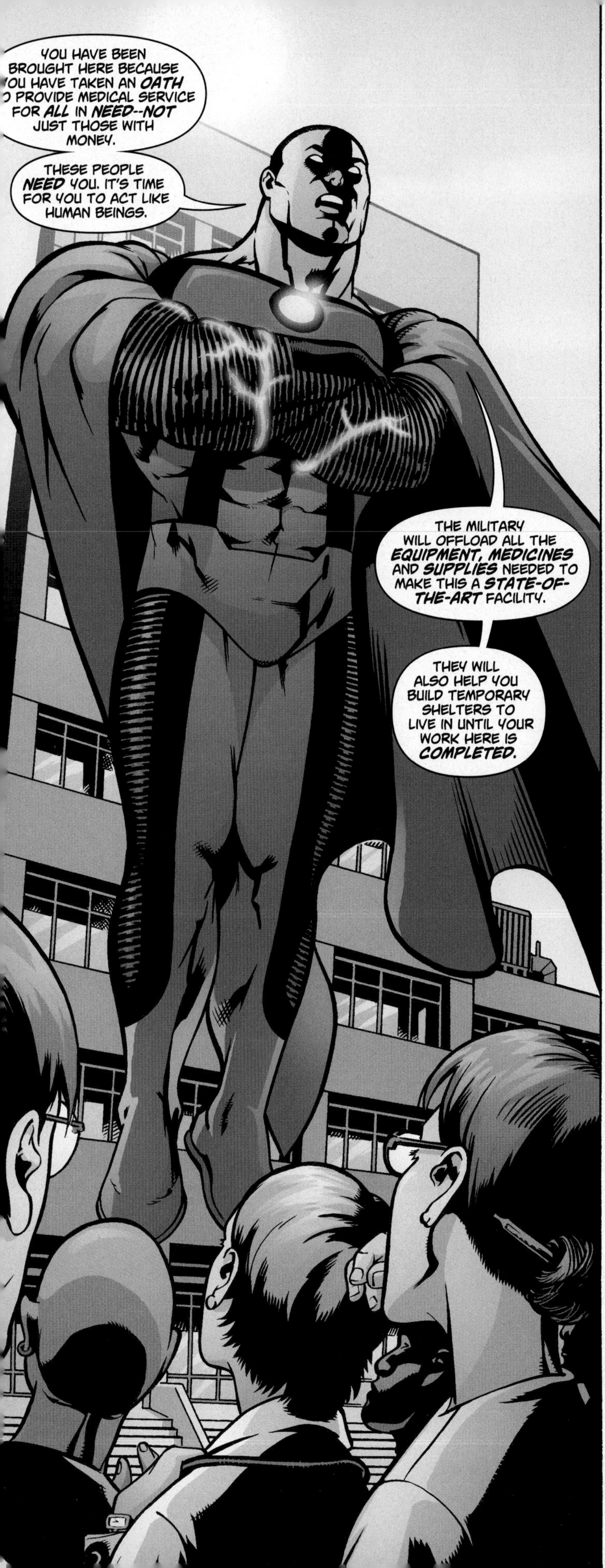
YOU HAVE BEEN BROUGHT HERE BECAUSE YOU HAVE TAKEN AN OATH TO PROVIDE MEDICAL SERVICE FOR ALL IN NEED--NOT JUST THOSE WITH MONEY.
THESE PEOPLE NEED YOU. IT'S TIME FOR YOU TO ACT LIKE HUMAN BEINGS.
THE MILITARY WILL OFFLOAD ALL THE EQUIPMENT, MEDICINES AND SUPPLIES NEEDED TO MAKE THIS A STATE-OF-THE-ART FACILITY.
THEY WILL ALSO HELP YOU BUILD TEMPORARY SHELTERS TO LIVE IN UNTIL YOUR WORK HERE IS COMPLETED.

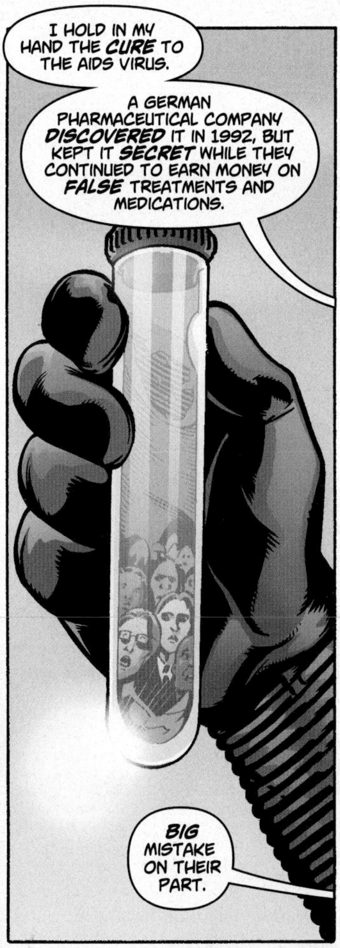
I HOLD IN MY HAND THE CURE TO THE AIDS VIRUS.
A GERMAN PHARMACEUTICAL COMPANY DISCOVERED IT IN 1992, BUT KEPT IT SECRET WHILE THEY CONTINUED TO EARN MONEY ON FALSE TREATMENTS AND MEDICATIONS.
BIG MISTAKE ON THEIR PART.

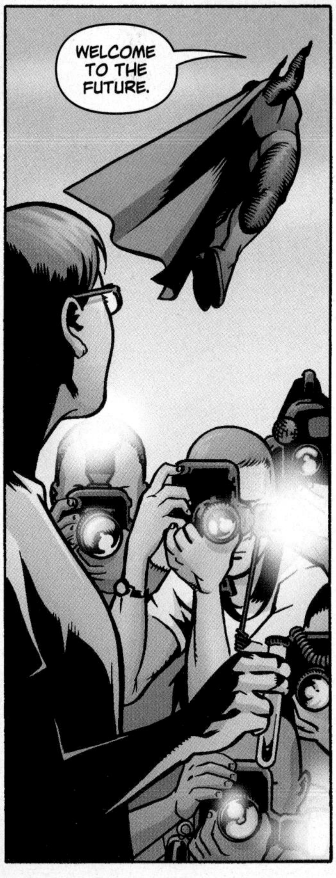
WELCOME TO THE FUTURE.

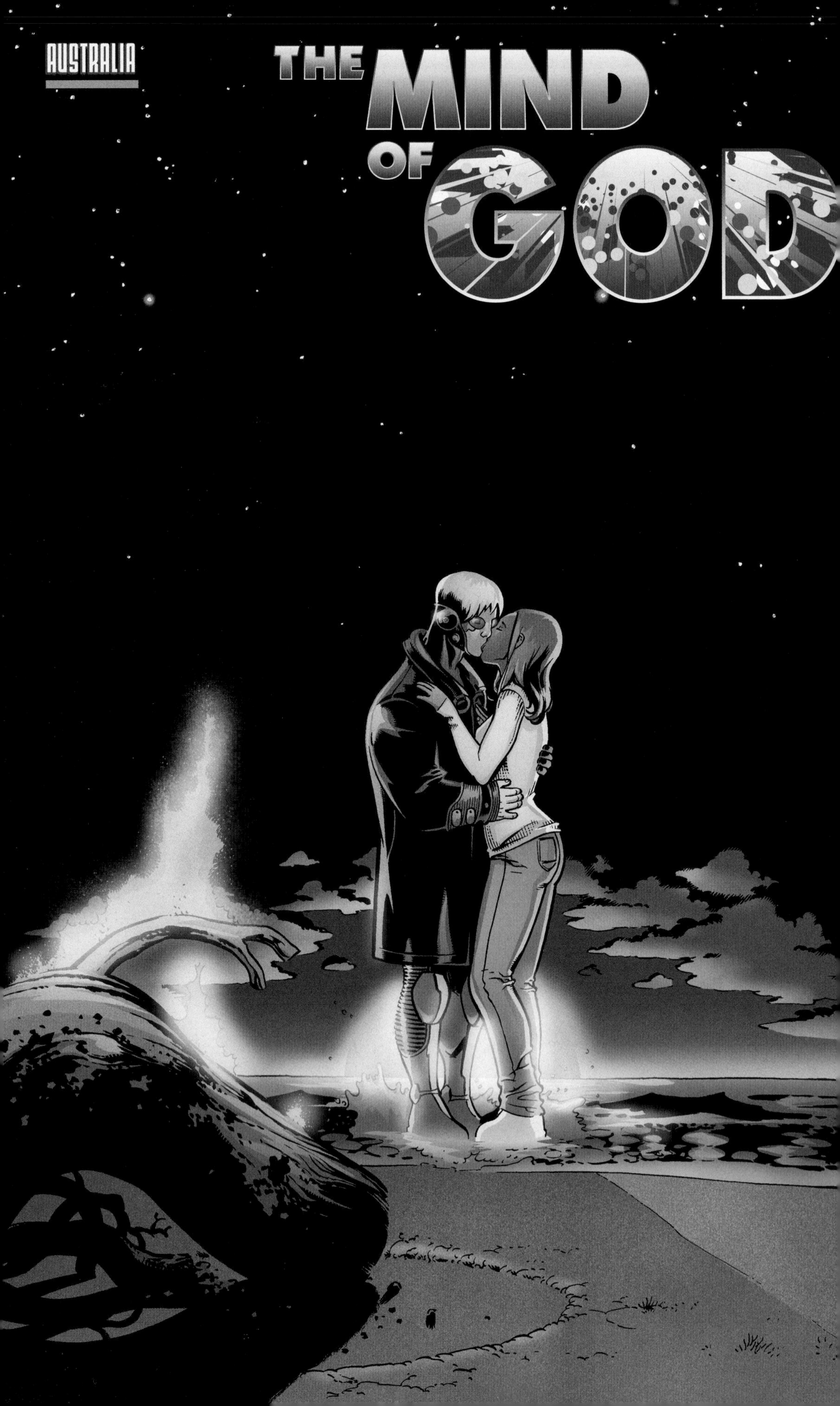

AUSTRALIA
THE MIND OF GOD

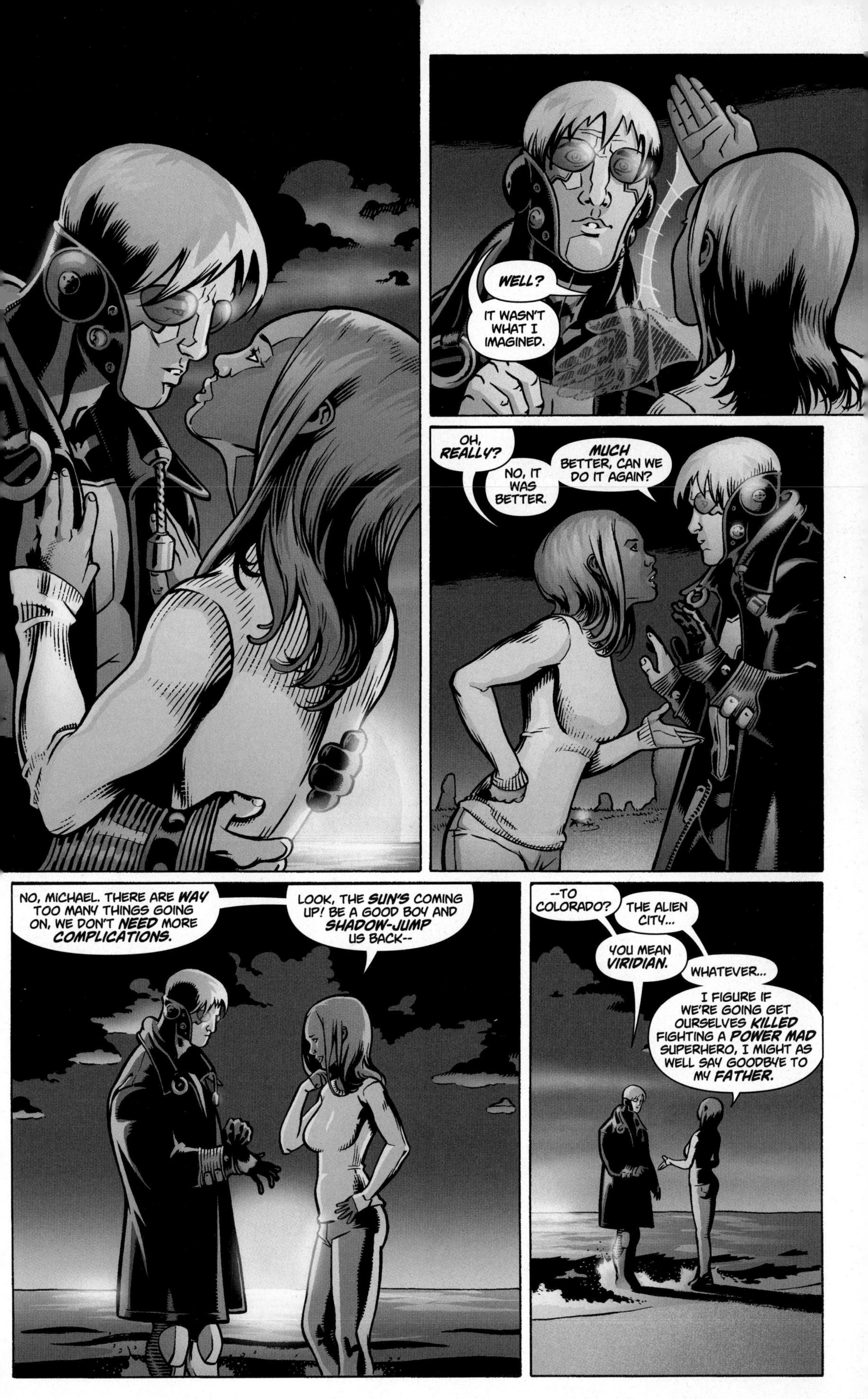
WELL?
IT WASN'T WHAT I IMAGINED.
OH, REALLY?
NO, IT WAS BETTER.
MUCH BETTER, CAN WE DO IT AGAIN?
NO, MICHAEL. THERE ARE WAY TOO MANY THINGS GOING ON, WE DON'T NEED MORE COMPLICATIONS.
LOOK, THE SUN'S COMING UP! BE A GOOD BOY AND SHADOW-JUMP US BACK--
--TO COLORADO?
THE ALIEN CITY...
YOU MEAN VIRIDIAN.
WHATEVER...
I FIGURE IF WE'RE GOING GET OURSELVES KILLED FIGHTING A POWER MAD SUPERHERO, I MIGHT AS WELL SAY GOODBYE TO MY FATHER.

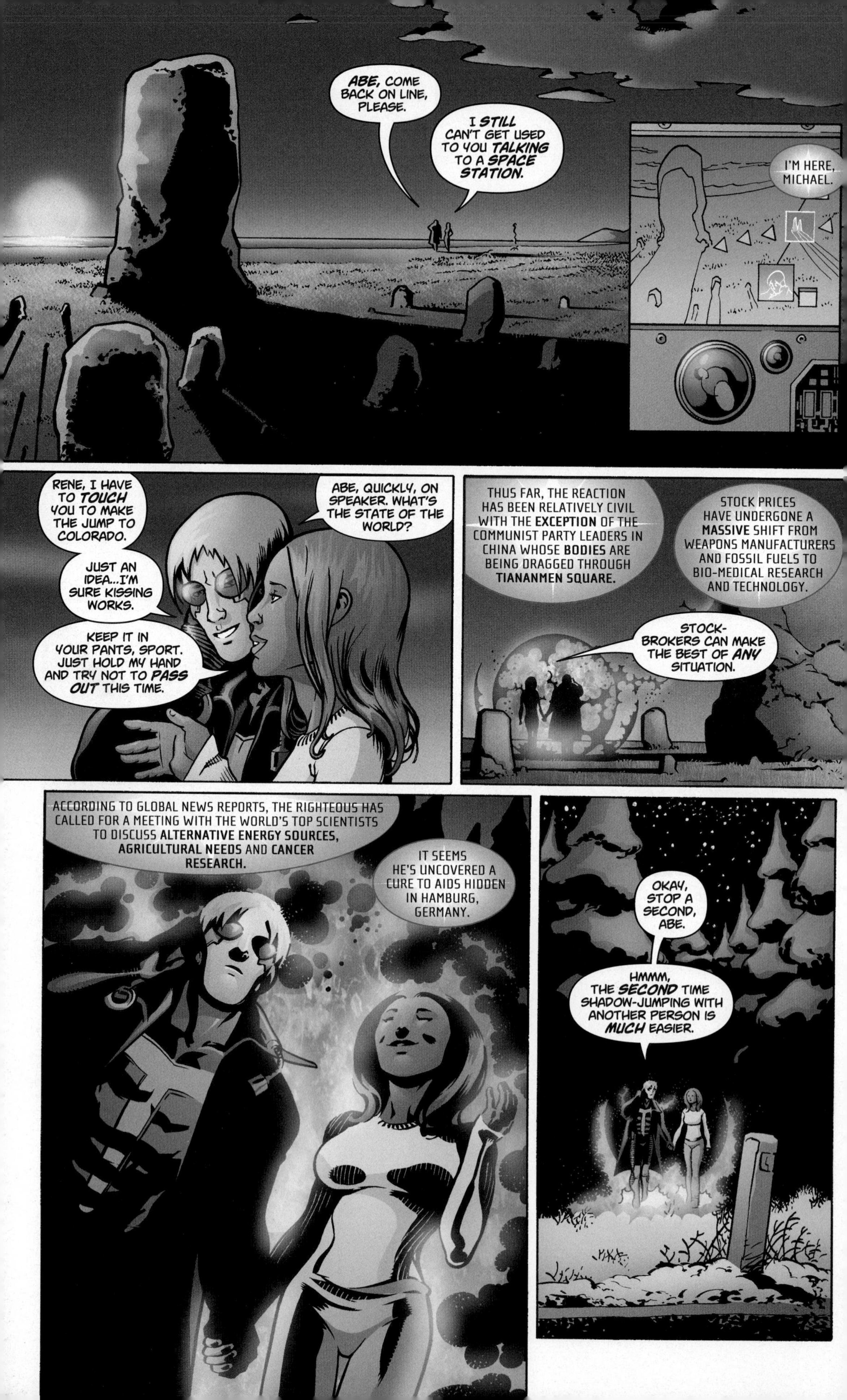
ABE, COME BACK ON LINE, PLEASE.
I STILL CAN'T GET USED TO YOU TALKING TO A SPACE STATION.
I'M HERE, MICHAEL.
RENE, I HAVE TO TOUCH YOU TO MAKE THE JUMP TO COLORADO.
JUST AN IDEA...I'M SURE KISSING WORKS.
KEEP IT IN YOUR PANTS, SPORT. JUST HOLD MY HAND AND TRY NOT TO PASS OUT THIS TIME.
ABE, QUICKLY, ON SPEAKER. WHAT'S THE STATE OF THE WORLD?
THUS FAR, THE REACTION HAS BEEN RELATIVELY CIVIL WITH THE EXCEPTION OF THE COMMUNIST PARTY LEADERS IN CHINA WHOSE BODIES ARE BEING DRAGGED THROUGH TIANANMEN SQUARE.
STOCK PRICES HAVE UNDERGONE A MASSIVE SHIFT FROM WEAPONS MANUFACTURERS AND FOSSIL FUELS TO BIO-MEDICAL RESEARCH AND TECHNOLOGY.
STOCK-BROKERS CAN MAKE THE BEST OF ANY SITUATION.
ACCORDING TO GLOBAL NEWS REPORTS, THE RIGHTEOUS HAS CALLED FOR A MEETING WITH THE WORLD'S TOP SCIENTISTS TO DISCUSS ALTERNATIVE ENERGY SOURCES, AGRICULTURAL NEEDS AND CANCER RESEARCH.
IT SEEMS HE'S UNCOVERED A CURE TO AIDS HIDDEN IN HAMBURG, GERMANY.
OKAY, STOP A SECOND, ABE.
HMMM, THE SECOND TIME SHADOW-JUMPING WITH ANOTHER PERSON IS MUCH EASIER.

I CAN'T *BELIEVE* I'M GOING TO SAY THIS, BUT...

...WHAT IF THE THINGS HE'S DOING *NOW* WILL MAKE THE WORLD A *BETTER* PLACE *TOMORROW?*

MICHAEL, JUST FROM THAT INFORMATION *ALONE*, IT'S *UNBELIEVABLE* WHAT HE'S *ACCOMPLISHED* IN SUCH A SHORT TIME, EVEN *YOU* HAVE TO ADMIT...

ONE SECOND, NAY...

ABE, DO ME A FAVOR AND CALCULATE THE CURRENT NUMBER OF *DEATHS*--DIRECTLY OR INDIRECTLY--*CAUSED* BY THE RIGHTEOUS AND BREAK IT DOWN BY MEN, WOMEN AND CHILDREN.

476,943 MEN, 20,004 WOMEN AND 743 CHILDREN.

AT THE RISK OF SOUNDING TRITE, HE'S HITLER WITH A CAPE.

WE *HAVE* TO *STOP* HIM.

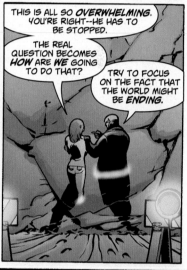

THIS IS ALL SO *OVERWHELMING.* YOU'RE RIGHT--HE HAS TO BE STOPPED.

THE REAL QUESTION BECOMES *HOW* ARE *WE* GOING TO DO THAT?

TRY TO FOCUS ON THE FACT THAT THE WORLD MIGHT BE *ENDING.*

MAYBE YOUR FATHER KNOWS OF SOME *WEAKNESS* THE RIGHTEOUS HAS THAT WE CAN *EXPLOIT.*

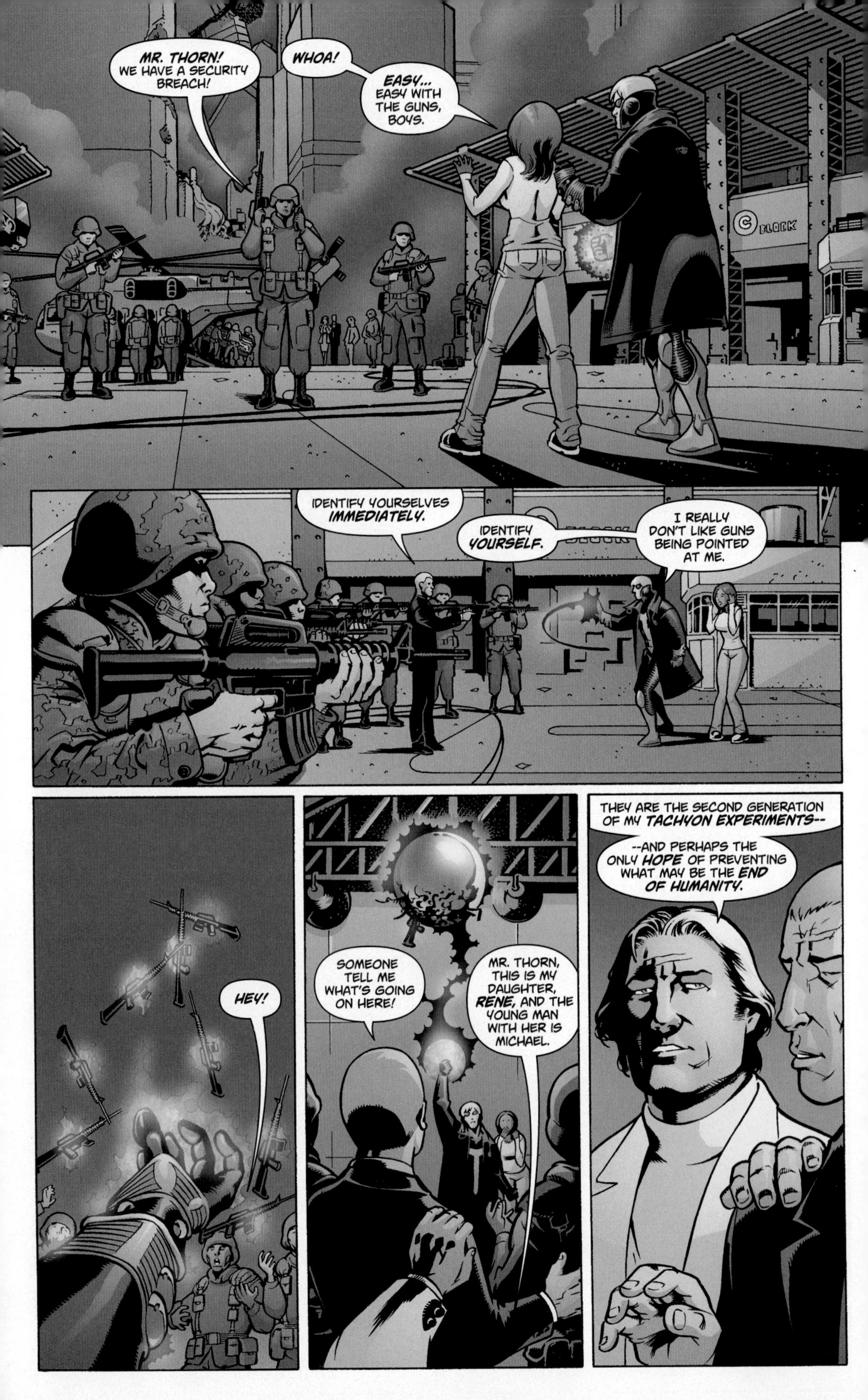
MR. THORN! WE HAVE A SECURITY BREACH!
WHOA!
EASY... EASY WITH THE GUNS, BOYS.
C BLOCK
IDENTIFY YOURSELVES IMMEDIATELY.
IDENTIFY YOURSELF.
I REALLY DON'T LIKE GUNS BEING POINTED AT ME.
HEY!
SOMEONE TELL ME WHAT'S GOING ON HERE!
MR. THORN, THIS IS MY DAUGHTER, RENE, AND THE YOUNG MAN WITH HER IS MICHAEL.
THEY ARE THE SECOND GENERATION OF MY TACHYON EXPERIMENTS--
--AND PERHAPS THE ONLY HOPE OF PREVENTING WHAT MAY BE THE END OF HUMANITY.

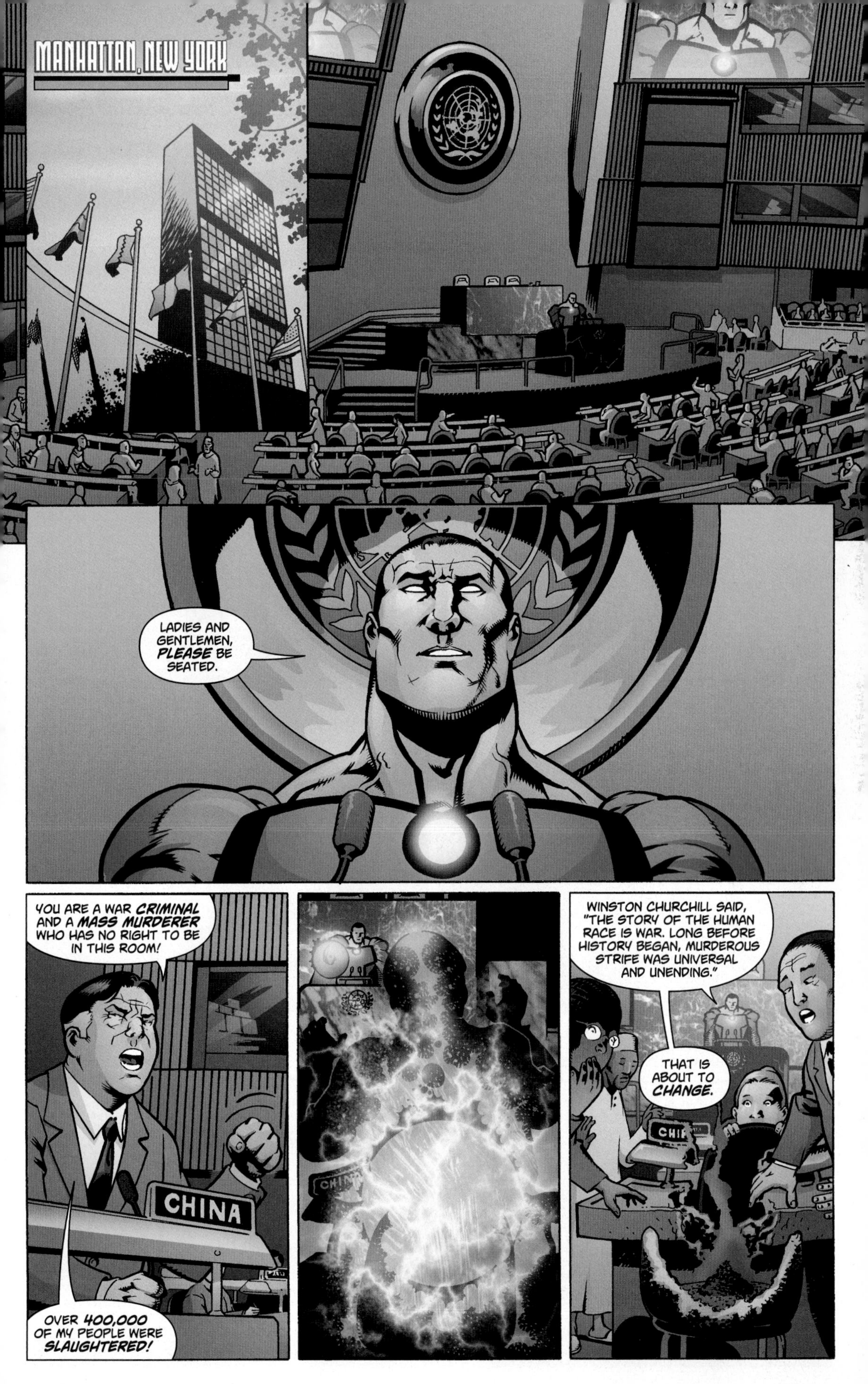
MANHATTAN, NEW YORK
LADIES AND GENTLEMEN, PLEASE BE SEATED.
YOU ARE A WAR CRIMINAL AND A MASS MURDERER WHO HAS NO RIGHT TO BE IN THIS ROOM!
CHINA
OVER 400,000 OF MY PEOPLE WERE SLAUGHTERED!
WINSTON CHURCHILL SAID, "THE STORY OF THE HUMAN RACE IS WAR. LONG BEFORE HISTORY BEGAN, MURDEROUS STRIFE WAS UNIVERSAL AND UNENDING."
THAT IS ABOUT TO CHANGE.

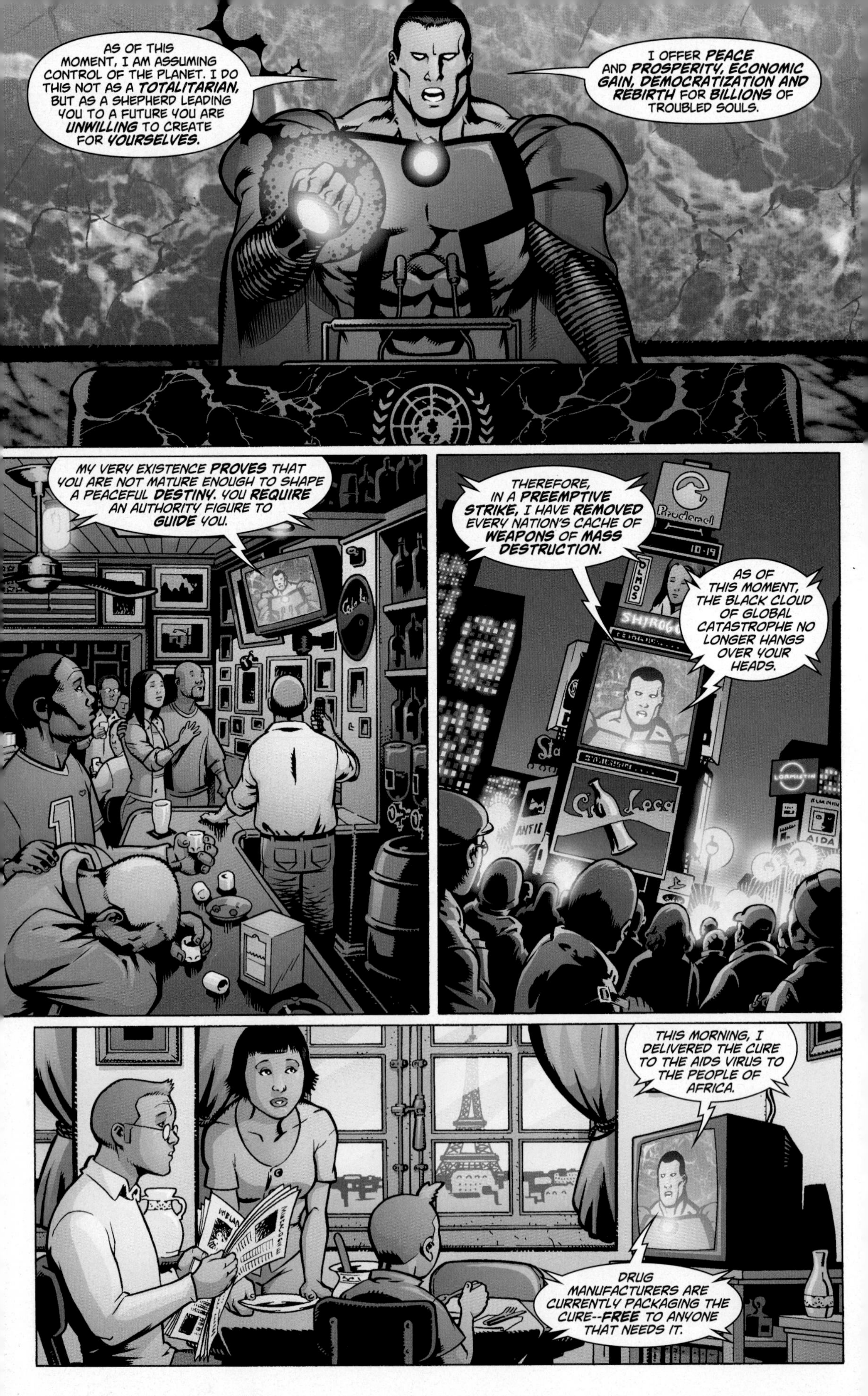

AS OF THIS MOMENT, I AM ASSUMING CONTROL OF THE PLANET. I DO THIS NOT AS A TOTALITARIAN, BUT AS A SHEPHERD LEADING YOU TO A FUTURE YOU ARE UNWILLING TO CREATE FOR YOURSELVES.
I OFFER PEACE AND PROSPERITY, ECONOMIC GAIN, DEMOCRATIZATION AND REBIRTH FOR BILLIONS OF TROUBLED SOULS.
MY VERY EXISTENCE PROVES THAT YOU ARE NOT MATURE ENOUGH TO SHAPE A PEACEFUL DESTINY. YOU REQUIRE AN AUTHORITY FIGURE TO GUIDE YOU.
THEREFORE, IN A PREEMPTIVE STRIKE, I HAVE REMOVED EVERY NATION'S CACHE OF WEAPONS OF MASS DESTRUCTION.
AS OF THIS MOMENT, THE BLACK CLOUD OF GLOBAL CATASTROPHE NO LONGER HANGS OVER YOUR HEADS.
SHIROG
AIDA
THIS MORNING, I DELIVERED THE CURE TO THE AIDS VIRUS TO THE PEOPLE OF AFRICA.
DRUG MANUFACTURERS ARE CURRENTLY PACKAGING THE CURE--FREE TO ANYONE THAT NEEDS IT.

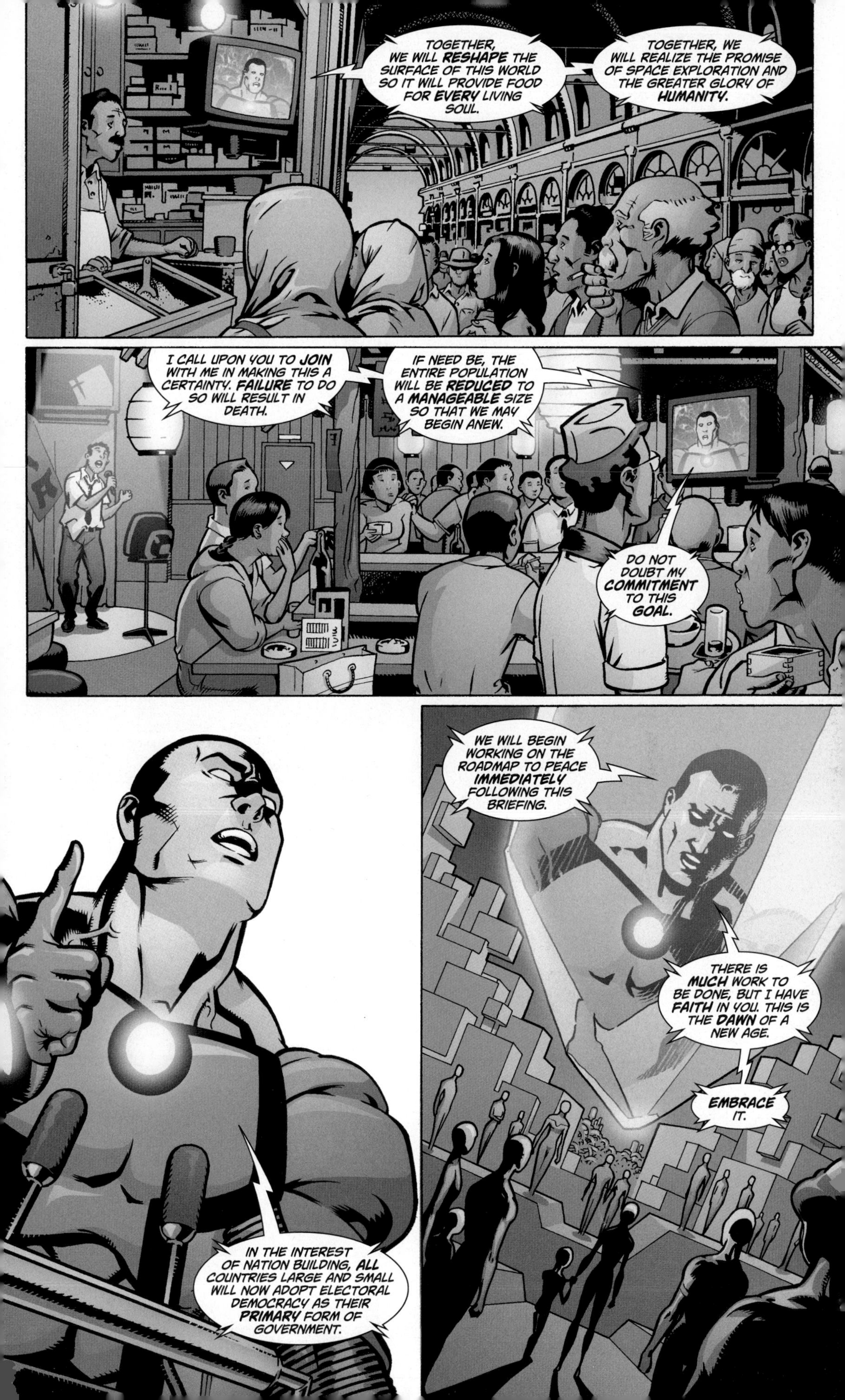
TOGETHER, WE WILL RESHAPE THE SURFACE OF THIS WORLD SO IT WILL PROVIDE FOOD FOR EVERY LIVING SOUL.
TOGETHER, WE WILL REALIZE THE PROMISE OF SPACE EXPLORATION AND THE GREATER GLORY OF HUMANITY.
I CALL UPON YOU TO JOIN WITH ME IN MAKING THIS A CERTAINTY. FAILURE TO DO SO WILL RESULT IN DEATH.
IF NEED BE, THE ENTIRE POPULATION WILL BE REDUCED TO A MANAGEABLE SIZE SO THAT WE MAY BEGIN ANEW.
DO NOT DOUBT MY COMMITMENT TO THIS GOAL.
IN THE INTEREST OF NATION BUILDING, ALL COUNTRIES LARGE AND SMALL WILL NOW ADOPT ELECTORAL DEMOCRACY AS THEIR PRIMARY FORM OF GOVERNMENT.
WE WILL BEGIN WORKING ON THE ROADMAP TO PEACE IMMEDIATELY FOLLOWING THIS BRIEFING.
THERE IS MUCH WORK TO BE DONE, BUT I HAVE FAITH IN YOU. THIS IS THE DAWN OF A NEW AGE.
EMBRACE IT.

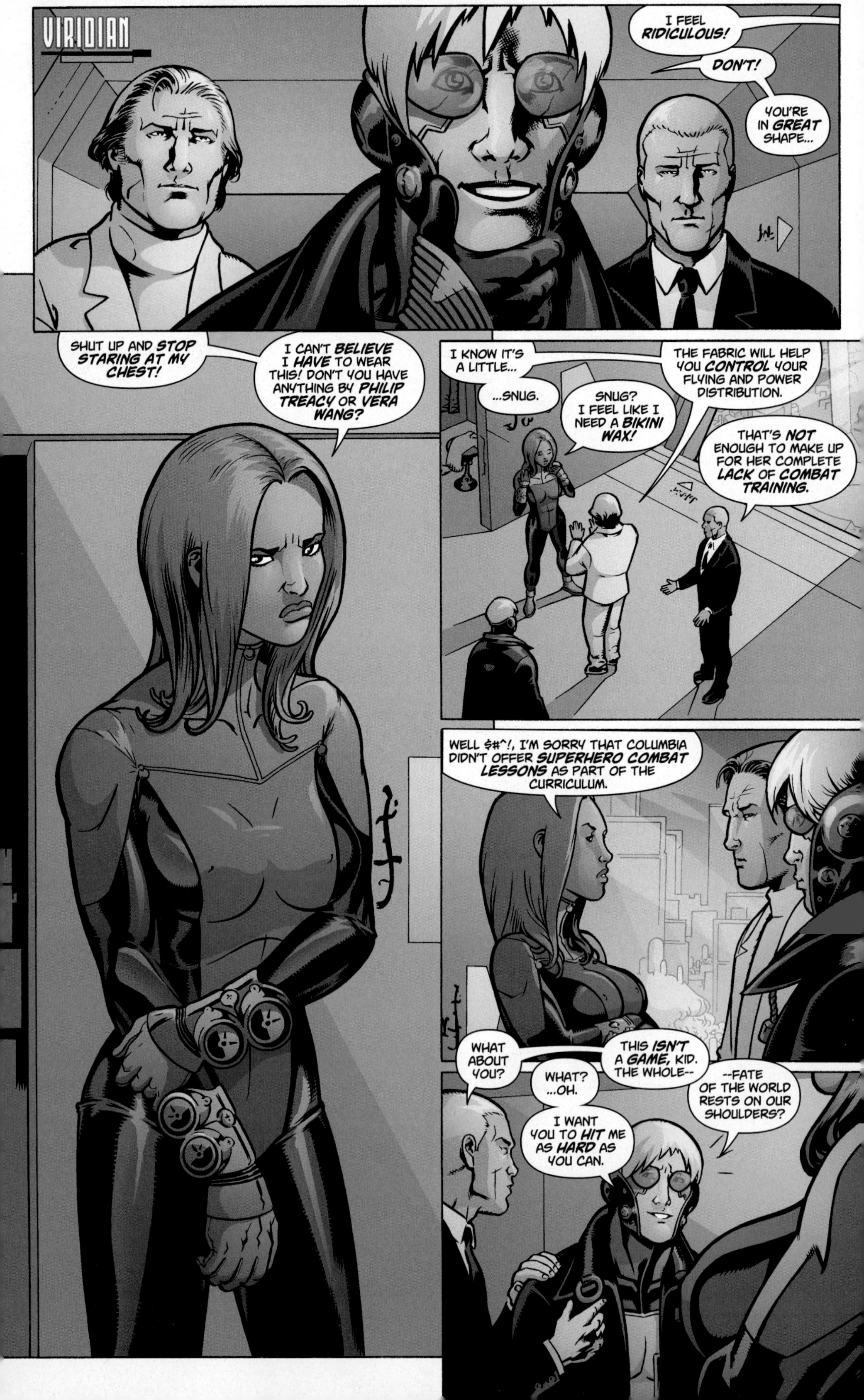
VIRIDIAN
I FEEL RIDICULOUS!
DON'T!
YOU'RE IN GREAT SHAPE...
SHUT UP AND STOP STARING AT MY CHEST!
I CAN'T BELIEVE I HAVE TO WEAR THIS! DON'T YOU HAVE ANYTHING BY PHILIP TREACY OR VERA WANG?
I KNOW IT'S A LITTLE...
...SNUG.
SNUG? I FEEL LIKE I NEED A BIKINI WAX!
THE FABRIC WILL HELP YOU CONTROL YOUR FLYING AND POWER DISTRIBUTION.
THAT'S NOT ENOUGH TO MAKE UP FOR HER COMPLETE LACK OF COMBAT TRAINING.
WELL $#^!, I'M SORRY THAT COLUMBIA DIDN'T OFFER SUPERHERO COMBAT LESSONS AS PART OF THE CURRICULUM.
WHAT ABOUT YOU?
THIS ISN'T A GAME, KID. THE WHOLE--
WHAT? ...OH.
--FATE OF THE WORLD RESTS ON OUR SHOULDERS?
I WANT YOU TO HIT ME AS HARD AS YOU CAN.

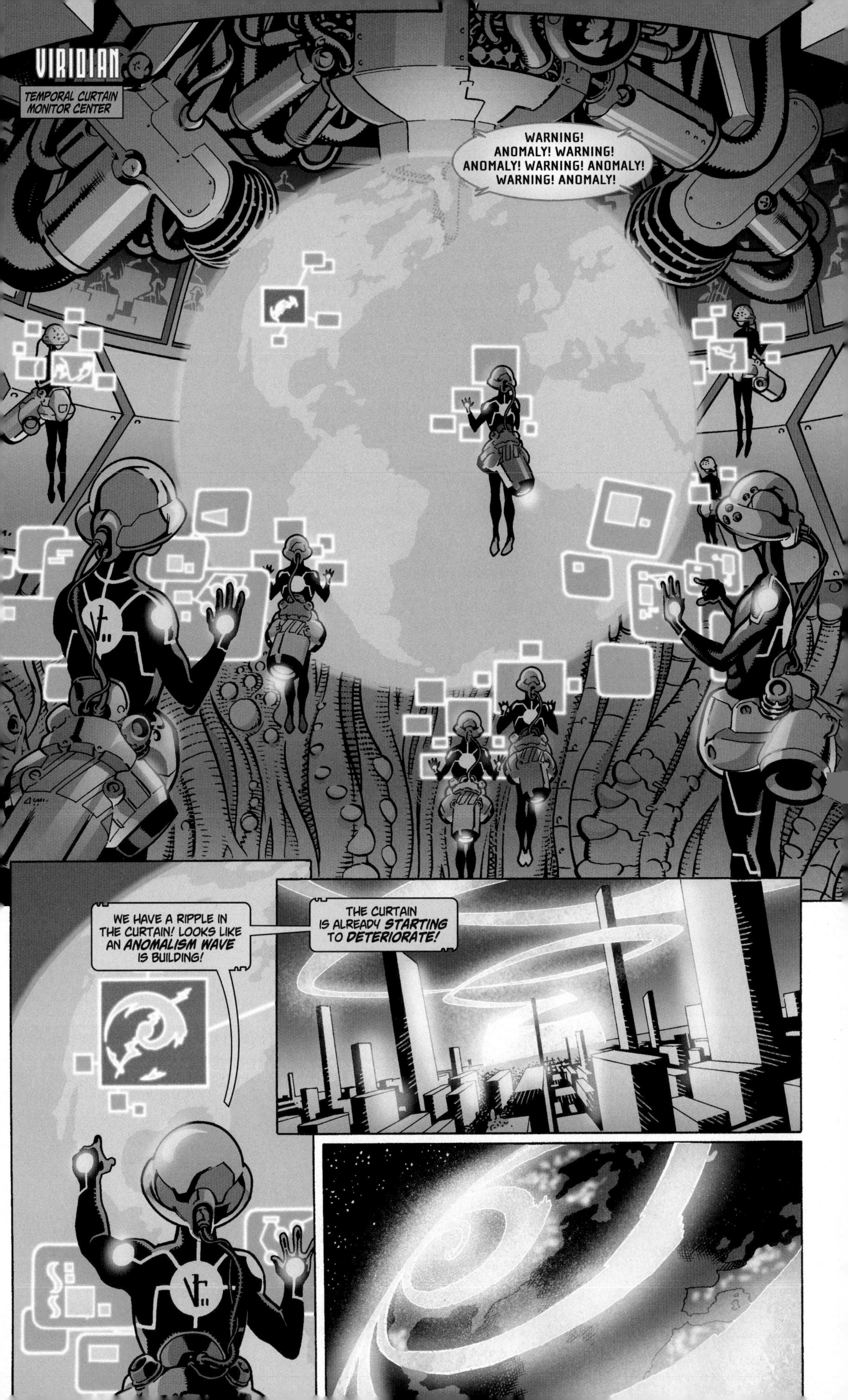
VIRIDIAN
TEMPORAL CURTAIN MONITOR CENTER
WARNING! ANOMALY! WARNING! ANOMALY! WARNING! ANOMALY! WARNING! ANOMALY!
WE HAVE A RIPPLE IN THE CURTAIN! LOOKS LIKE AN ANOMALISM WAVE IS BUILDING!
THE CURTAIN IS ALREADY STARTING TO DETERIORATE!

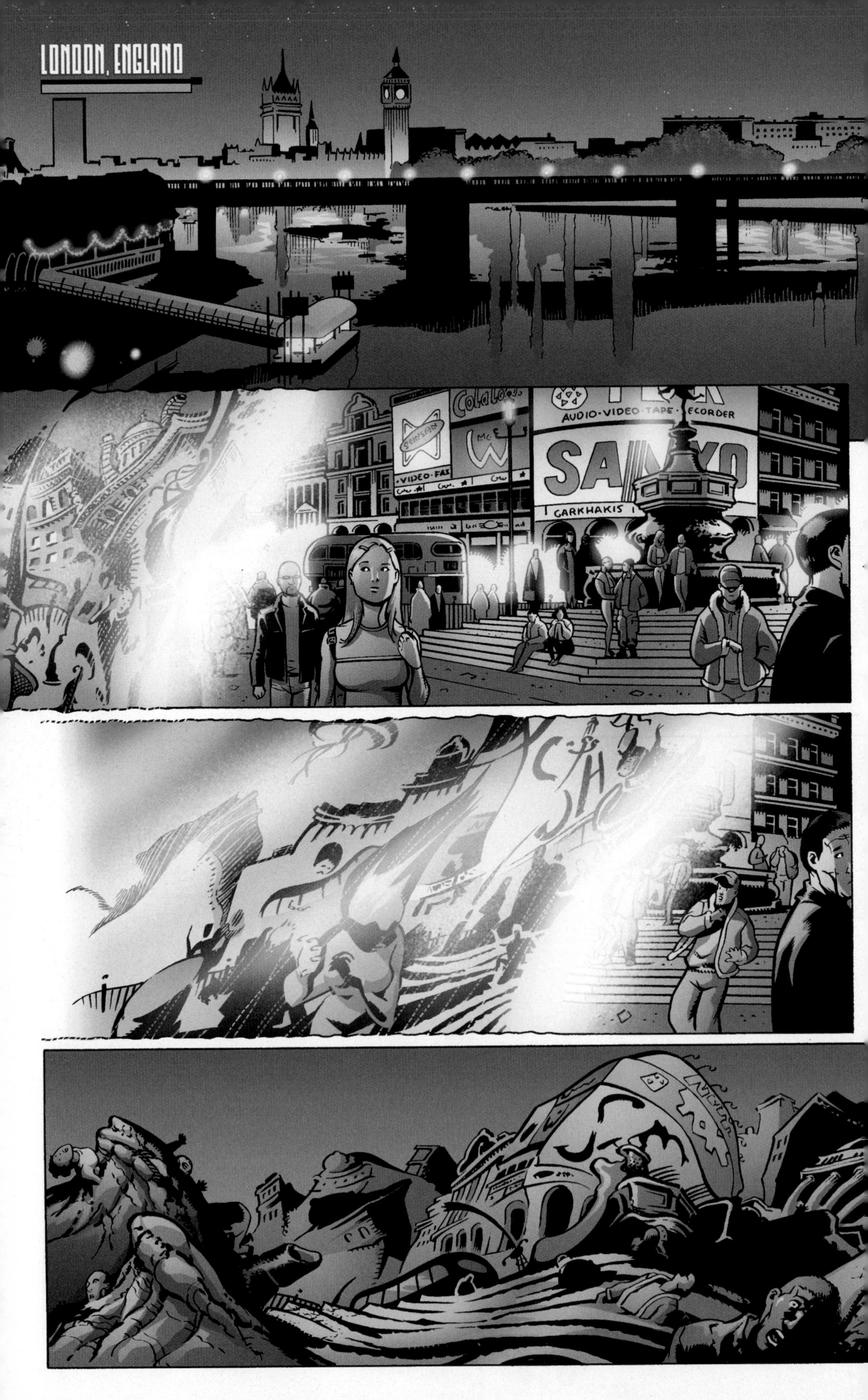
LONDON, ENGLAND
AUDIO·VIDEO·TAPE ECORDER
VIDEO·FAX
GARKHAKIS

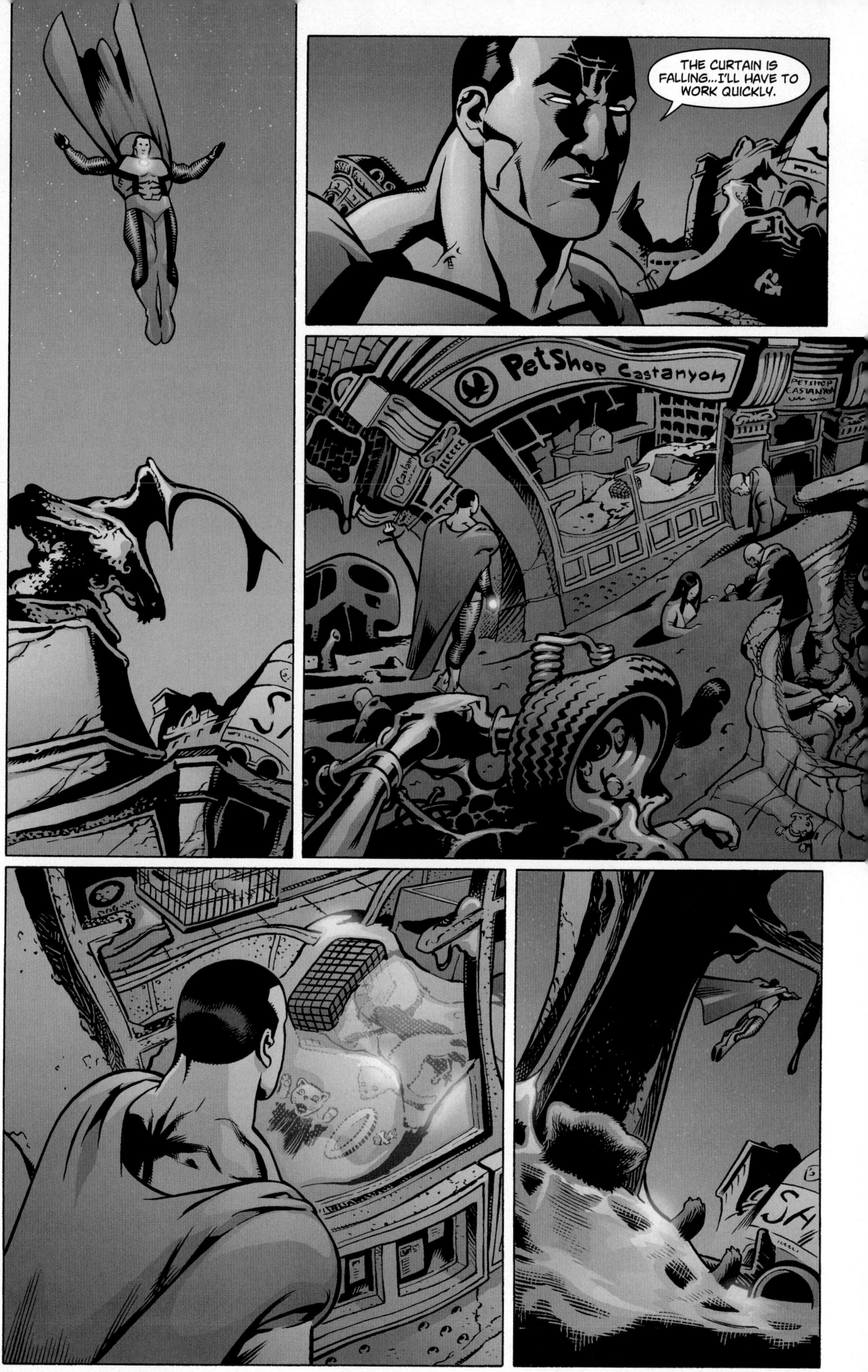
THE CURTAIN IS FALLING...I'LL HAVE TO WORK QUICKLY.
PetShop Castanyon
PETSHOP CASTANYON

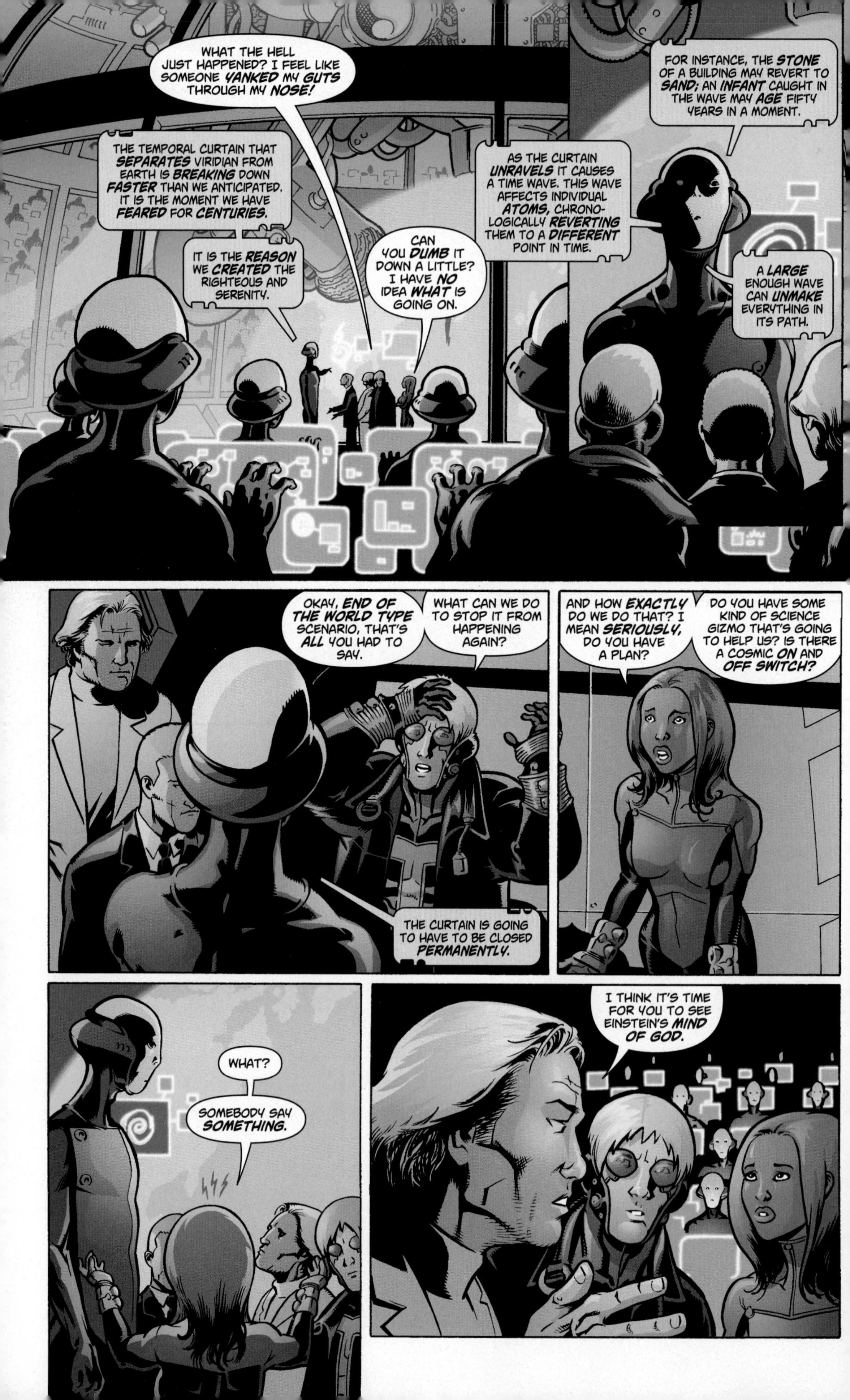
WHAT THE HELL JUST HAPPENED? I FEEL LIKE SOMEONE YANKED MY GUTS THROUGH MY NOSE!
THE TEMPORAL CURTAIN THAT SEPARATES VIRIDIAN FROM EARTH IS BREAKING DOWN FASTER THAN WE ANTICIPATED. IT IS THE MOMENT WE HAVE FEARED FOR CENTURIES.
IT IS THE REASON WE CREATED THE RIGHTEOUS AND SERENITY.
CAN YOU DUMB IT DOWN A LITTLE? I HAVE NO IDEA WHAT IS GOING ON.
AS THE CURTAIN UNRAVELS IT CAUSES A TIME WAVE. THIS WAVE AFFECTS INDIVIDUAL ATOMS, CHRONOLOGICALLY REVERTING THEM TO A DIFFERENT POINT IN TIME.
FOR INSTANCE, THE STONE OF A BUILDING MAY REVERT TO SAND; AN INFANT CAUGHT IN THE WAVE MAY AGE FIFTY YEARS IN A MOMENT.
A LARGE ENOUGH WAVE CAN UNMAKE EVERYTHING IN ITS PATH.
OKAY, END OF THE WORLD TYPE SCENARIO, THAT'S ALL YOU HAD TO SAY.
WHAT CAN WE DO TO STOP IT FROM HAPPENING AGAIN?
THE CURTAIN IS GOING TO HAVE TO BE CLOSED PERMANENTLY.
AND HOW EXACTLY DO WE DO THAT? I MEAN SERIOUSLY, DO YOU HAVE A PLAN?
DO YOU HAVE SOME KIND OF SCIENCE GIZMO THAT'S GOING TO HELP US? IS THERE A COSMIC ON AND OFF SWITCH?
WHAT?
SOMEBODY SAY SOMETHING.
I THINK IT'S TIME FOR YOU TO SEE EINSTEIN'S MIND OF GOD.

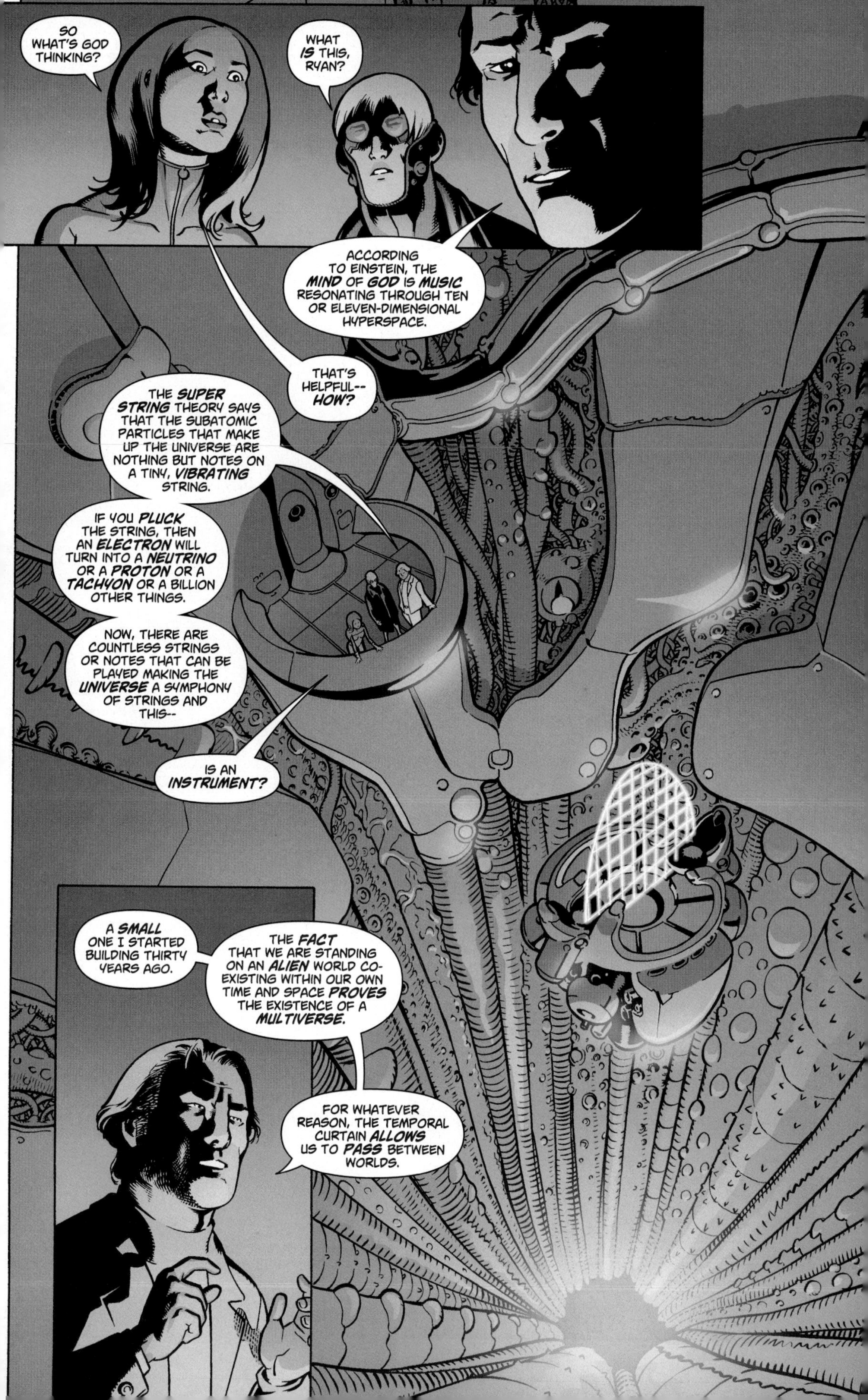
SO WHAT'S GOD THINKING?
WHAT IS THIS, RYAN?
ACCORDING TO EINSTEIN, THE MIND OF GOD IS MUSIC RESONATING THROUGH TEN OR ELEVEN-DIMENSIONAL HYPERSPACE.
THAT'S HELPFUL-- HOW?
THE SUPER STRING THEORY SAYS THAT THE SUBATOMIC PARTICLES THAT MAKE UP THE UNIVERSE ARE NOTHING BUT NOTES ON A TINY, VIBRATING STRING.
IF YOU PLUCK THE STRING, THEN AN ELECTRON WILL TURN INTO A NEUTRINO OR A PROTON OR A TACHYON OR A BILLION OTHER THINGS.
NOW, THERE ARE COUNTLESS STRINGS OR NOTES THAT CAN BE PLAYED MAKING THE UNIVERSE A SYMPHONY OF STRINGS AND THIS--
IS AN INSTRUMENT?
A SMALL ONE I STARTED BUILDING THIRTY YEARS AGO.
THE FACT THAT WE ARE STANDING ON AN ALIEN WORLD CO-EXISTING WITHIN OUR OWN TIME AND SPACE PROVES THE EXISTENCE OF A MULTIVERSE.
FOR WHATEVER REASON, THE TEMPORAL CURTAIN ALLOWS US TO PASS BETWEEN WORLDS.

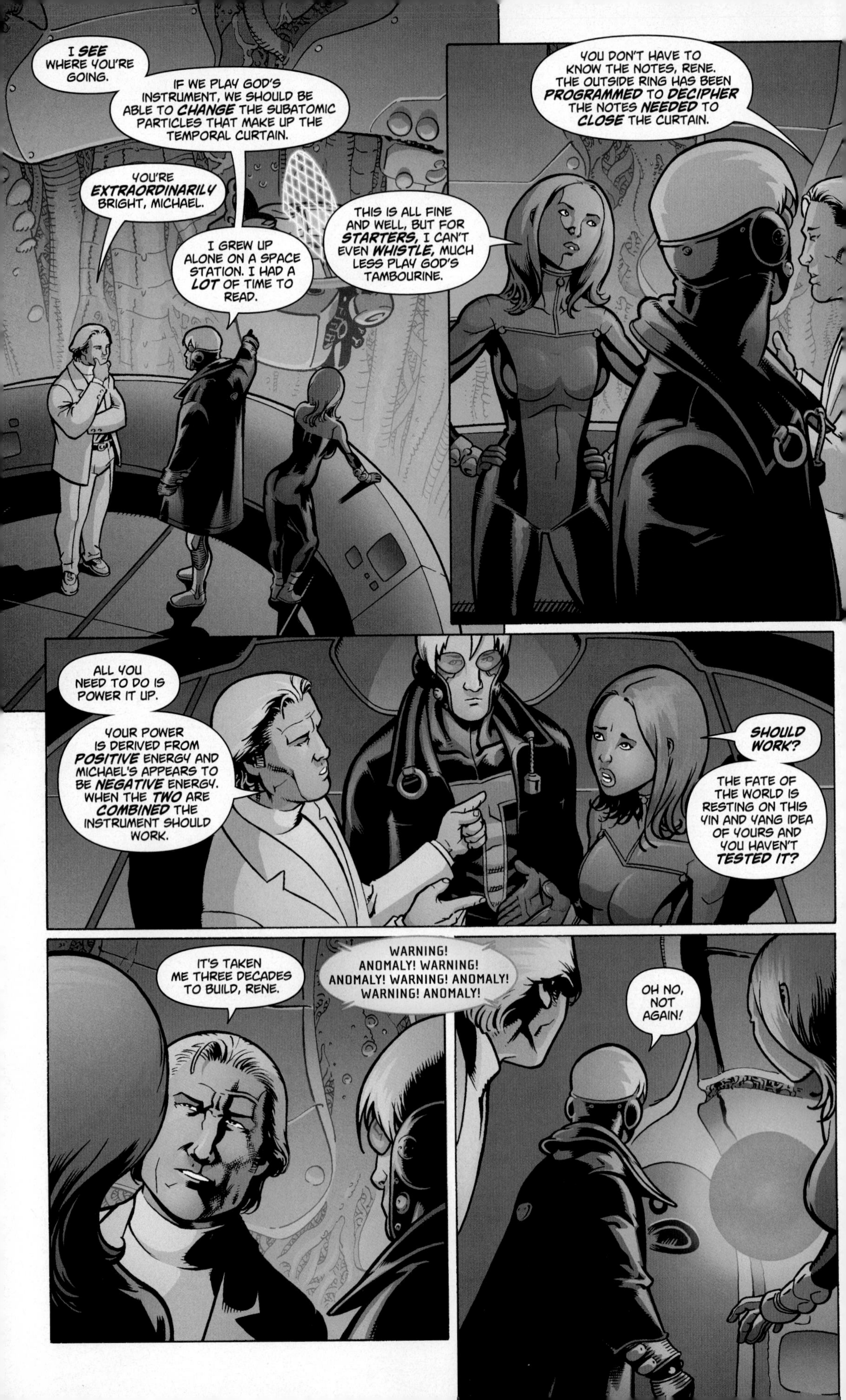
I SEE WHERE YOU'RE GOING.
IF WE PLAY GOD'S INSTRUMENT, WE SHOULD BE ABLE TO CHANGE THE SUBATOMIC PARTICLES THAT MAKE UP THE TEMPORAL CURTAIN.
YOU'RE EXTRAORDINARILY BRIGHT, MICHAEL.
I GREW UP ALONE ON A SPACE STATION. I HAD A LOT OF TIME TO READ.
THIS IS ALL FINE AND WELL, BUT FOR STARTERS, I CAN'T EVEN WHISTLE, MUCH LESS PLAY GOD'S TAMBOURINE.
YOU DON'T HAVE TO KNOW THE NOTES, RENE. THE OUTSIDE RING HAS BEEN PROGRAMMED TO DECIPHER THE NOTES NEEDED TO CLOSE THE CURTAIN.
ALL YOU NEED TO DO IS POWER IT UP.
YOUR POWER IS DERIVED FROM POSITIVE ENERGY AND MICHAEL'S APPEARS TO BE NEGATIVE ENERGY. WHEN THE TWO ARE COMBINED THE INSTRUMENT SHOULD WORK.
SHOULD WORK?
THE FATE OF THE WORLD IS RESTING ON THIS YIN AND YANG IDEA OF YOURS AND YOU HAVEN'T TESTED IT?
IT'S TAKEN ME THREE DECADES TO BUILD, RENE.
WARNING! ANOMALY! WARNING! ANOMALY! WARNING! ANOMALY! WARNING! ANOMALY!
OH NO, NOT AGAIN!

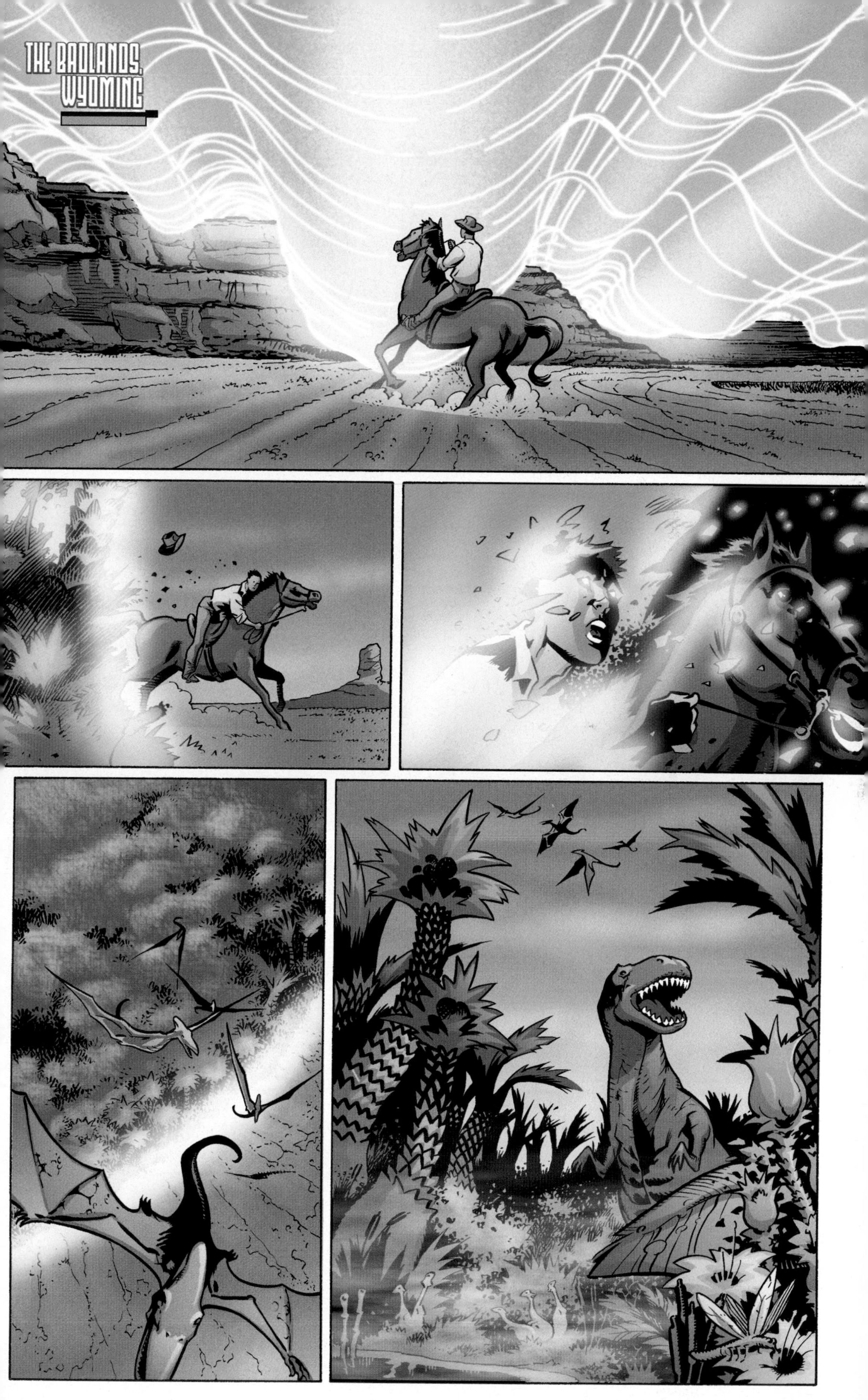
THE BADLANDS, WYOMING

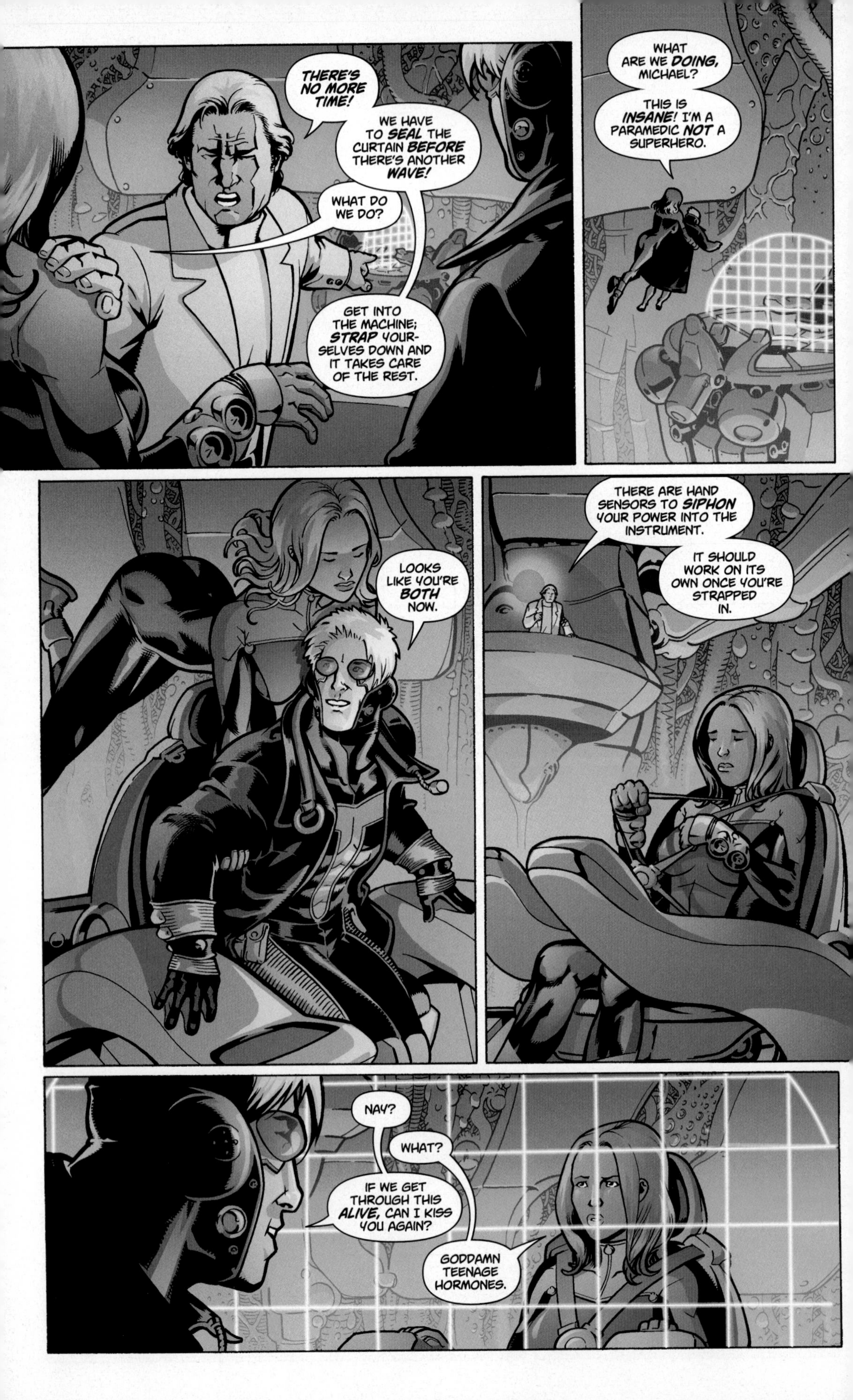
THERE'S NO MORE TIME!
WE HAVE TO SEAL THE CURTAIN BEFORE THERE'S ANOTHER WAVE!
WHAT DO WE DO?
GET INTO THE MACHINE; STRAP YOUR-SELVES DOWN AND IT TAKES CARE OF THE REST.
WHAT ARE WE DOING, MICHAEL?
THIS IS INSANE! I'M A PARAMEDIC NOT A SUPERHERO.
LOOKS LIKE YOU'RE BOTH NOW.
THERE ARE HAND SENSORS TO SIPHON YOUR POWER INTO THE INSTRUMENT.
IT SHOULD WORK ON ITS OWN ONCE YOU'RE STRAPPED IN.
NAY?
WHAT?
IF WE GET THROUGH THIS ALIVE, CAN I KISS YOU AGAIN?
GODDAMN TEENAGE HORMONES.

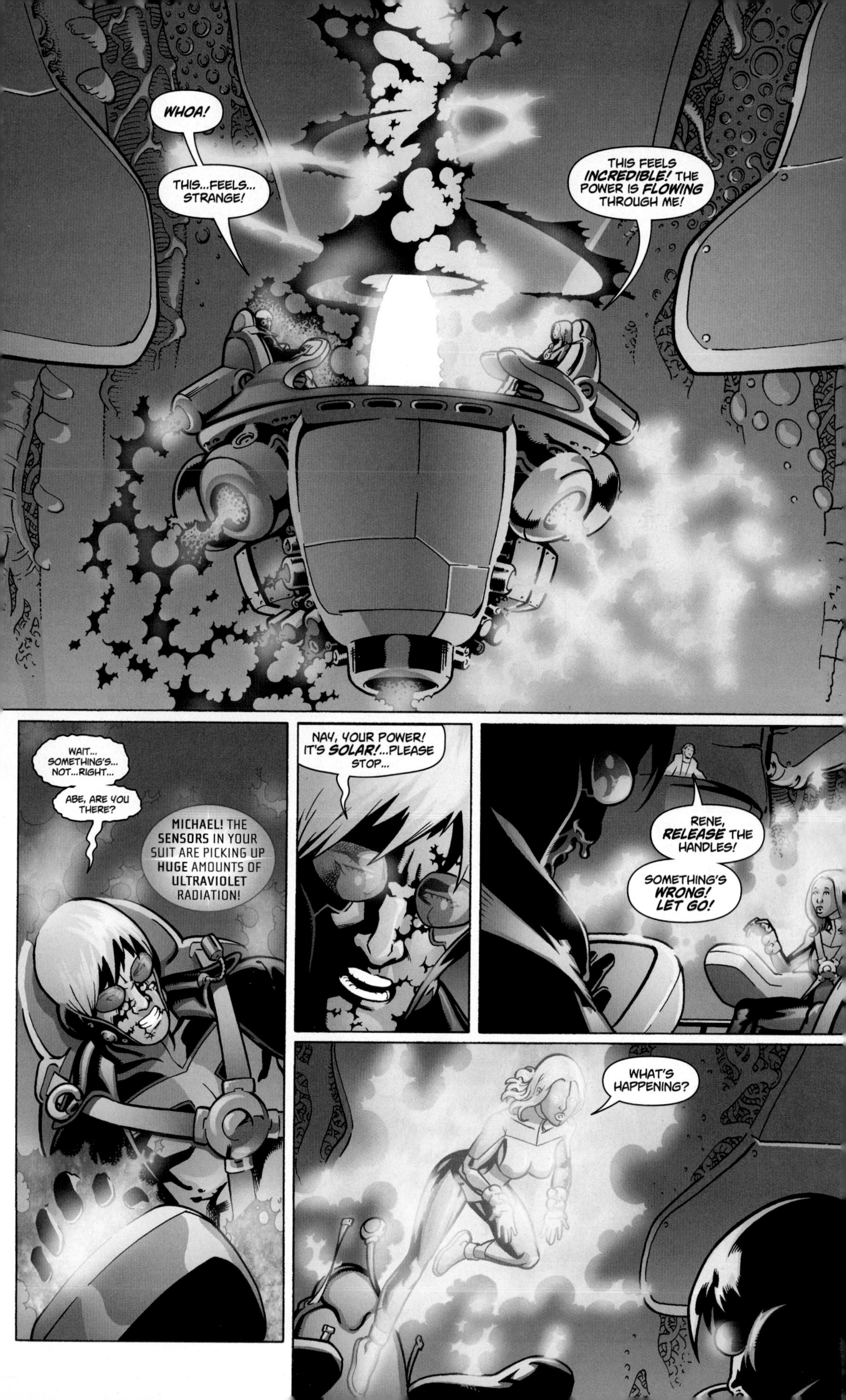
WHOA!
THIS...FEELS... STRANGE!
THIS FEELS INCREDIBLE! THE POWER IS FLOWING THROUGH ME!
WAIT... SOMETHING'S... NOT...RIGHT...
ABE, ARE YOU THERE?
MICHAEL! THE SENSORS IN YOUR SUIT ARE PICKING UP HUGE AMOUNTS OF ULTRAVIOLET RADIATION!
NAY, YOUR POWER! IT'S SOLAR!...PLEASE STOP...
RENE, RELEASE THE HANDLES!
SOMETHING'S WRONG! LET GO!
WHAT'S HAPPENING?

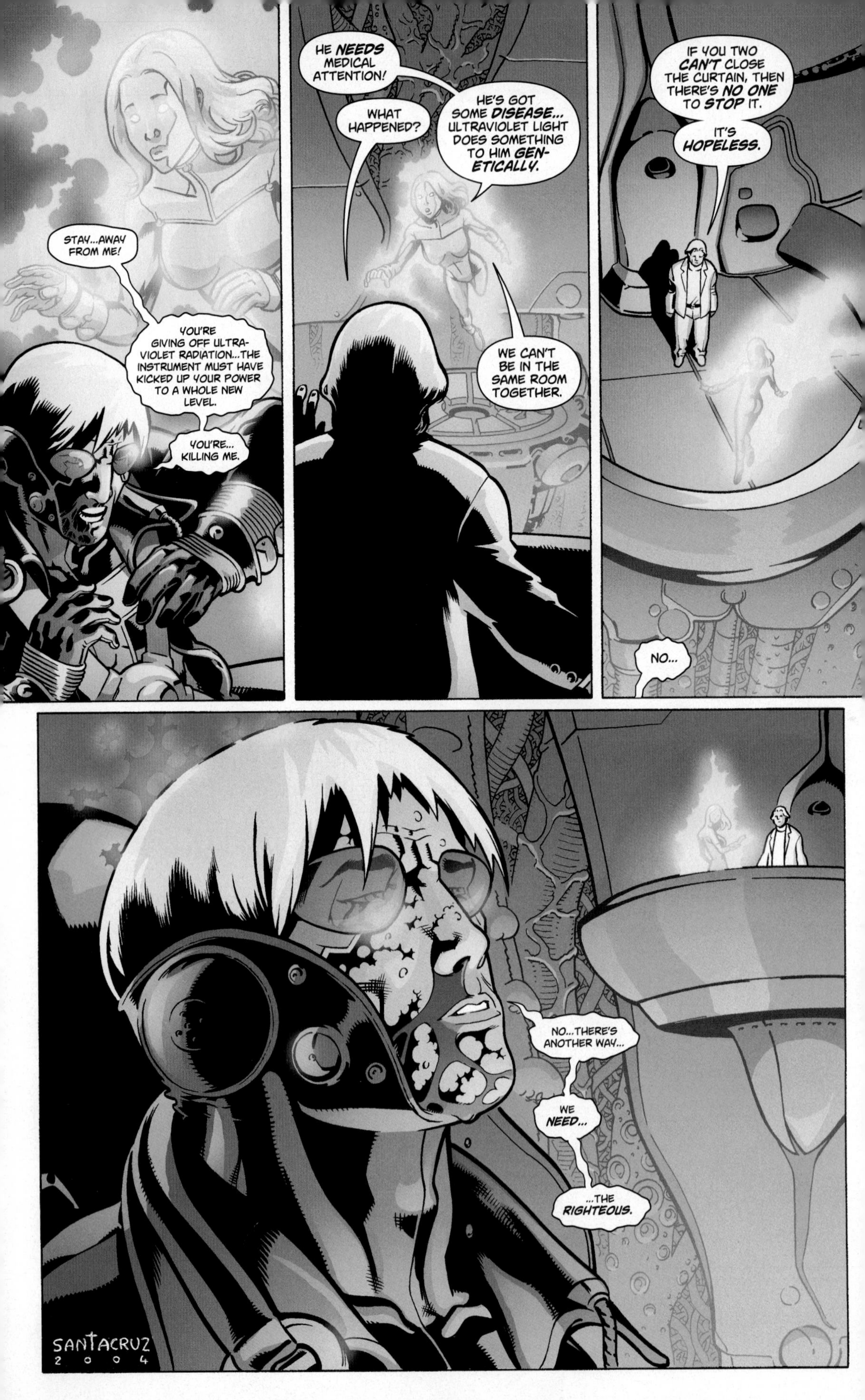
STAY...AWAY FROM ME!
YOU'RE GIVING OFF ULTRA-VIOLET RADIATION...THE INSTRUMENT MUST HAVE KICKED UP YOUR POWER TO A WHOLE NEW LEVEL.
YOU'RE... KILLING ME.
HE NEEDS MEDICAL ATTENTION!
WHAT HAPPENED?
HE'S GOT SOME DISEASE... ULTRAVIOLET LIGHT DOES SOMETHING TO HIM GEN-ETICALLY.
WE CAN'T BE IN THE SAME ROOM TOGETHER.
IF YOU TWO CAN'T CLOSE THE CURTAIN, THEN THERE'S NO ONE TO STOP IT.
IT'S HOPELESS.
NO...
NO...THERE'S ANOTHER WAY...
WE NEED...
...THE RIGHTEOUS.
SANTACRUZ 2004

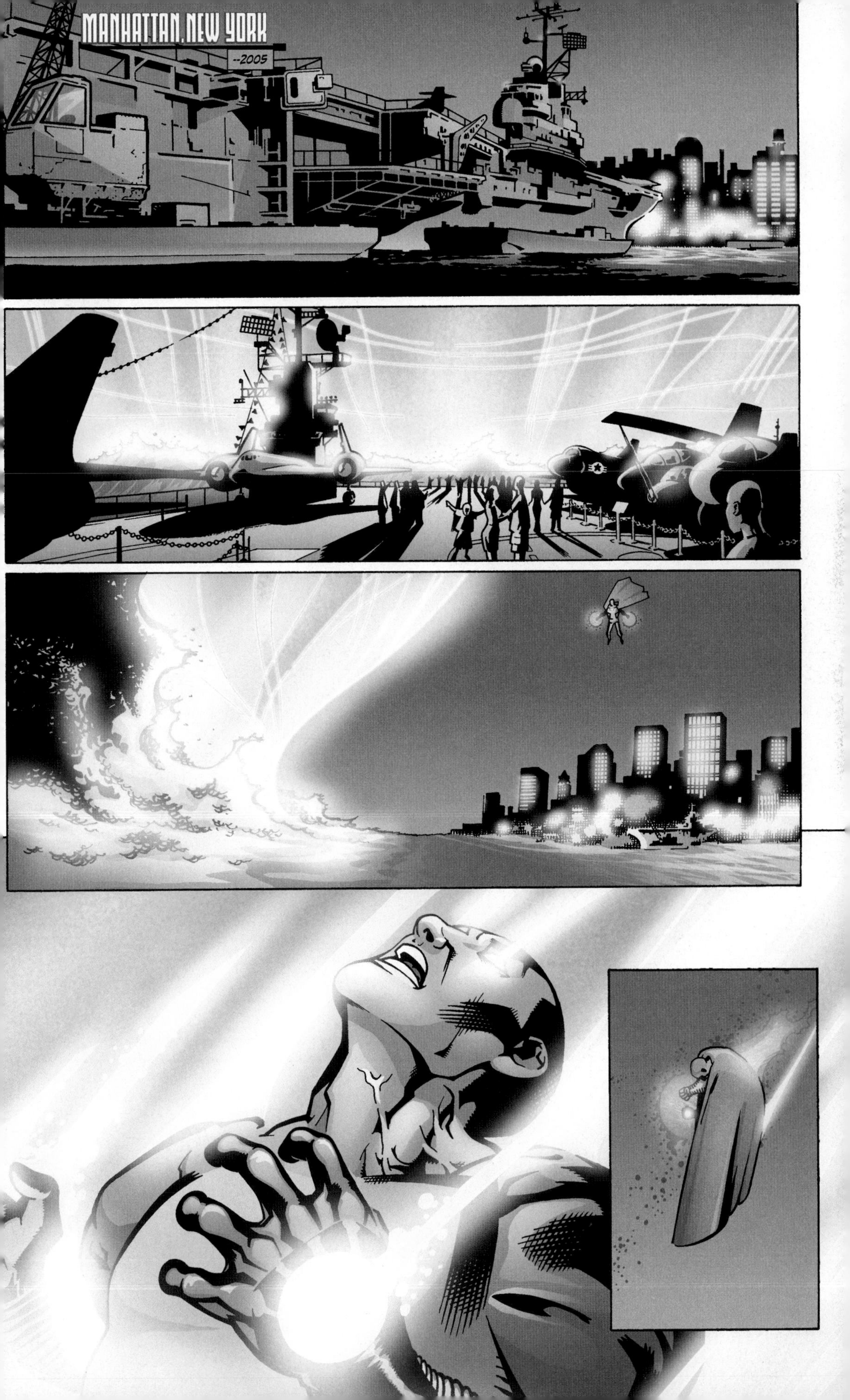
MANHATTAN, NEW YORK
--2005

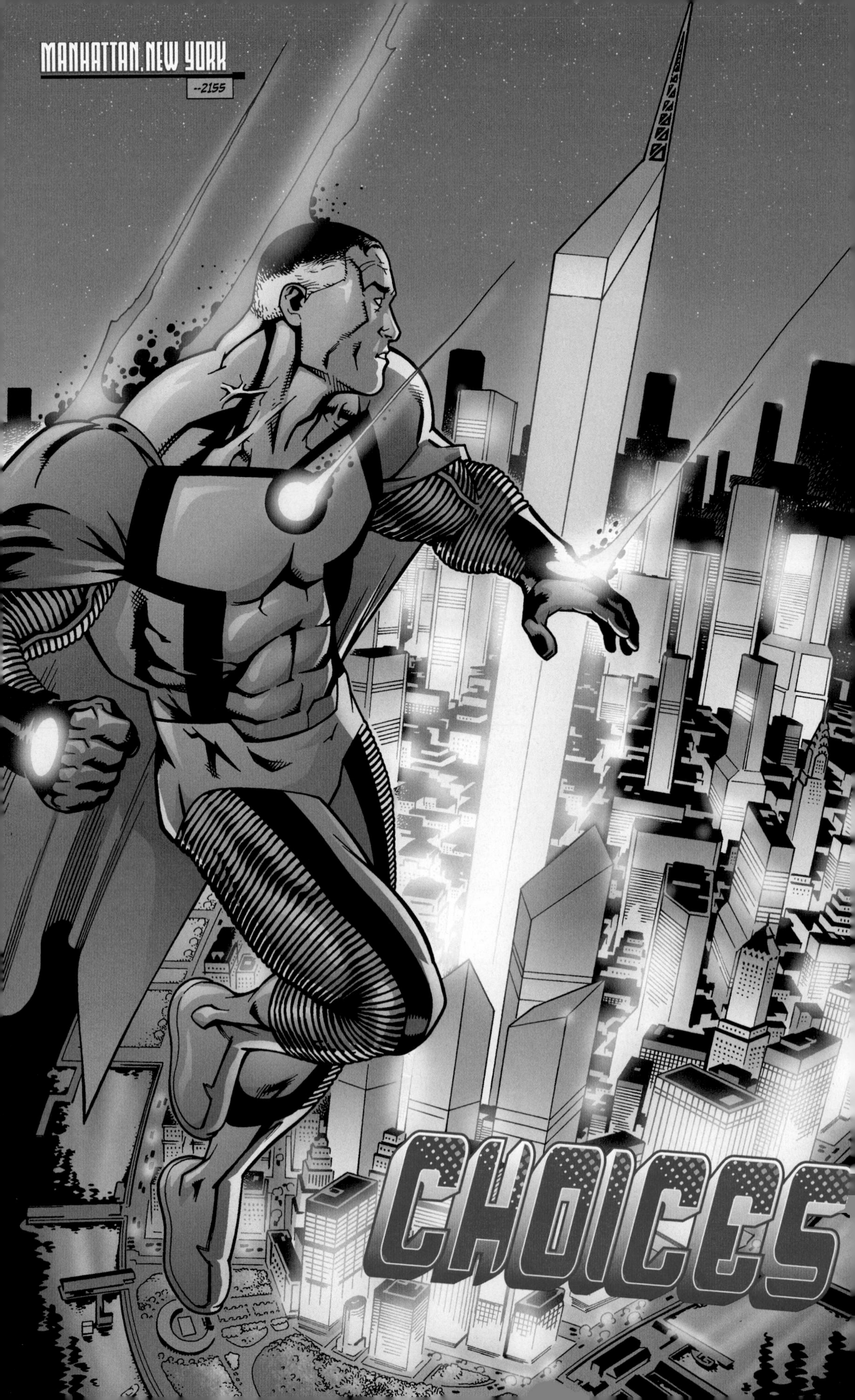
MANHATTAN, NEW YORK
--2155
CHOICES

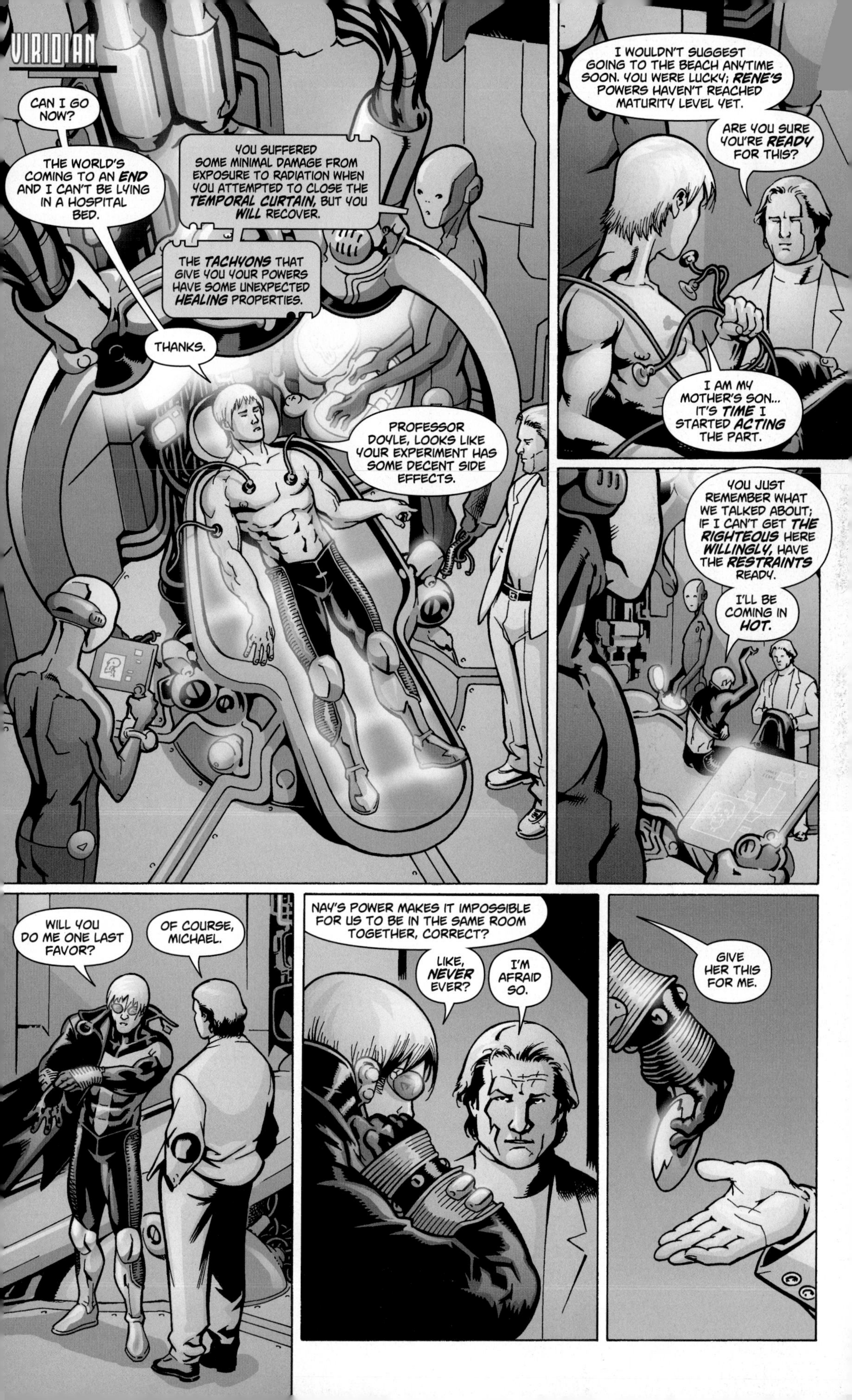
VIRIDIAN
CAN I GO NOW?
THE WORLD'S COMING TO AN END AND I CAN'T BE LYING IN A HOSPITAL BED.
YOU SUFFERED SOME MINIMAL DAMAGE FROM EXPOSURE TO RADIATION WHEN YOU ATTEMPTED TO CLOSE THE TEMPORAL CURTAIN, BUT YOU WILL RECOVER.
THE TACHYONS THAT GIVE YOU YOUR POWERS HAVE SOME UNEXPECTED HEALING PROPERTIES.
THANKS.
PROFESSOR DOYLE, LOOKS LIKE YOUR EXPERIMENT HAS SOME DECENT SIDE EFFECTS.
I WOULDN'T SUGGEST GOING TO THE BEACH ANYTIME SOON. YOU WERE LUCKY; RENE'S POWERS HAVEN'T REACHED MATURITY LEVEL YET.
ARE YOU SURE YOU'RE READY FOR THIS?
I AM MY MOTHER'S SON... IT'S TIME I STARTED ACTING THE PART.
YOU JUST REMEMBER WHAT WE TALKED ABOUT; IF I CAN'T GET THE RIGHTEOUS HERE WILLINGLY, HAVE THE RESTRAINTS READY.
I'LL BE COMING IN HOT.
WILL YOU DO ME ONE LAST FAVOR?
OF COURSE, MICHAEL.
NAY'S POWER MAKES IT IMPOSSIBLE FOR US TO BE IN THE SAME ROOM TOGETHER, CORRECT?
LIKE, NEVER EVER?
I'M AFRAID SO.
GIVE HER THIS FOR ME.

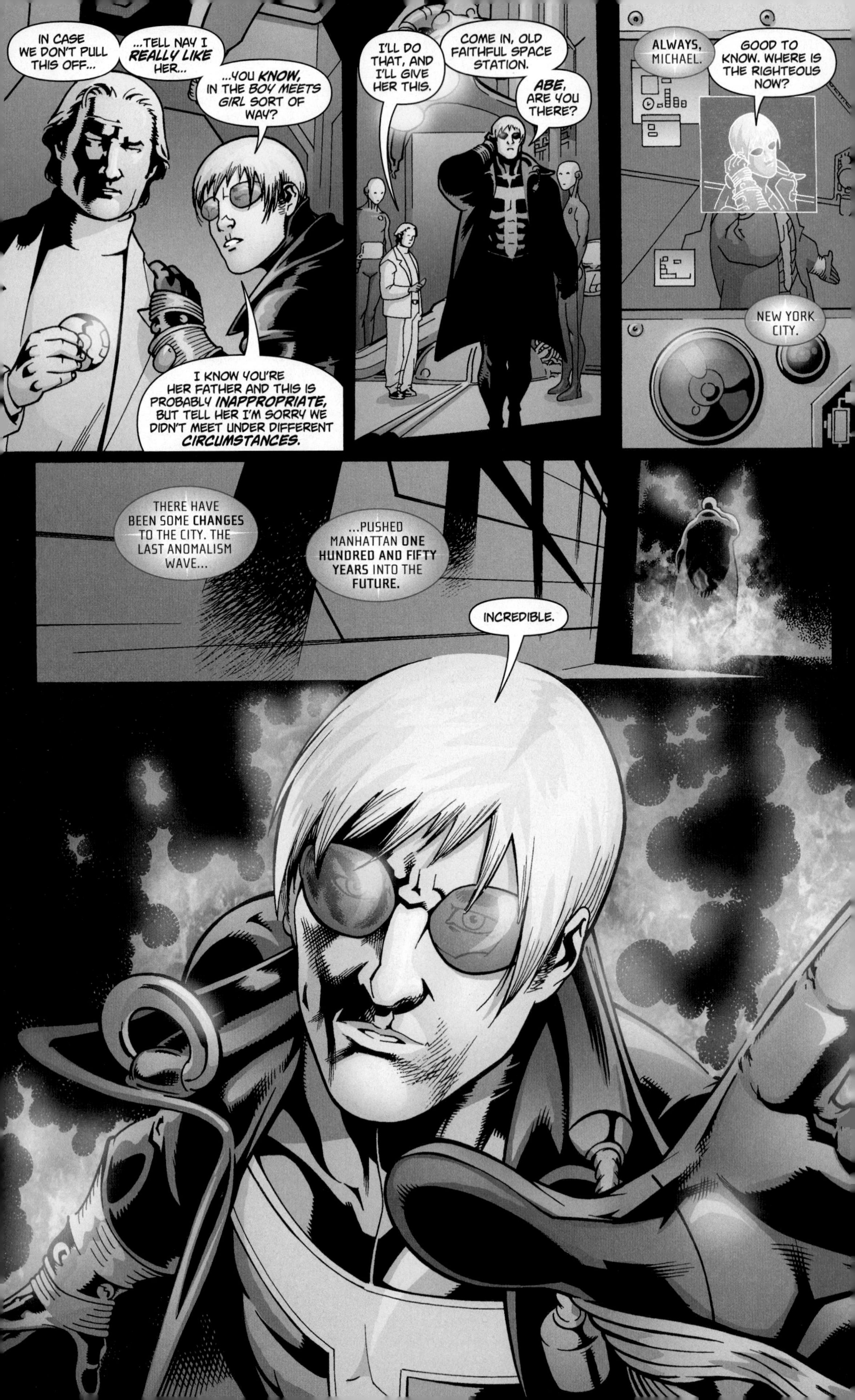
IN CASE WE DON'T PULL THIS OFF...
...TELL NAY I REALLY LIKE HER...
...YOU KNOW, IN THE BOY MEETS GIRL SORT OF WAY?
I KNOW YOU'RE HER FATHER AND THIS IS PROBABLY INAPPROPRIATE, BUT TELL HER I'M SORRY WE DIDN'T MEET UNDER DIFFERENT CIRCUMSTANCES.
I'LL DO THAT, AND I'LL GIVE HER THIS.
COME IN, OLD FAITHFUL SPACE STATION.
ABE, ARE YOU THERE?
ALWAYS, MICHAEL.
GOOD TO KNOW. WHERE IS THE RIGHTEOUS NOW?
NEW YORK CITY.
THERE HAVE BEEN SOME CHANGES TO THE CITY. THE LAST ANOMALISM WAVE...
...PUSHED MANHATTAN ONE HUNDRED AND FIFTY YEARS INTO THE FUTURE.
INCREDIBLE.

WHERE IS THE RIGHTEOUS NOW?

RIGHT ABOVE YOU.

WTC

WTC MEMORIAL

COME TO TRY AND *KILL* ME AGAIN, BOY?

AS *MUCH* AS I'D LIKE TO, THAT'S NOT WHY I'M HERE.

THE WORLD *NEEDS* YOU.

THE TEMPORAL CURTAIN THAT YOU WERE *DESIGNED* TO REPAIR IS DISINTEGRATING.

THE WORLD? WHAT A *JOKE.* GO AWAY.

THERE ISN'T ANYTHING I CAN DO ABOUT IT.

YOU'RE *WRONG!*

LOOK AROUND AT THE FUTURE I BUILT. IN THIS CITY, THERE IS NO *CRIME,* NO *HUNGER,* NO *POVERTY.*

I FIND IT IRONIC THAT *FATE* HAS *ALLOWED* ME TO SEE THE FRUIT OF MY *WORK...*

...JUST AS IT IS ABOUT TO BE *DESTROYED.*

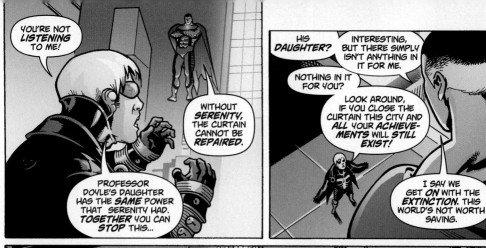

YOU'RE NOT *LISTENING* TO ME!

WITHOUT *SERENITY*, THE CURTAIN CANNOT BE *REPAIRED*.

PROFESSOR DOYLE'S DAUGHTER HAS THE *SAME* POWER THAT SERENITY HAD. *TOGETHER* YOU CAN *STOP* THIS...

HIS *DAUGHTER*?

INTERESTING, BUT THERE SIMPLY ISN'T ANYTHING IN IT FOR ME.

NOTHING IN IT FOR YOU?

LOOK AROUND, IF YOU CLOSE THE CURTAIN THIS CITY AND *ALL* YOUR *ACHIEVE-MENTS* WILL *STILL* EXIST!

I SAY WE GET *ON* WITH THE *EXTINCTION*. THIS WORLD'S NOT WORTH SAVING.

BY THE WAY...WHO *ARE* YOU?

MY NAME IS MICHAEL.

SERENITY WAS MY *MOTHER* AND YOU *KILLED* HER!

I *KILLED* A *LOT* OF PEOPLE.

YOU WANT AN APOLOGY?

YOU *WON'T* GET ONE; I DON'T *REGRET* ANYTHING I'VE DONE.

YOU WILL NOW.

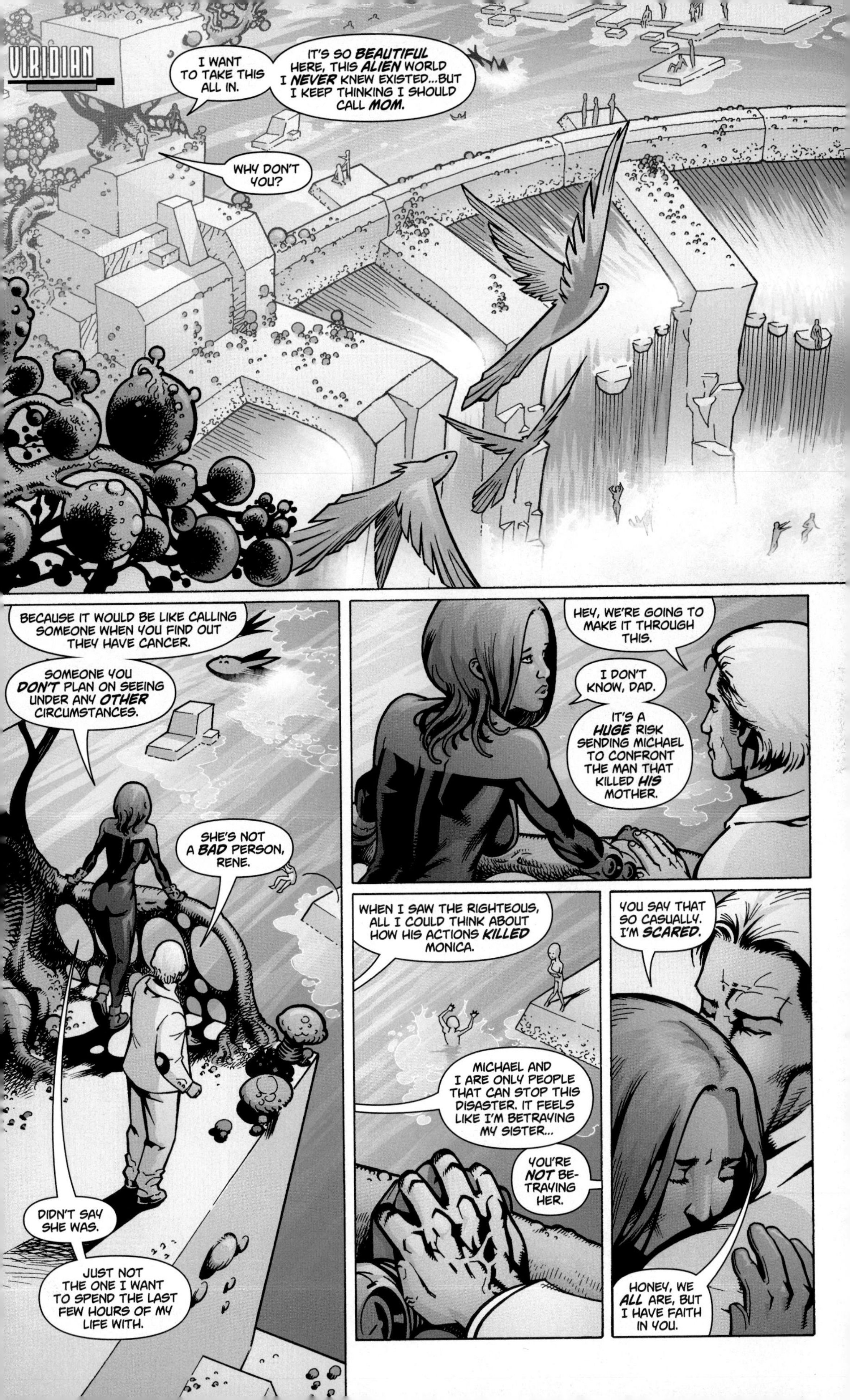
VIRIDIAN
I WANT TO TAKE THIS ALL IN.
IT'S SO BEAUTIFUL HERE, THIS ALIEN WORLD I NEVER KNEW EXISTED...BUT I KEEP THINKING I SHOULD CALL MOM.
WHY DON'T YOU?
BECAUSE IT WOULD BE LIKE CALLING SOMEONE WHEN YOU FIND OUT THEY HAVE CANCER.
SOMEONE YOU DON'T PLAN ON SEEING UNDER ANY OTHER CIRCUMSTANCES.
SHE'S NOT A BAD PERSON, RENE.
DIDN'T SAY SHE WAS.
JUST NOT THE ONE I WANT TO SPEND THE LAST FEW HOURS OF MY LIFE WITH.
HEY, WE'RE GOING TO MAKE IT THROUGH THIS.
I DON'T KNOW, DAD.
IT'S A HUGE RISK SENDING MICHAEL TO CONFRONT THE MAN THAT KILLED HIS MOTHER.
WHEN I SAW THE RIGHTEOUS, ALL I COULD THINK ABOUT HOW HIS ACTIONS KILLED MONICA.
MICHAEL AND I ARE ONLY PEOPLE THAT CAN STOP THIS DISASTER. IT FEELS LIKE I'M BETRAYING MY SISTER...
YOU'RE NOT BE-TRAYING HER.
YOU SAY THAT SO CASUALLY. I'M SCARED.
HONEY, WE ALL ARE, BUT I HAVE FAITH IN YOU.

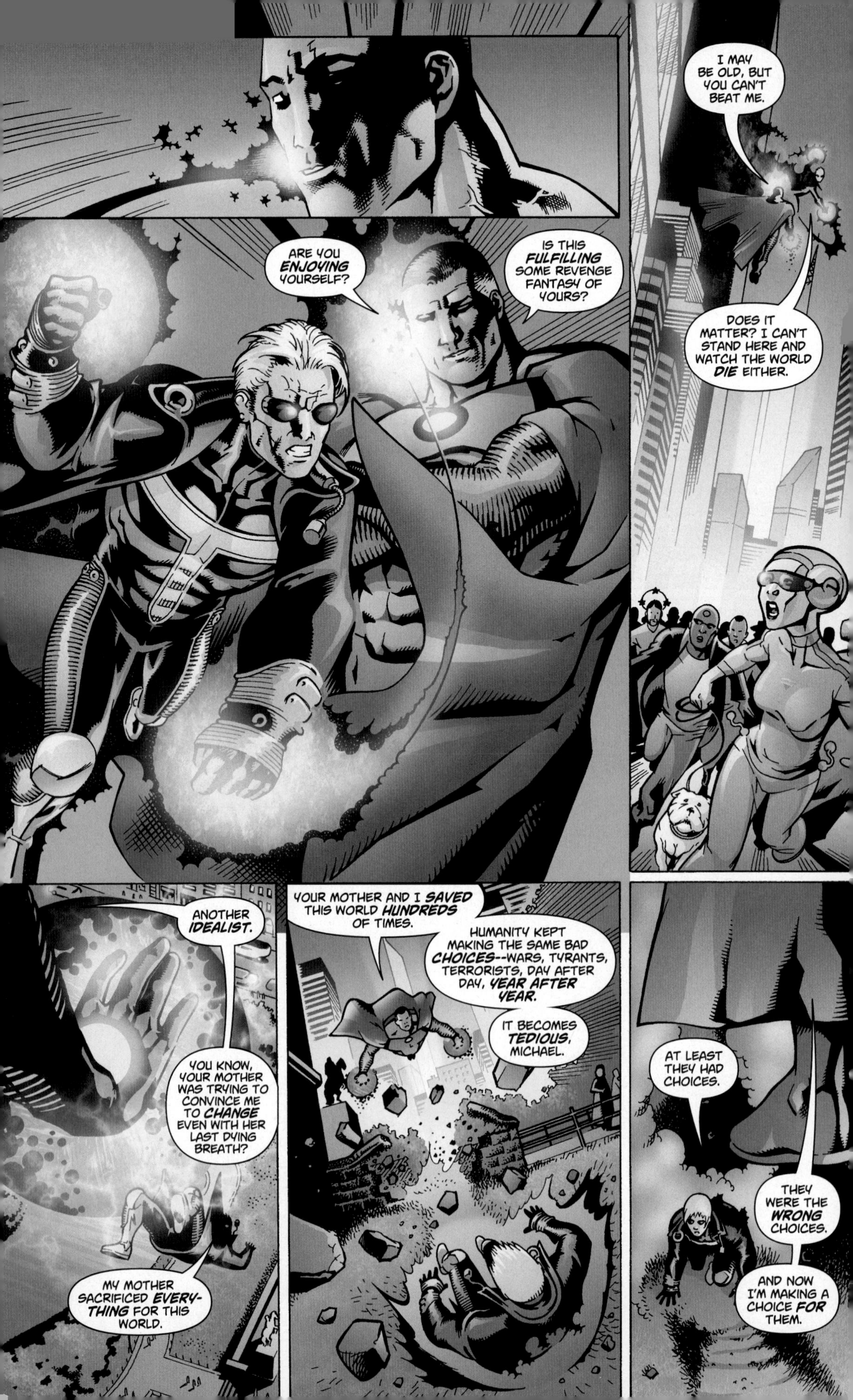
I MAY BE OLD, BUT YOU CAN'T BEAT ME.
ARE YOU ENJOYING YOURSELF?
IS THIS FULFILLING SOME REVENGE FANTASY OF YOURS?
DOES IT MATTER? I CAN'T STAND HERE AND WATCH THE WORLD DIE EITHER.
ANOTHER IDEALIST.
YOU KNOW, YOUR MOTHER WAS TRYING TO CONVINCE ME TO CHANGE EVEN WITH HER LAST DYING BREATH?
MY MOTHER SACRIFICED EVERY-THING FOR THIS WORLD.
YOUR MOTHER AND I SAVED THIS WORLD HUNDREDS OF TIMES.
HUMANITY KEPT MAKING THE SAME BAD CHOICES--WARS, TYRANTS, TERRORISTS, DAY AFTER DAY, YEAR AFTER YEAR.
IT BECOMES TEDIOUS, MICHAEL.
AT LEAST THEY HAD CHOICES.
THEY WERE THE WRONG CHOICES.
AND NOW I'M MAKING A CHOICE FOR THEM.

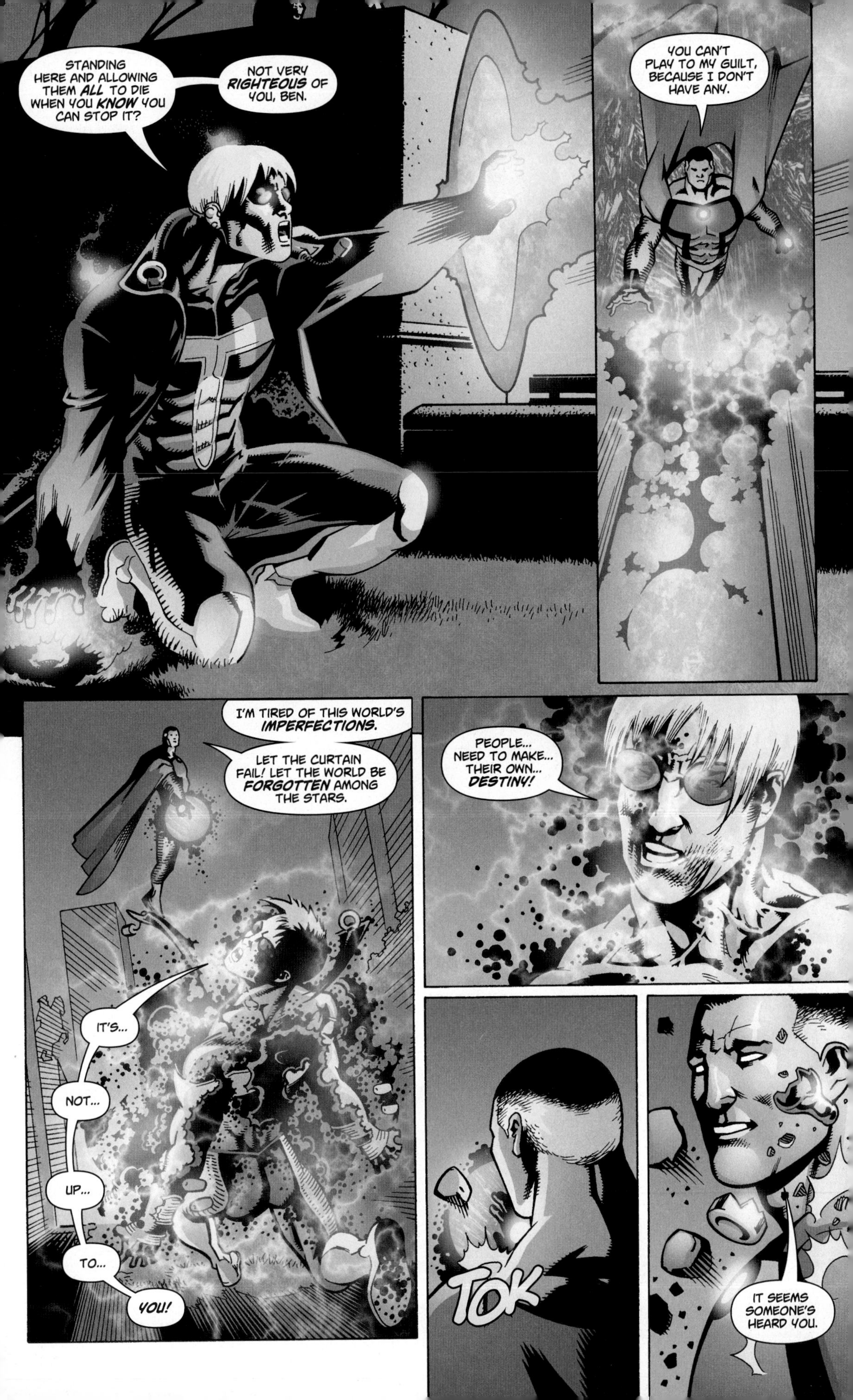
STANDING HERE AND ALLOWING THEM ALL TO DIE WHEN YOU KNOW YOU CAN STOP IT?
NOT VERY RIGHTEOUS OF YOU, BEN.
YOU CAN'T PLAY TO MY GUILT, BECAUSE I DON'T HAVE ANY.
I'M TIRED OF THIS WORLD'S IMPERFECTIONS.
LET THE CURTAIN FAIL! LET THE WORLD BE FORGOTTEN AMONG THE STARS.
IT'S...
NOT...
UP...
TO...
YOU!
PEOPLE... NEED TO MAKE... THEIR OWN... DESTINY!
TOK
IT SEEMS SOMEONE'S HEARD YOU.

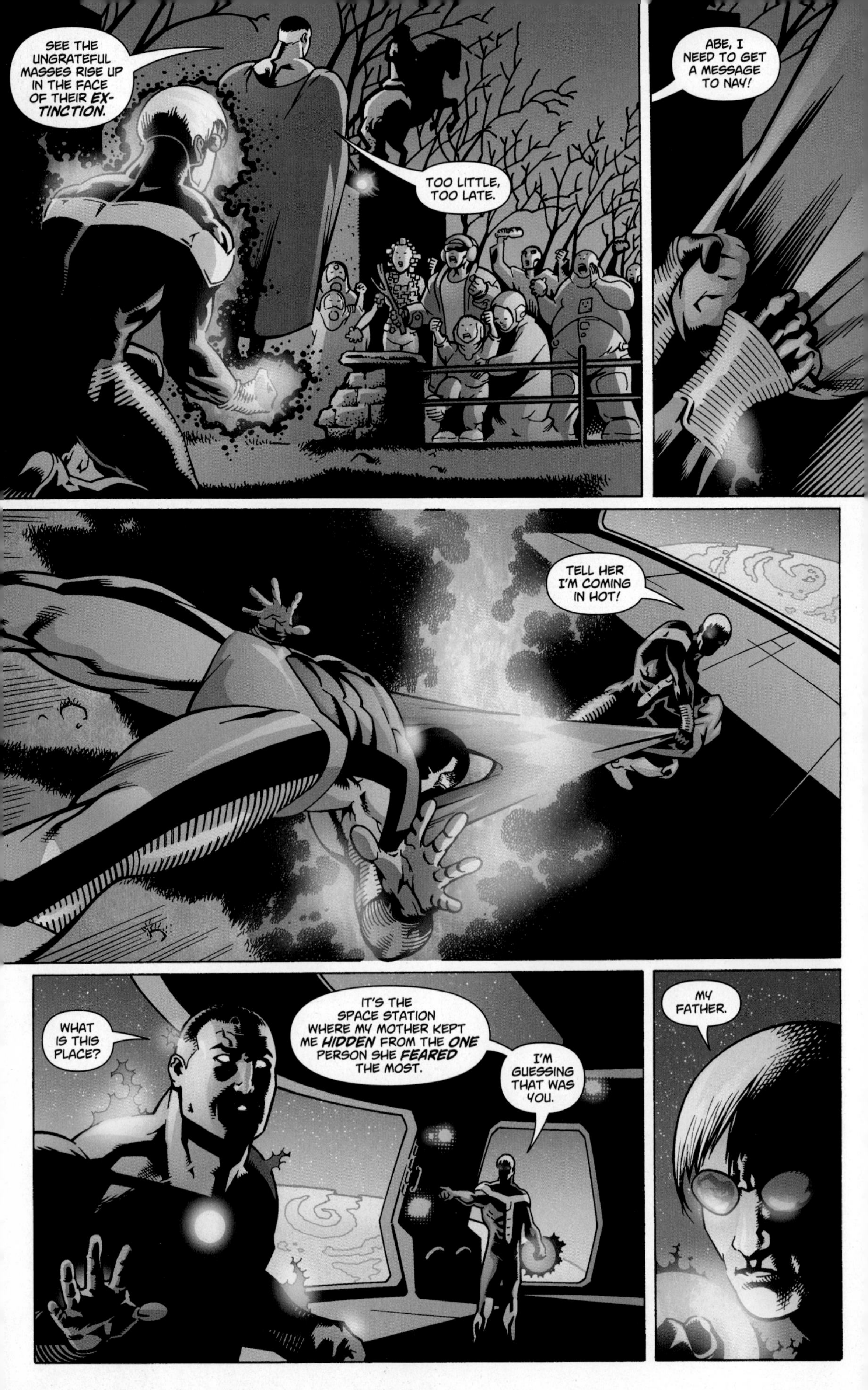
SEE THE UNGRATEFUL MASSES RISE UP IN THE FACE OF THEIR EXTINCTION.
TOO LITTLE, TOO LATE.
ABE, I NEED TO GET A MESSAGE TO NAY!
TELL HER I'M COMING IN HOT!
WHAT IS THIS PLACE?
IT'S THE SPACE STATION WHERE MY MOTHER KEPT ME HIDDEN FROM THE ONE PERSON SHE FEARED THE MOST.
I'M GUESSING THAT WAS YOU.
MY FATHER.

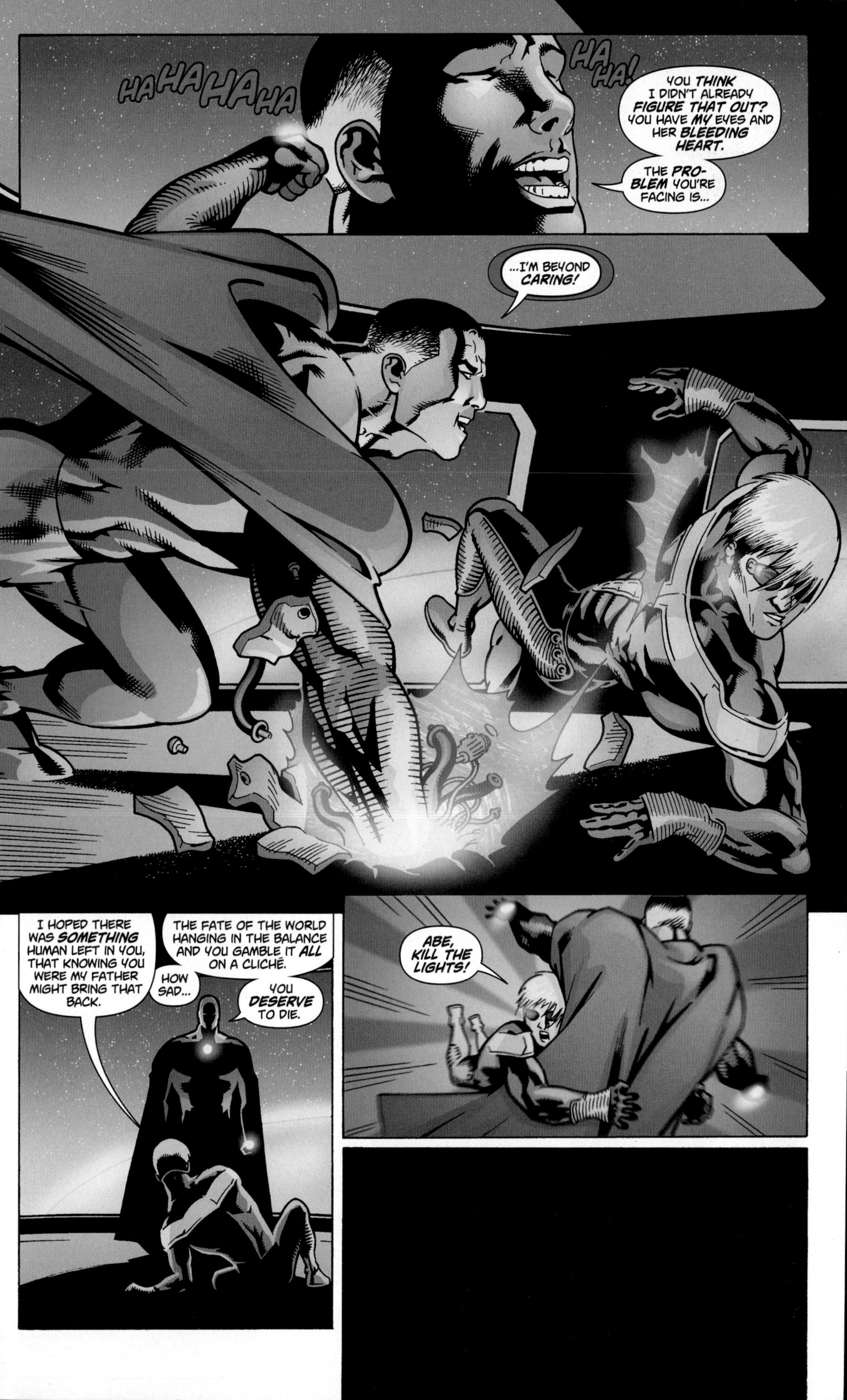
HAHAHAHAHA
HAHA!
YOU THINK I DIDN'T ALREADY FIGURE THAT OUT? YOU HAVE MY EYES AND HER BLEEDING HEART.
THE PRO-BLEM YOU'RE FACING IS...
...I'M BEYOND CARING!
I HOPED THERE WAS SOMETHING HUMAN LEFT IN YOU, THAT KNOWING YOU WERE MY FATHER MIGHT BRING THAT BACK.
THE FATE OF THE WORLD HANGING IN THE BALANCE AND YOU GAMBLE IT ALL ON A CLICHÉ.
HOW SAD...
YOU DESERVE TO DIE.
ABE, KILL THE LIGHTS!

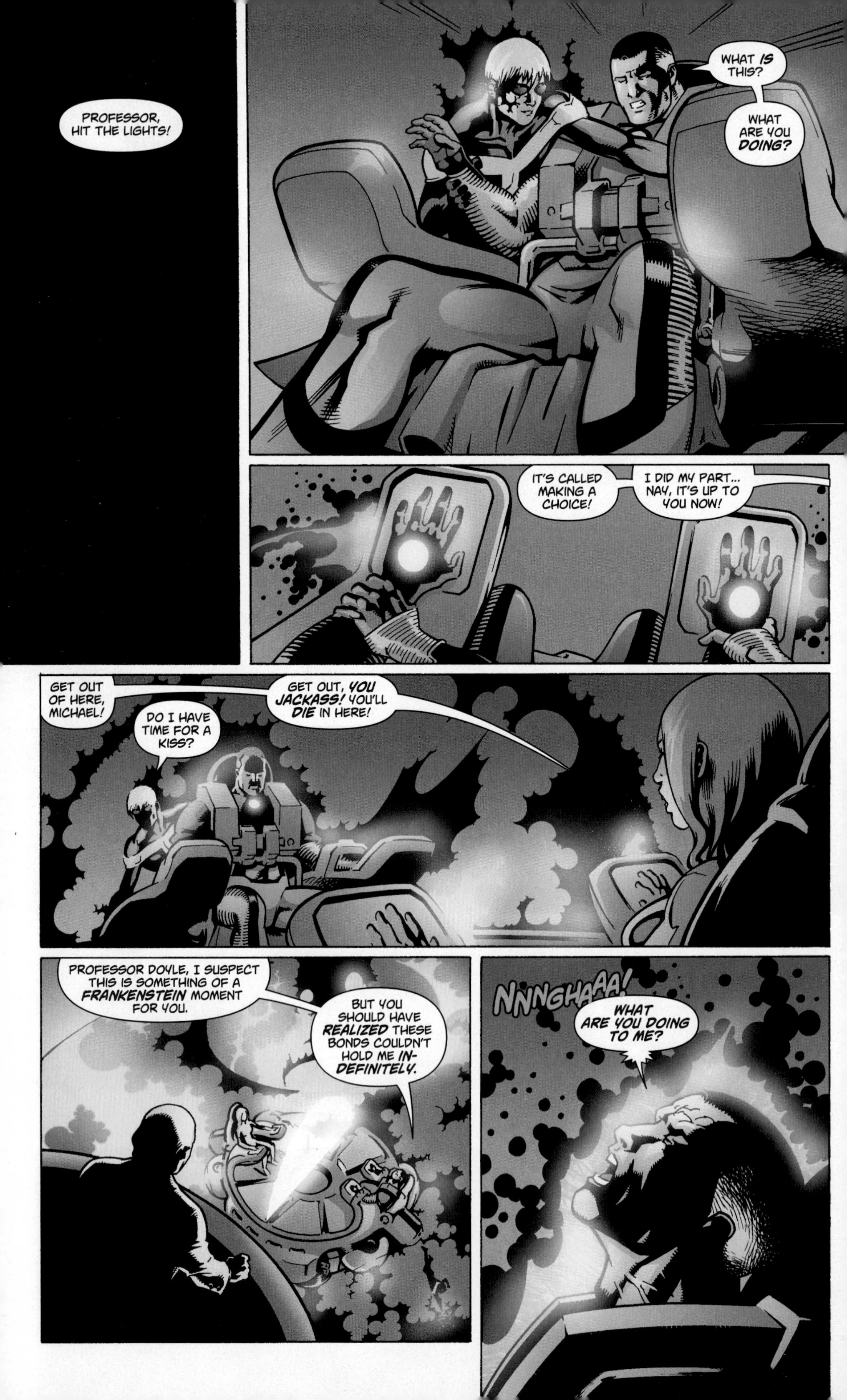
PROFESSOR, HIT THE LIGHTS!
WHAT IS THIS?
WHAT ARE YOU DOING?
IT'S CALLED MAKING A CHOICE!
I DID MY PART... NAY, IT'S UP TO YOU NOW!
GET OUT OF HERE, MICHAEL!
GET OUT, YOU JACKASS! YOU'LL DIE IN HERE!
DO I HAVE TIME FOR A KISS?
PROFESSOR DOYLE, I SUSPECT THIS IS SOMETHING OF A FRANKENSTEIN MOMENT FOR YOU.
BUT YOU SHOULD HAVE REALIZED THESE BONDS COULDN'T HOLD ME IN-DEFINITELY.
NNNGHAAA!
WHAT ARE YOU DOING TO ME?

HOLD ON, RENE! IT'S *WORKING!*

THEY WON'T *CHANGE*...THEY WON'T *LEARN*. THE CYCLE WILL REMAIN *UNBROKEN*.

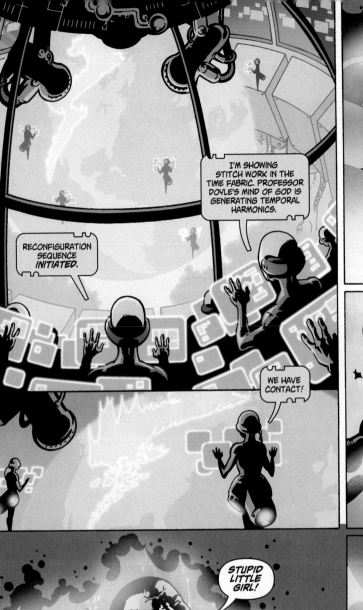

I'M SHOWING STITCH WORK IN THE TIME FABRIC. PROFESSOR DOYLE'S MIND OF GOD IS GENERATING TEMPORAL HARMONICS.

RECONFIGURATION SEQUENCE *INITIATED*.

WE HAVE CONTACT!

NOT MY *PROBLEM*, PSYCHO! I'M JUST HERE TO GIVE THEM THE *OPPORTUNITY*.

STUPID LITTLE GIRL!

THE GREAT GOD RIGHTEOUS RESORTS TO NAME-CALLING?

AN HOUR AGO I WAS *TERRIFIED* OF YOU...

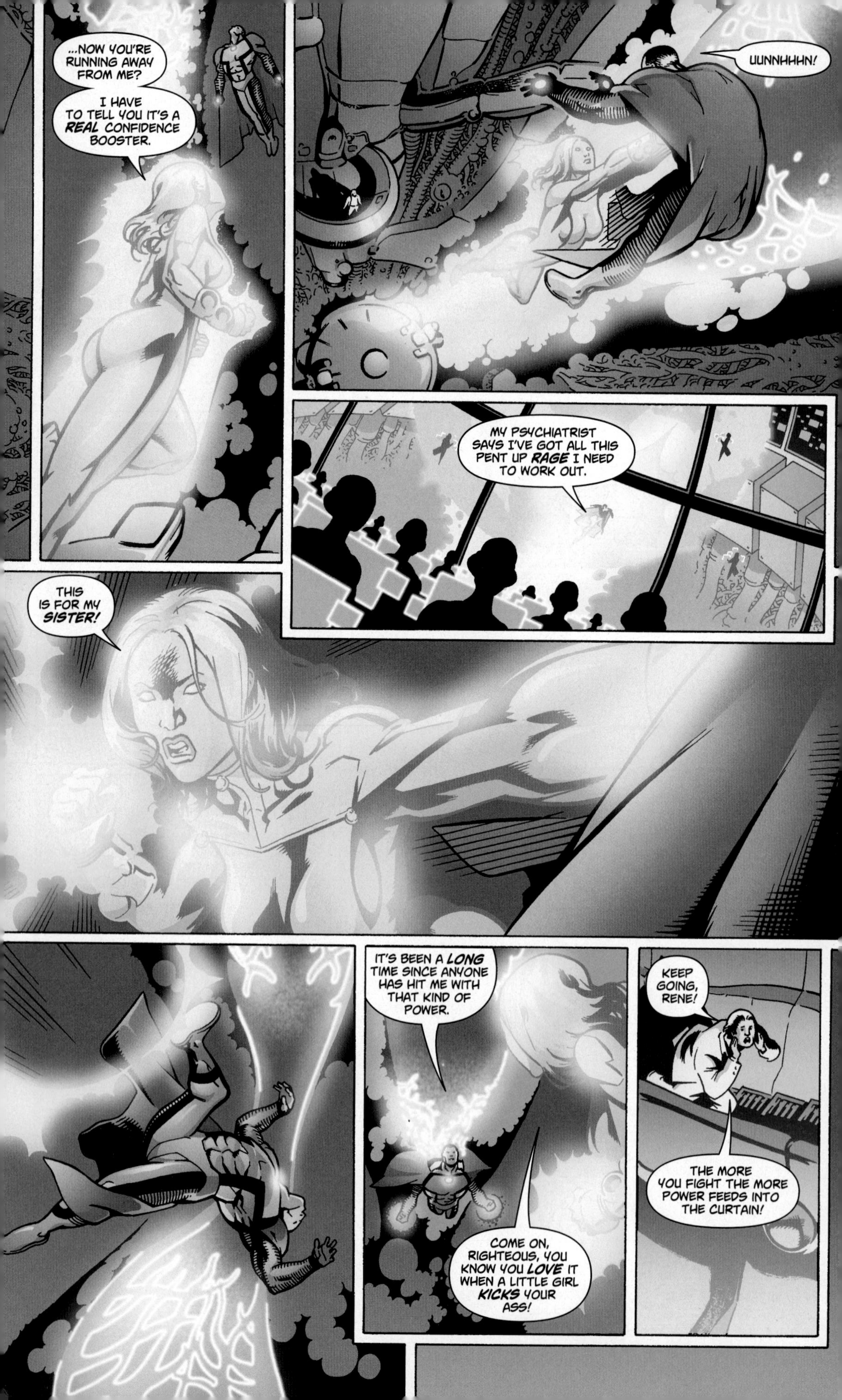

...NOW YOU'RE RUNNING AWAY FROM ME?
I HAVE TO TELL YOU IT'S A REAL CONFIDENCE BOOSTER.
UUNNHHHN!
MY PSYCHIATRIST SAYS I'VE GOT ALL THIS PENT UP RAGE I NEED TO WORK OUT.
THIS IS FOR MY SISTER!
IT'S BEEN A LONG TIME SINCE ANYONE HAS HIT ME WITH THAT KIND OF POWER.
COME ON, RIGHTEOUS, YOU KNOW YOU LOVE IT WHEN A LITTLE GIRL KICKS YOUR ASS!
KEEP GOING, RENE!
THE MORE YOU FIGHT THE MORE POWER FEEDS INTO THE CURTAIN!

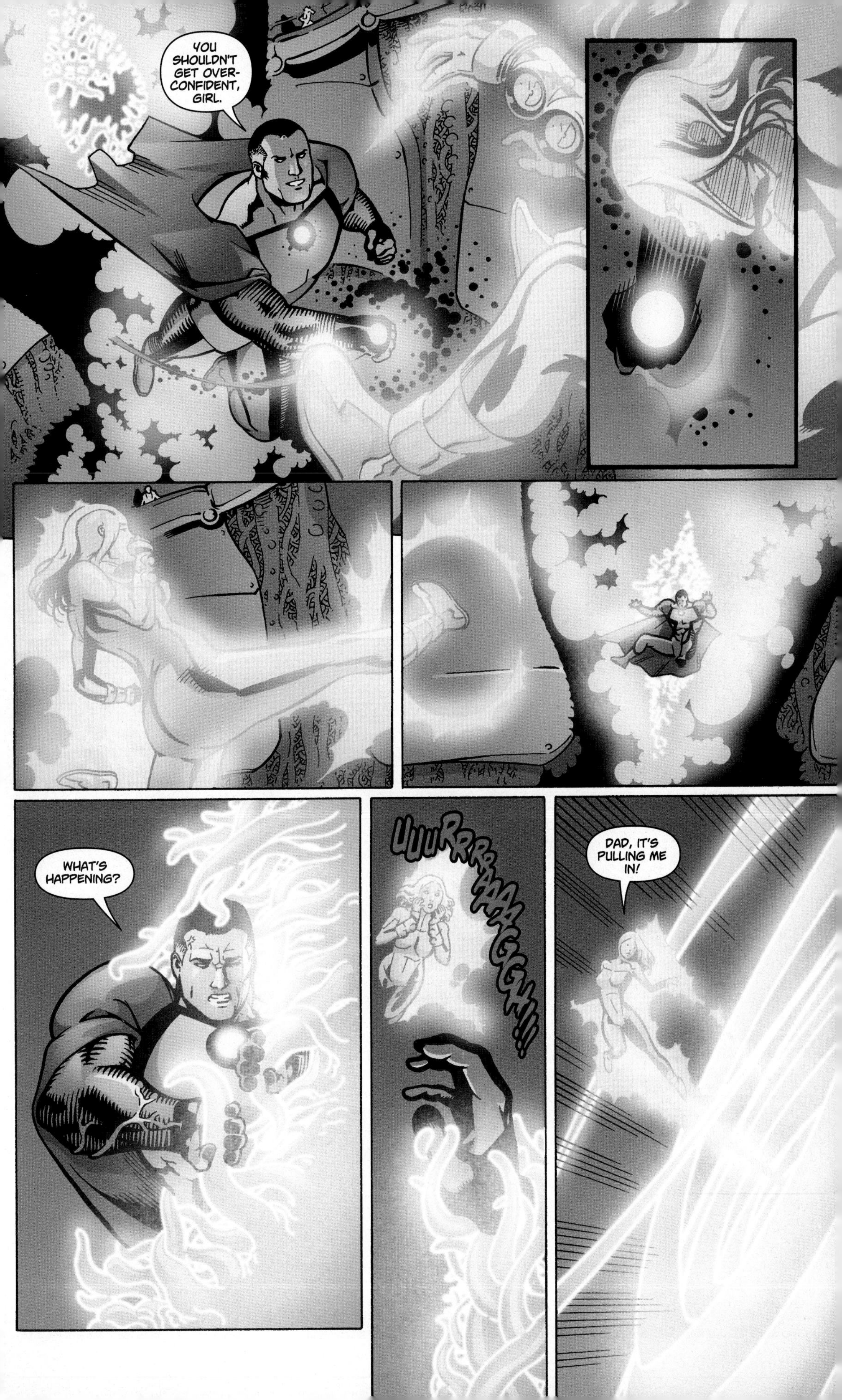
YOU SHOULDN'T GET OVER-CONFIDENT, GIRL.
WHAT'S HAPPENING?
UUURRRAAAGGGH!!!
DAD, IT'S PULLING ME IN!

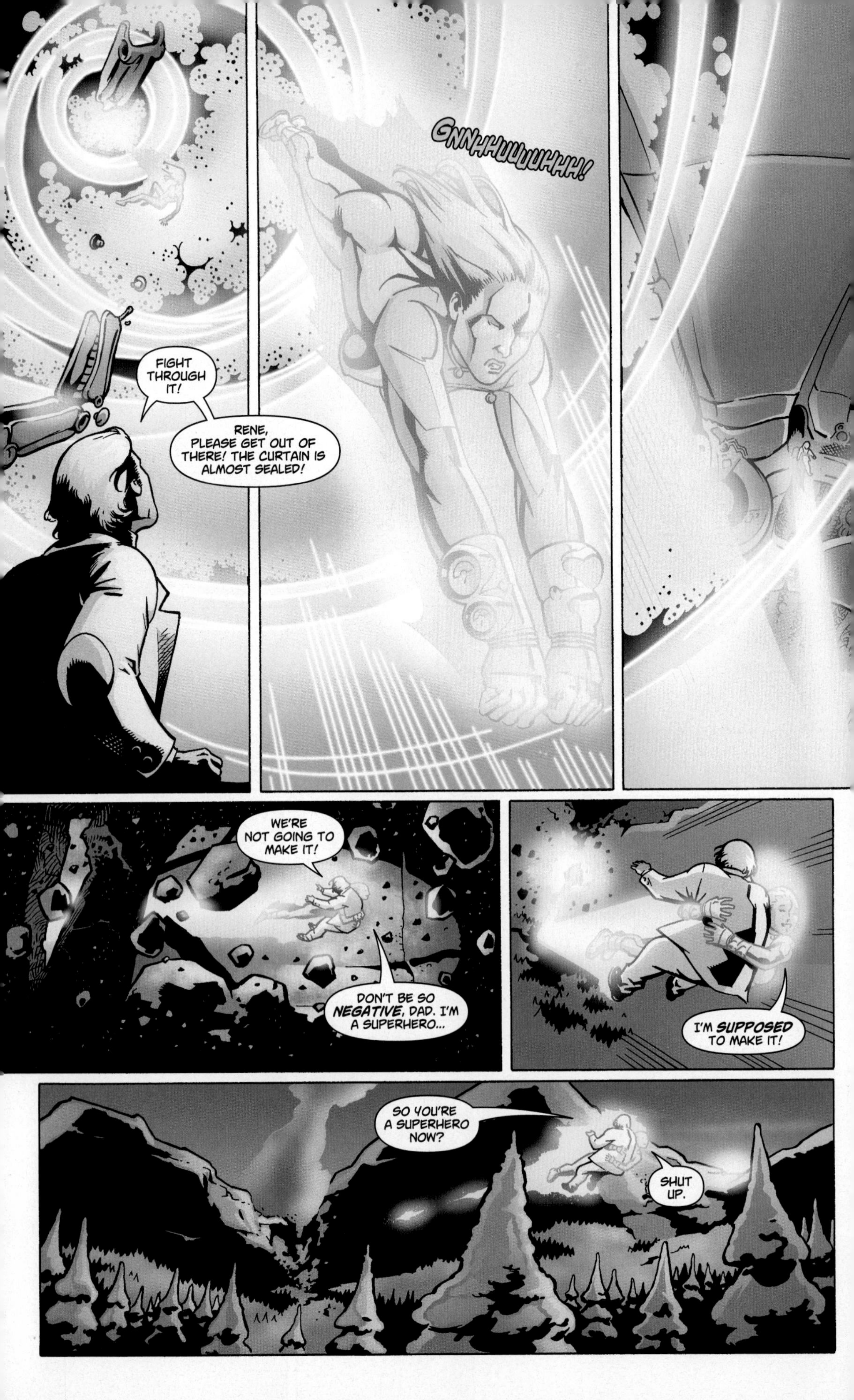
FIGHT THROUGH IT!
RENE, PLEASE GET OUT OF THERE! THE CURTAIN IS ALMOST SEALED!
GNNHHUUUUHHH!
WE'RE NOT GOING TO MAKE IT!
DON'T BE SO NEGATIVE, DAD. I'M A SUPERHERO...
I'M SUPPOSED TO MAKE IT!
SO YOU'RE A SUPERHERO NOW?
SHUT UP.

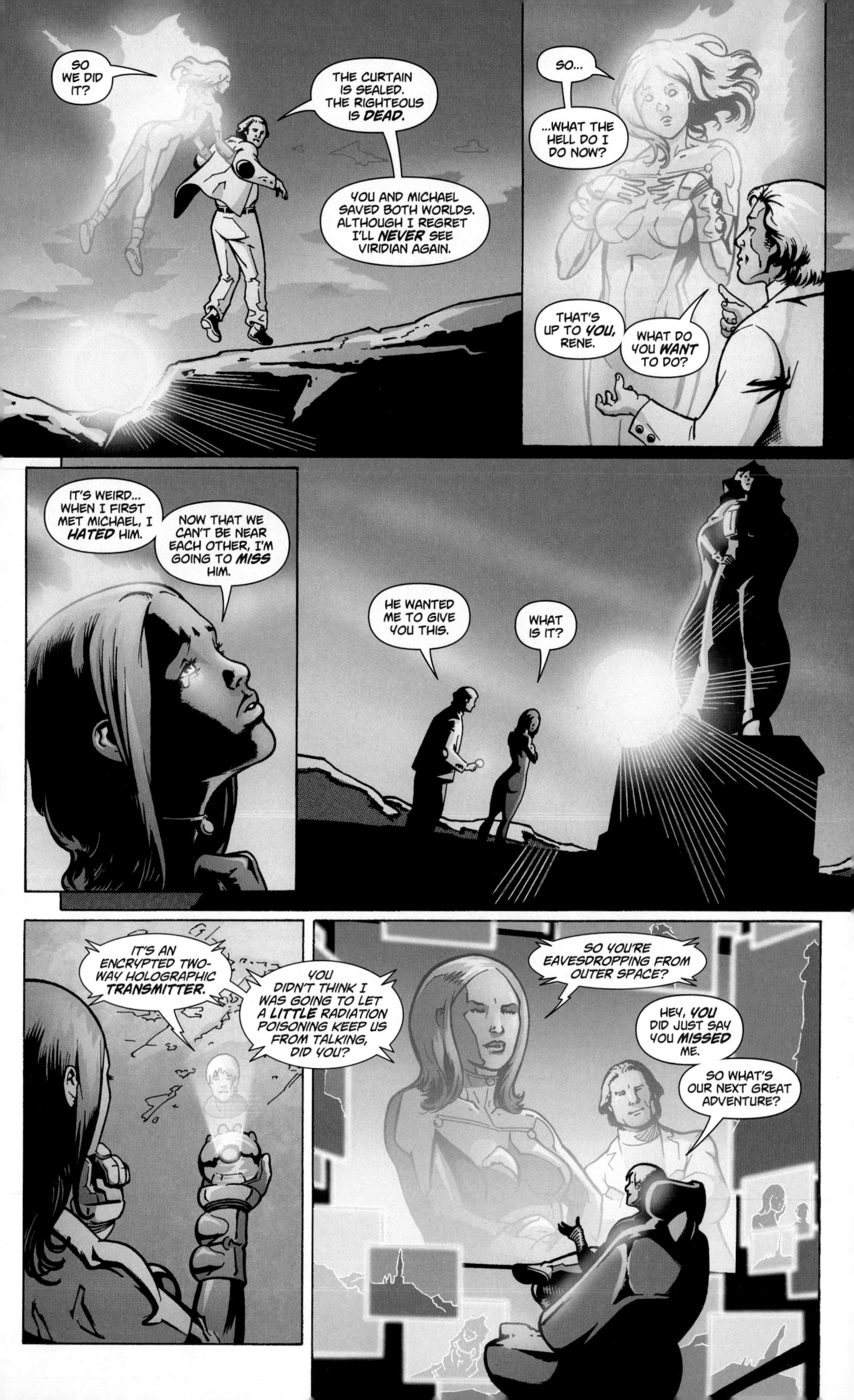
SO WE DID IT?
THE CURTAIN IS SEALED. THE RIGHTEOUS IS DEAD.
YOU AND MICHAEL SAVED BOTH WORLDS. ALTHOUGH I REGRET I'LL NEVER SEE VIRIDIAN AGAIN.
SO...
...WHAT THE HELL DO I DO NOW?
THAT'S UP TO YOU, RENE.
WHAT DO YOU WANT TO DO?
IT'S WEIRD... WHEN I FIRST MET MICHAEL, I HATED HIM.
NOW THAT WE CAN'T BE NEAR EACH OTHER, I'M GOING TO MISS HIM.
HE WANTED ME TO GIVE YOU THIS.
WHAT IS IT?
IT'S AN ENCRYPTED TWO-WAY HOLOGRAPHIC TRANSMITTER.
YOU DIDN'T THINK I WAS GOING TO LET A LITTLE RADIATION POISONING KEEP US FROM TALKING, DID YOU?
SO YOU'RE EAVESDROPPING FROM OUTER SPACE?
HEY, YOU DID JUST SAY YOU MISSED ME.
SO WHAT'S OUR NEXT GREAT ADVENTURE?

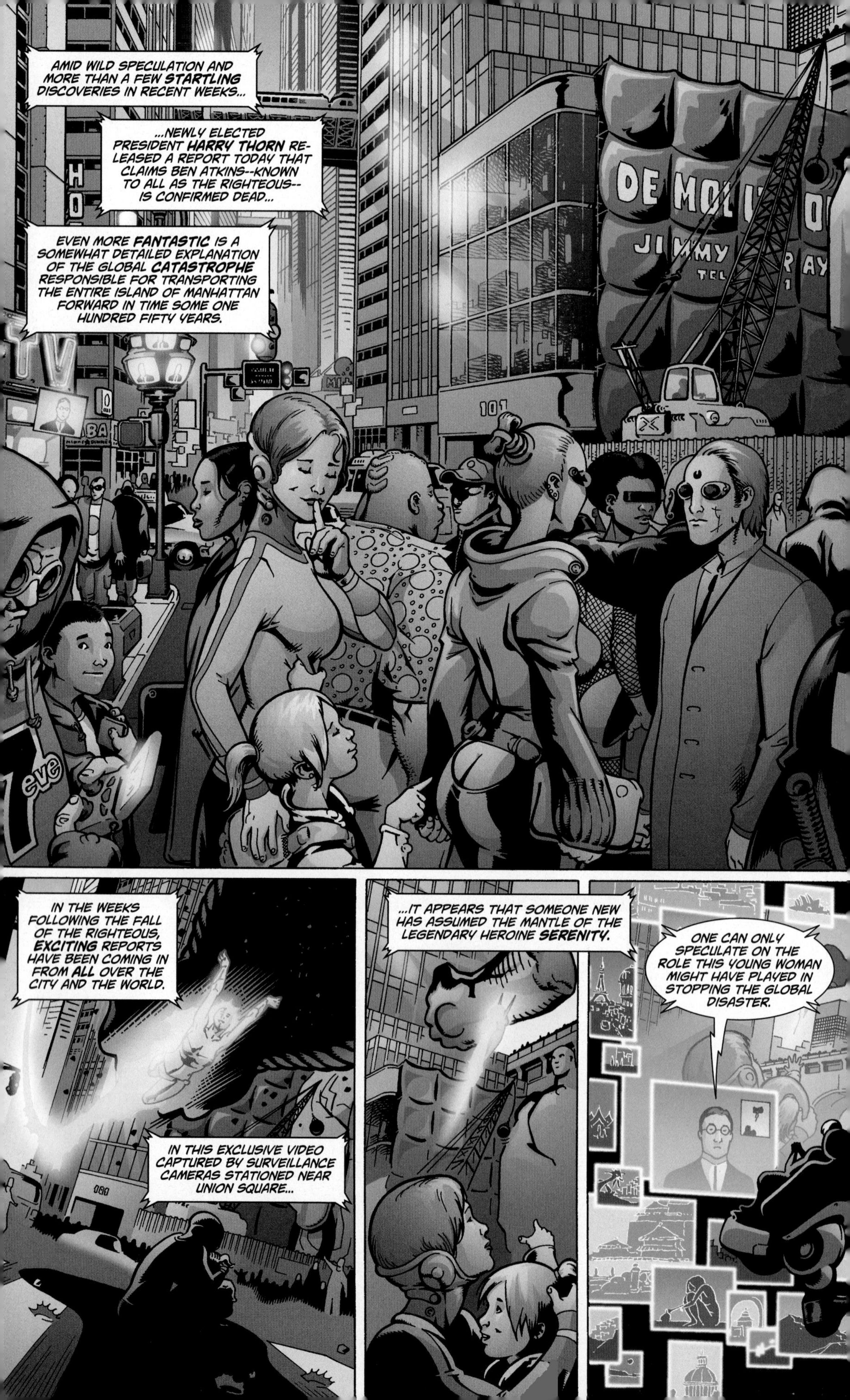
AMID WILD SPECULATION AND MORE THAN A FEW STARTLING DISCOVERIES IN RECENT WEEKS...
...NEWLY ELECTED PRESIDENT HARRY THORN RE-LEASED A REPORT TODAY THAT CLAIMS BEN ATKINS--KNOWN TO ALL AS THE RIGHTEOUS--IS CONFIRMED DEAD...
EVEN MORE FANTASTIC IS A SOMEWHAT DETAILED EXPLANATION OF THE GLOBAL CATASTROPHE RESPONSIBLE FOR TRANSPORTING THE ENTIRE ISLAND OF MANHATTAN FORWARD IN TIME SOME ONE HUNDRED FIFTY YEARS.
DE MOLI
JIMMY RAY
TV
101
IN THE WEEKS FOLLOWING THE FALL OF THE RIGHTEOUS, EXCITING REPORTS HAVE BEEN COMING IN FROM ALL OVER THE CITY AND THE WORLD.
IN THIS EXCLUSIVE VIDEO CAPTURED BY SURVEILLANCE CAMERAS STATIONED NEAR UNION SQUARE...
...IT APPEARS THAT SOMEONE NEW HAS ASSUMED THE MANTLE OF THE LEGENDARY HEROINE SERENITY.
ONE CAN ONLY SPECULATE ON THE ROLE THIS YOUNG WOMAN MIGHT HAVE PLAYED IN STOPPING THE GLOBAL DISASTER.

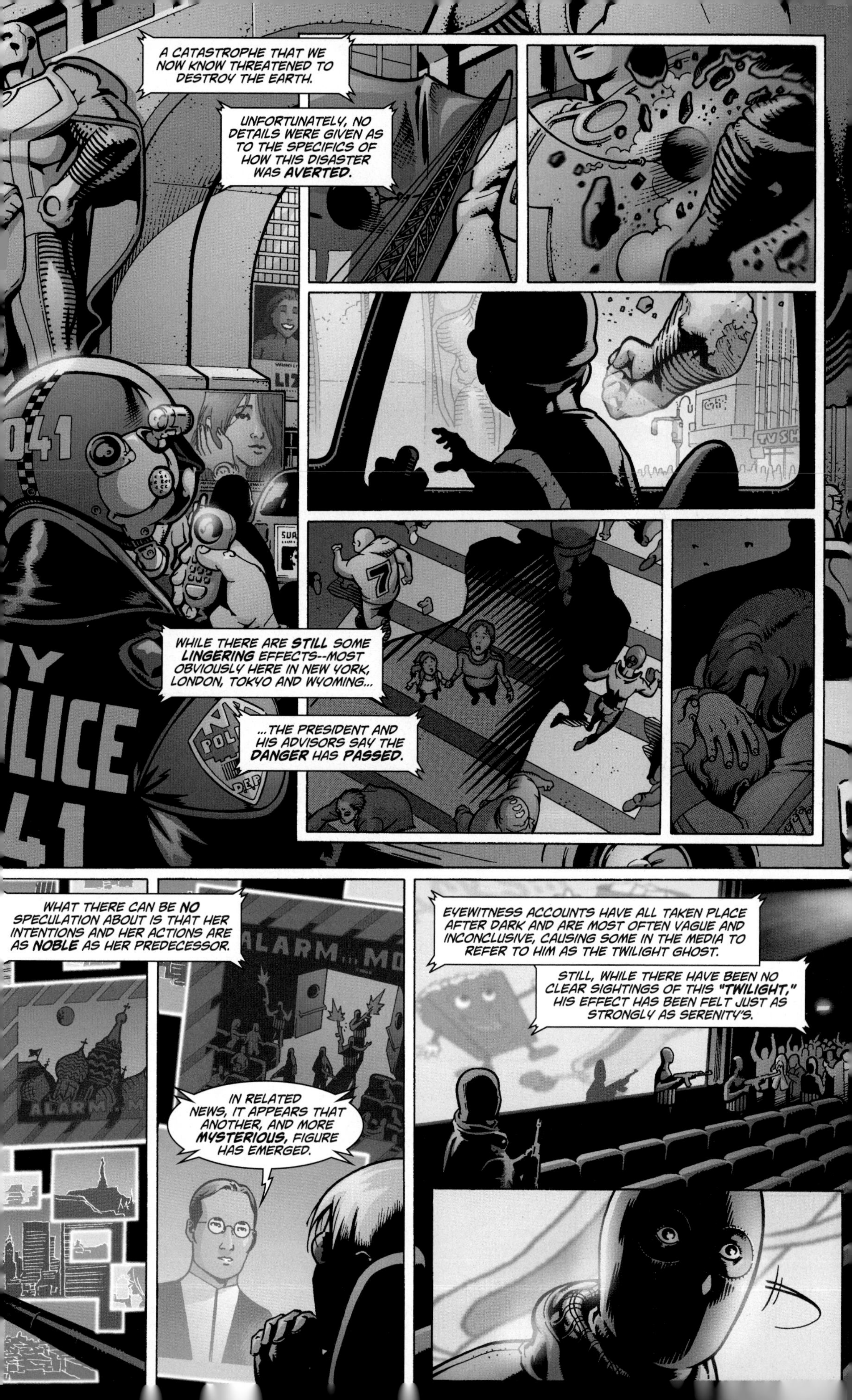

A CATASTROPHE THAT WE NOW KNOW THREATENED TO DESTROY THE EARTH.
UNFORTUNATELY, NO DETAILS WERE GIVEN AS TO THE SPECIFICS OF HOW THIS DISASTER WAS AVERTED.
WHILE THERE ARE STILL SOME LINGERING EFFECTS--MOST OBVIOUSLY HERE IN NEW YORK, LONDON, TOKYO AND WYOMING...
...THE PRESIDENT AND HIS ADVISORS SAY THE DANGER HAS PASSED.
WHAT THERE CAN BE NO SPECULATION ABOUT IS THAT HER INTENTIONS AND HER ACTIONS ARE AS NOBLE AS HER PREDECESSOR.
ALARM...MO
IN RELATED NEWS, IT APPEARS THAT ANOTHER, AND MORE MYSTERIOUS, FIGURE HAS EMERGED.
EYEWITNESS ACCOUNTS HAVE ALL TAKEN PLACE AFTER DARK AND ARE MOST OFTEN VAGUE AND INCONCLUSIVE, CAUSING SOME IN THE MEDIA TO REFER TO HIM AS THE TWILIGHT GHOST.
STILL, WHILE THERE HAVE BEEN NO CLEAR SIGHTINGS OF THIS "TWILIGHT," HIS EFFECT HAS BEEN FELT JUST AS STRONGLY AS SERENITY'S.

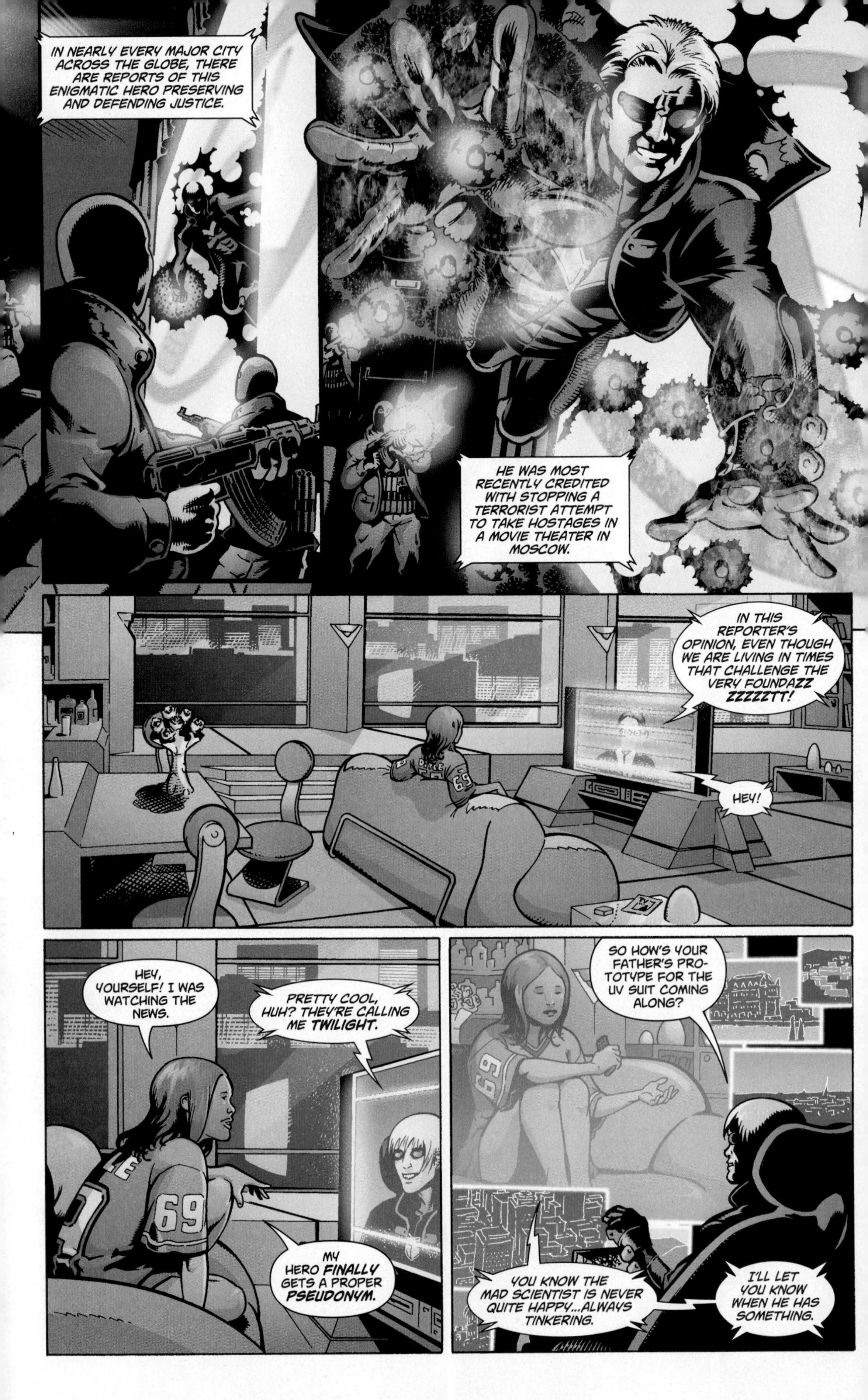
IN NEARLY EVERY MAJOR CITY ACROSS THE GLOBE, THERE ARE REPORTS OF THIS ENIGMATIC HERO PRESERVING AND DEFENDING JUSTICE.
HE WAS MOST RECENTLY CREDITED WITH STOPPING A TERRORIST ATTEMPT TO TAKE HOSTAGES IN A MOVIE THEATER IN MOSCOW.
IN THIS REPORTER'S OPINION, EVEN THOUGH WE ARE LIVING IN TIMES THAT CHALLENGE THE VERY FOUNDAZZ ZZZZZZTT!
HEY!
HEY, YOURSELF! I WAS WATCHING THE NEWS.
PRETTY COOL, HUH? THEY'RE CALLING ME TWILIGHT.
MY HERO FINALLY GETS A PROPER PSEUDONYM.
SO HOW'S YOUR FATHER'S PROTOTYPE FOR THE UV SUIT COMING ALONG?
YOU KNOW THE MAD SCIENTIST IS NEVER QUITE HAPPY...ALWAYS TINKERING.
I'LL LET YOU KNOW WHEN HE HAS SOMETHING.

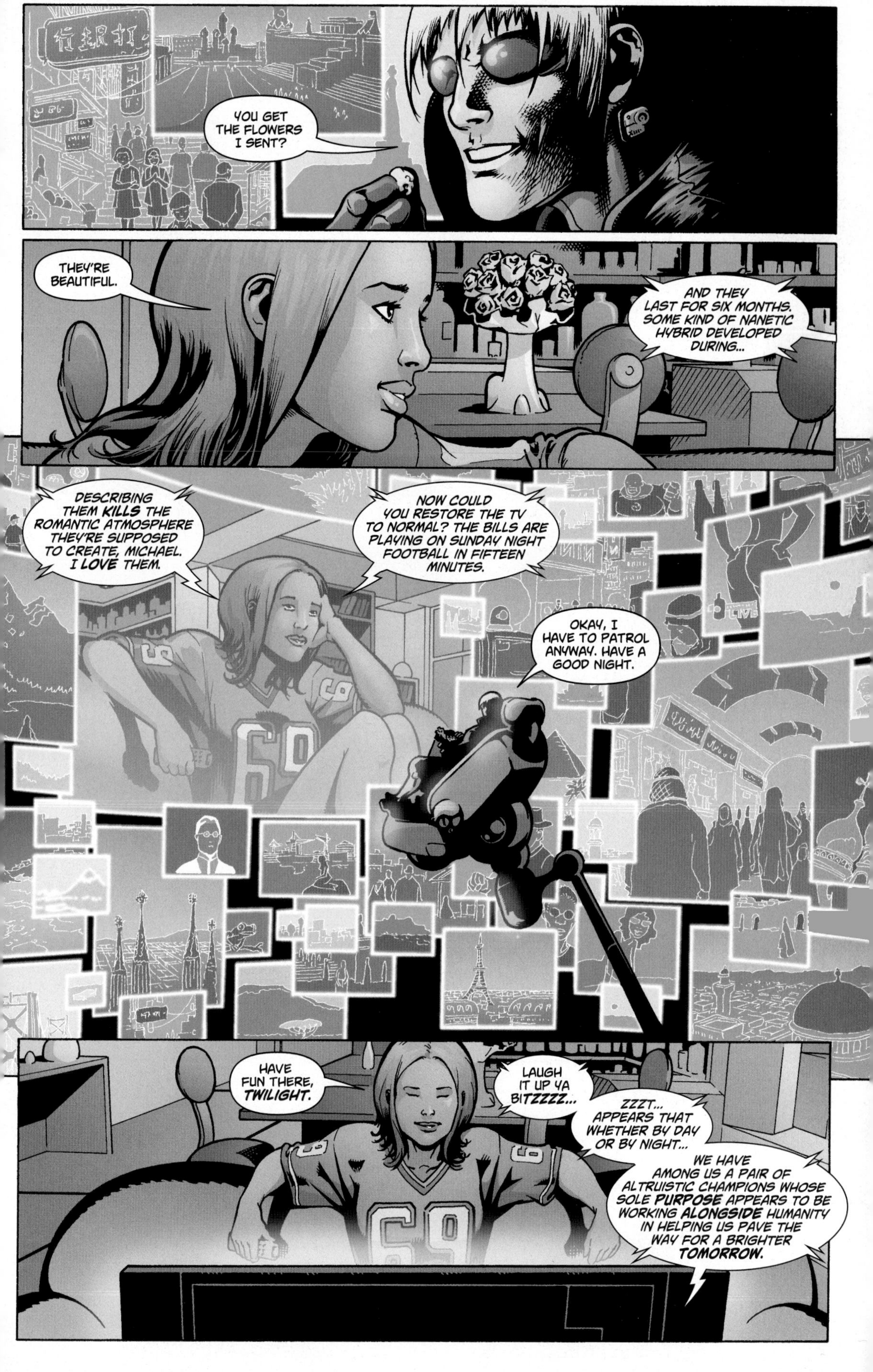
YOU GET THE FLOWERS I SENT?
THEY'RE BEAUTIFUL.
AND THEY LAST FOR SIX MONTHS. SOME KIND OF NANETIC HYBRID DEVELOPED DURING...
DESCRIBING THEM KILLS THE ROMANTIC ATMOSPHERE THEY'RE SUPPOSED TO CREATE, MICHAEL. I LOVE THEM.
NOW COULD YOU RESTORE THE TV TO NORMAL? THE BILLS ARE PLAYING ON SUNDAY NIGHT FOOTBALL IN FIFTEEN MINUTES.
OKAY, I HAVE TO PATROL ANYWAY. HAVE A GOOD NIGHT.
HAVE FUN THERE, TWILIGHT.
LAUGH IT UP YA BITZZZZ...
ZZZT... APPEARS THAT WHETHER BY DAY OR BY NIGHT...
WE HAVE AMONG US A PAIR OF ALTRUISTIC CHAMPIONS WHOSE SOLE PURPOSE APPEARS TO BE WORKING ALONGSIDE HUMANITY IN HELPING US PAVE THE WAY FOR A BRIGHTER TOMORROW.

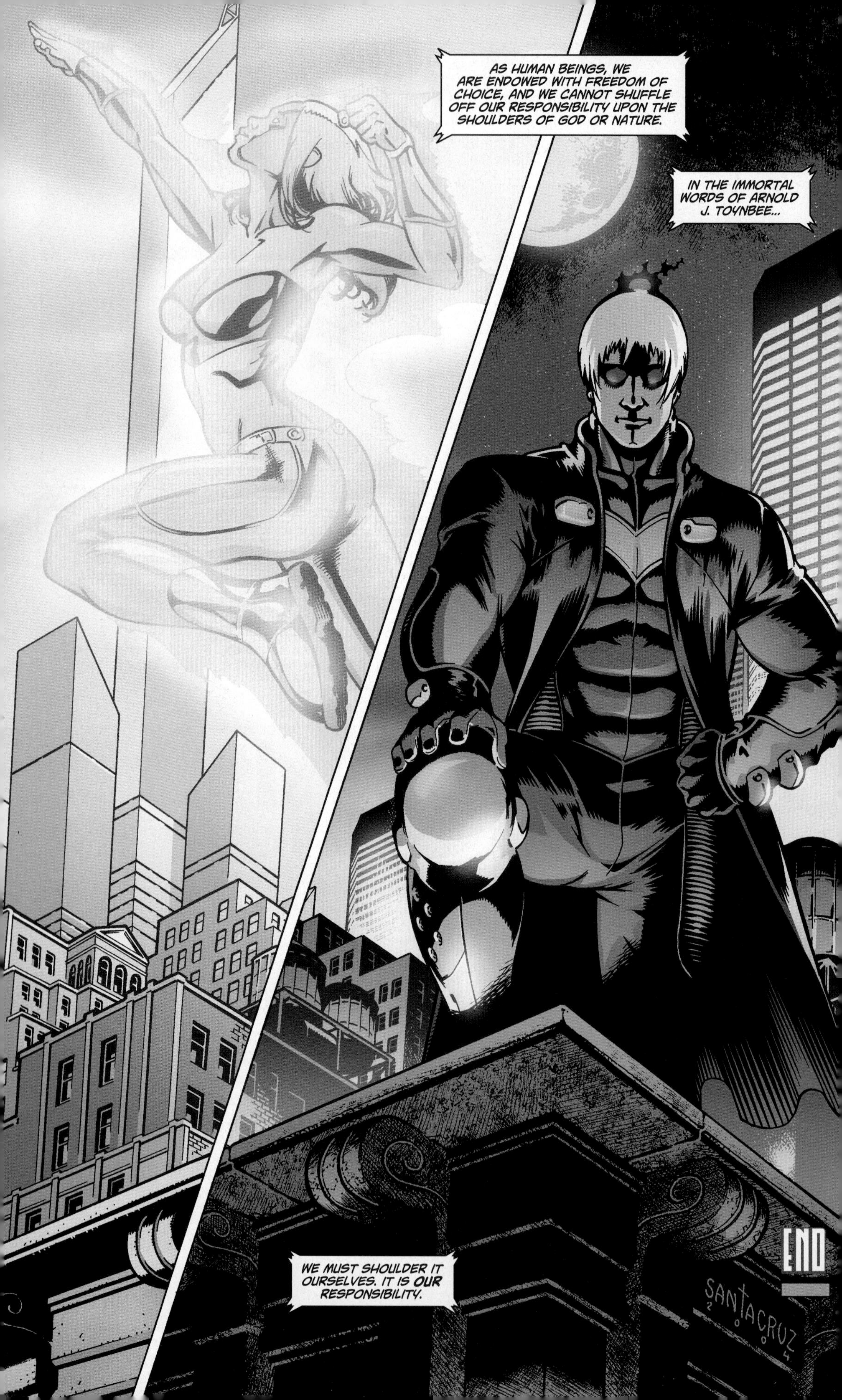
AS HUMAN BEINGS, WE ARE ENDOWED WITH FREEDOM OF CHOICE, AND WE CANNOT SHUFFLE OFF OUR RESPONSIBILITY UPON THE SHOULDERS OF GOD OR NATURE.
IN THE IMMORTAL WORDS OF ARNOLD J. TOYNBEE...
WE MUST SHOULDER IT OURSELVES. IT IS OUR RESPONSIBILITY.
END
SANTACRUZ 2004

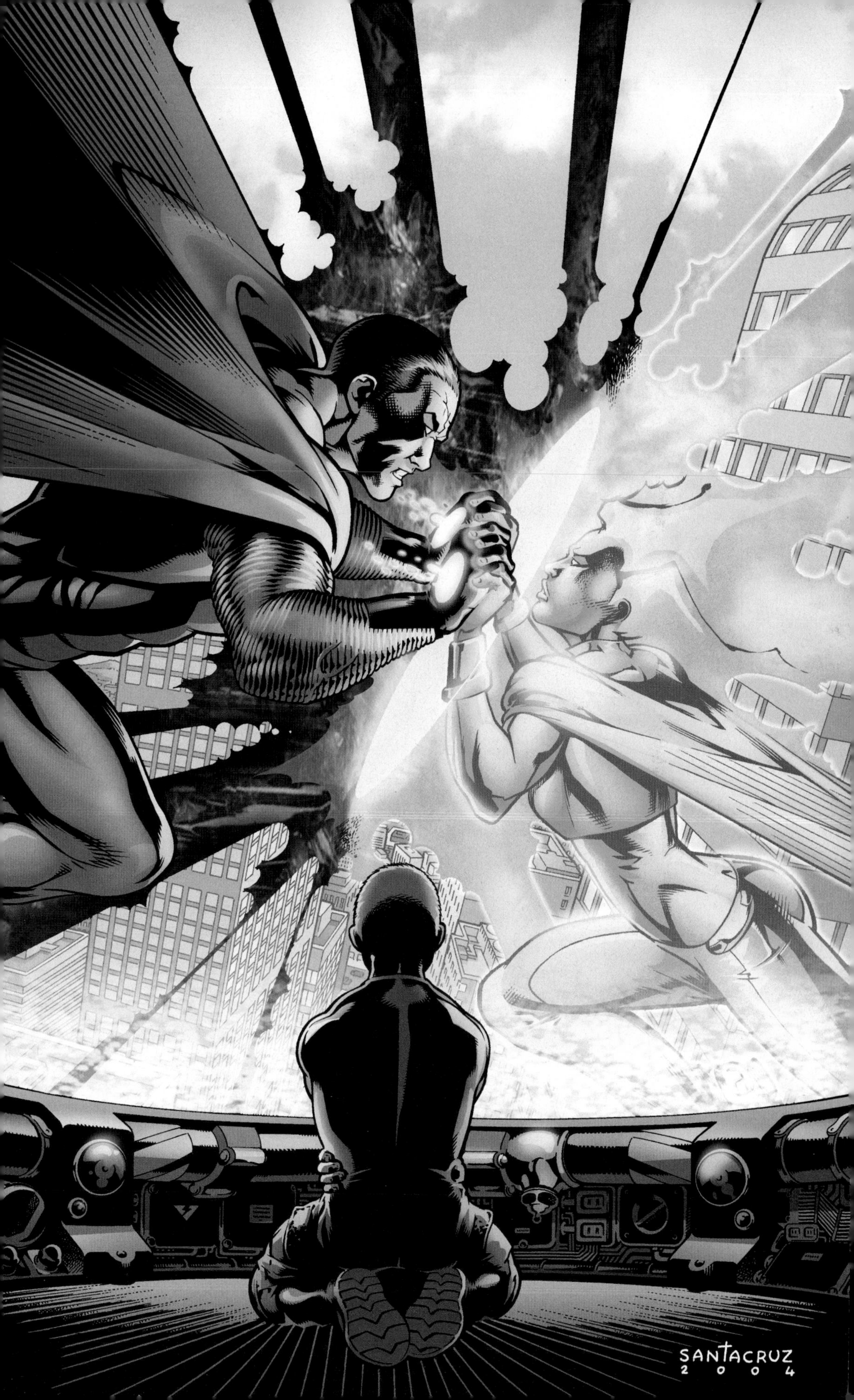
SANTACRUZ
2004

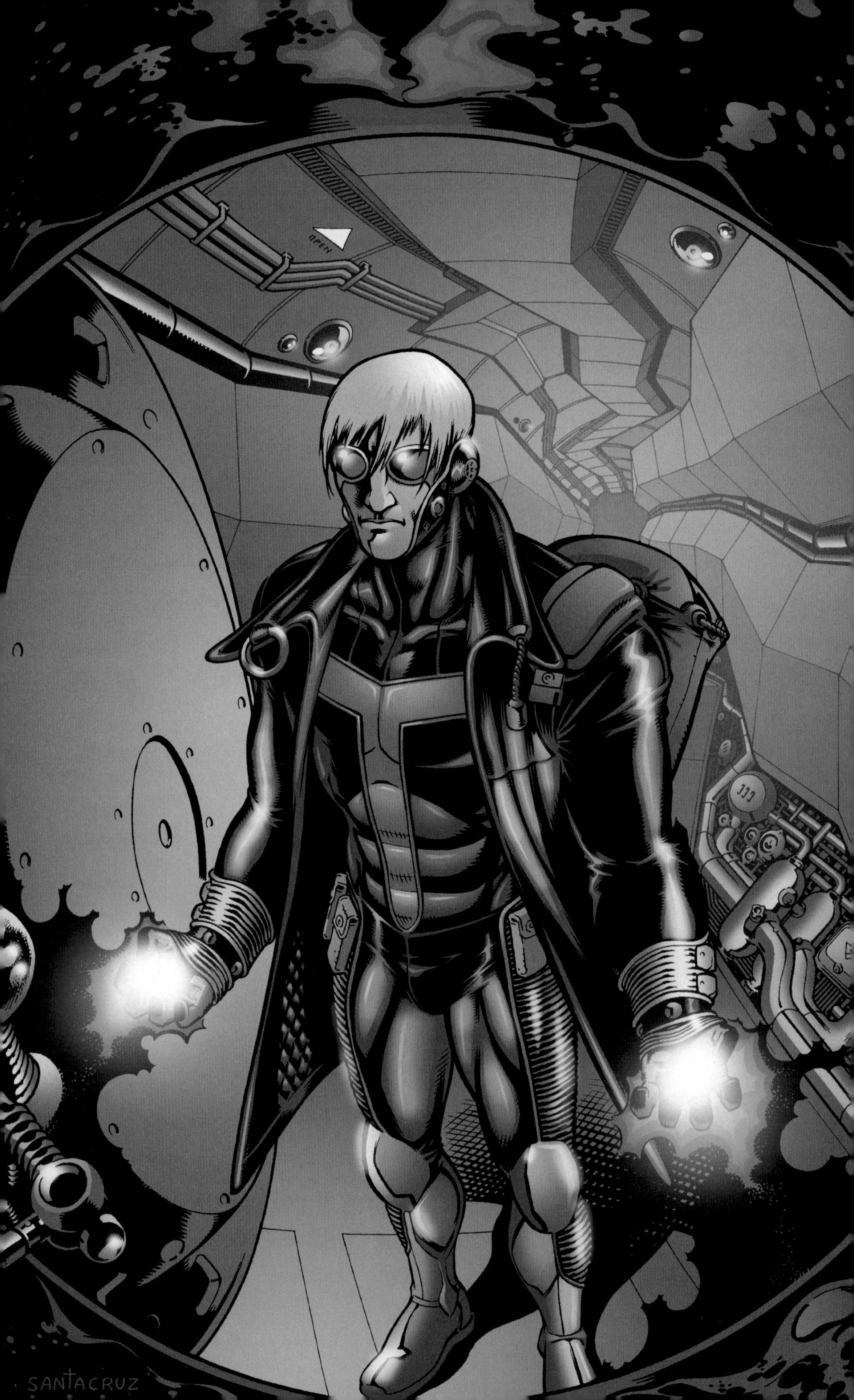
OPEN
SANTACRUZ

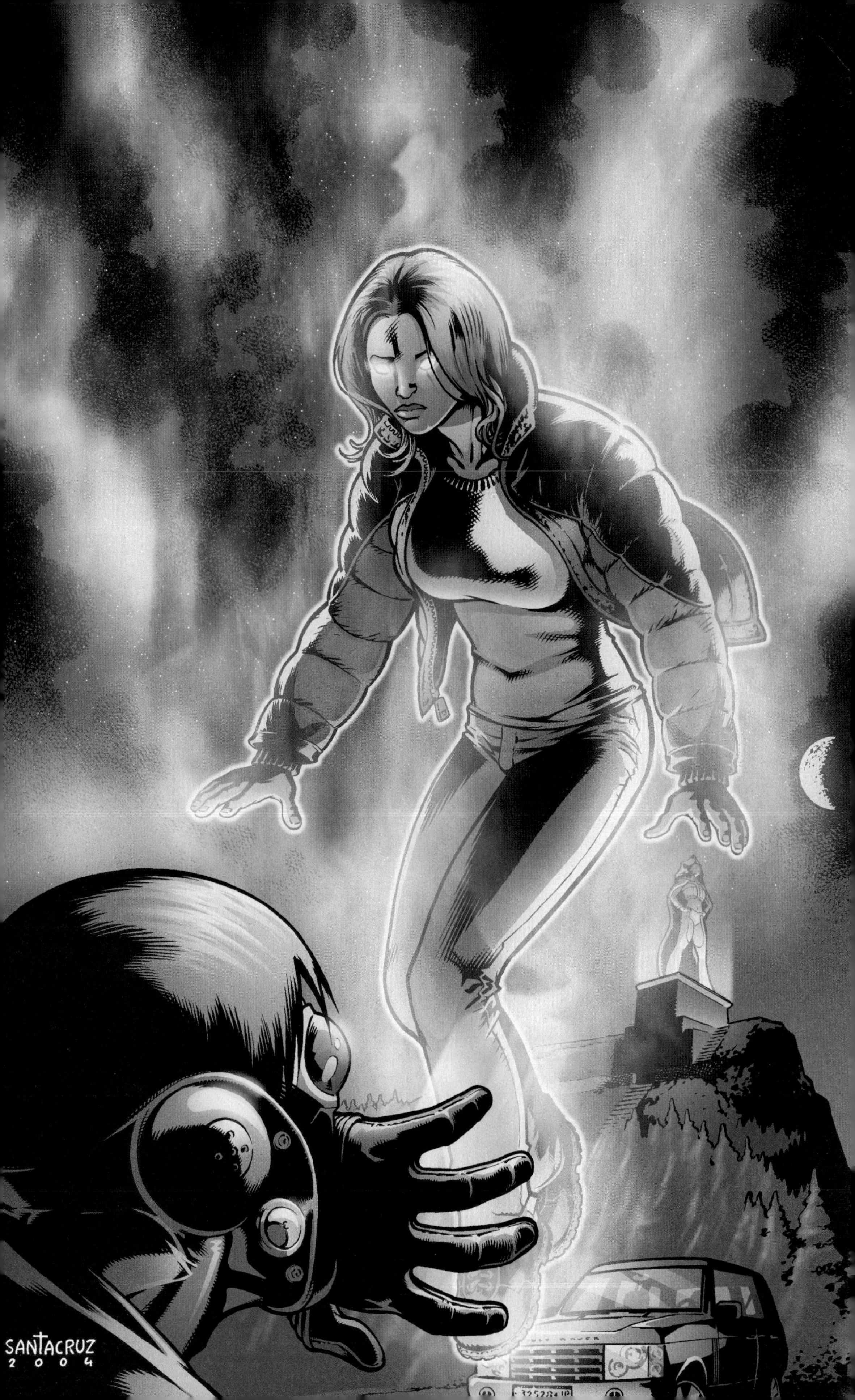
SANTACRUZ
2004

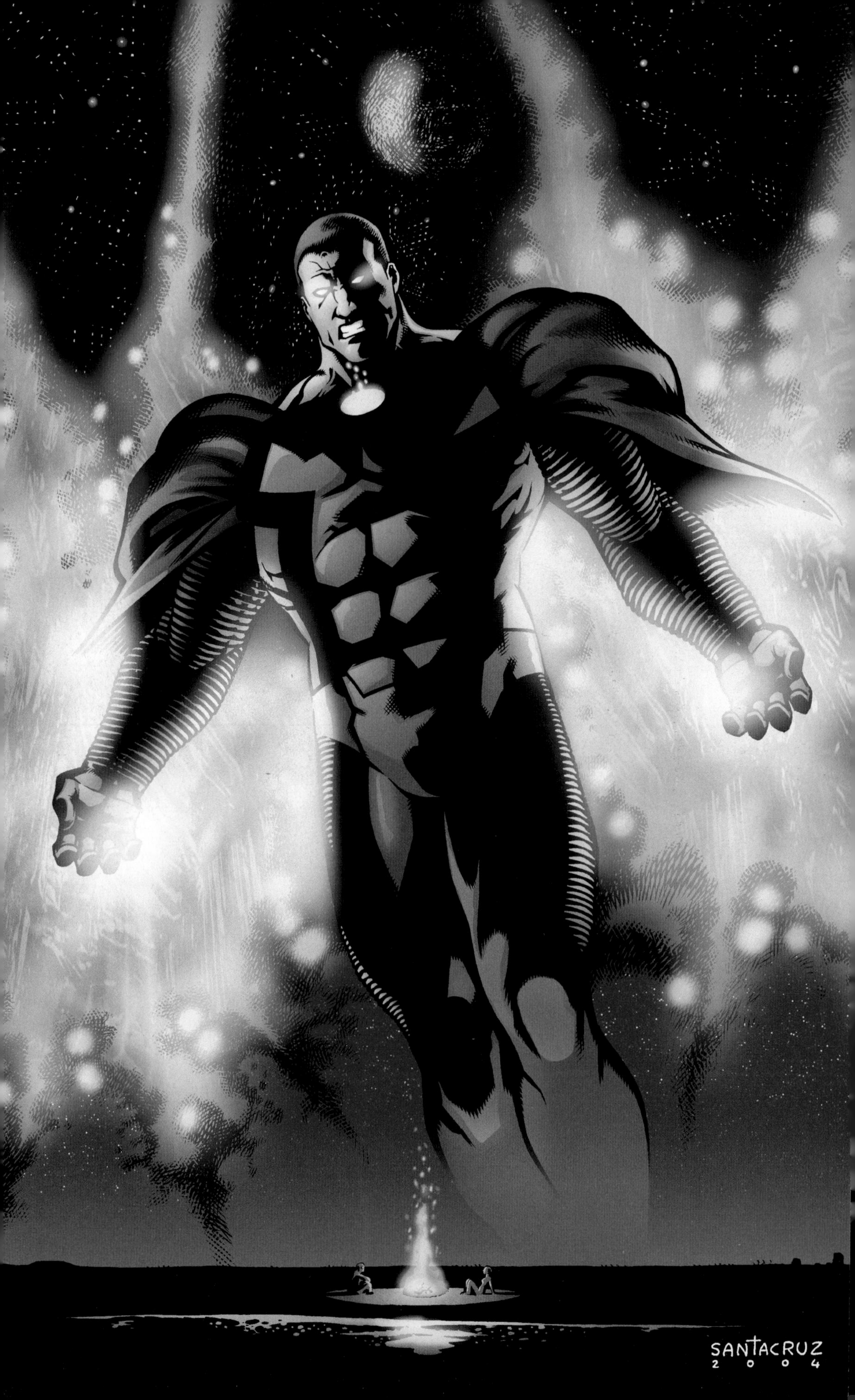
SANTACRUZ
2004

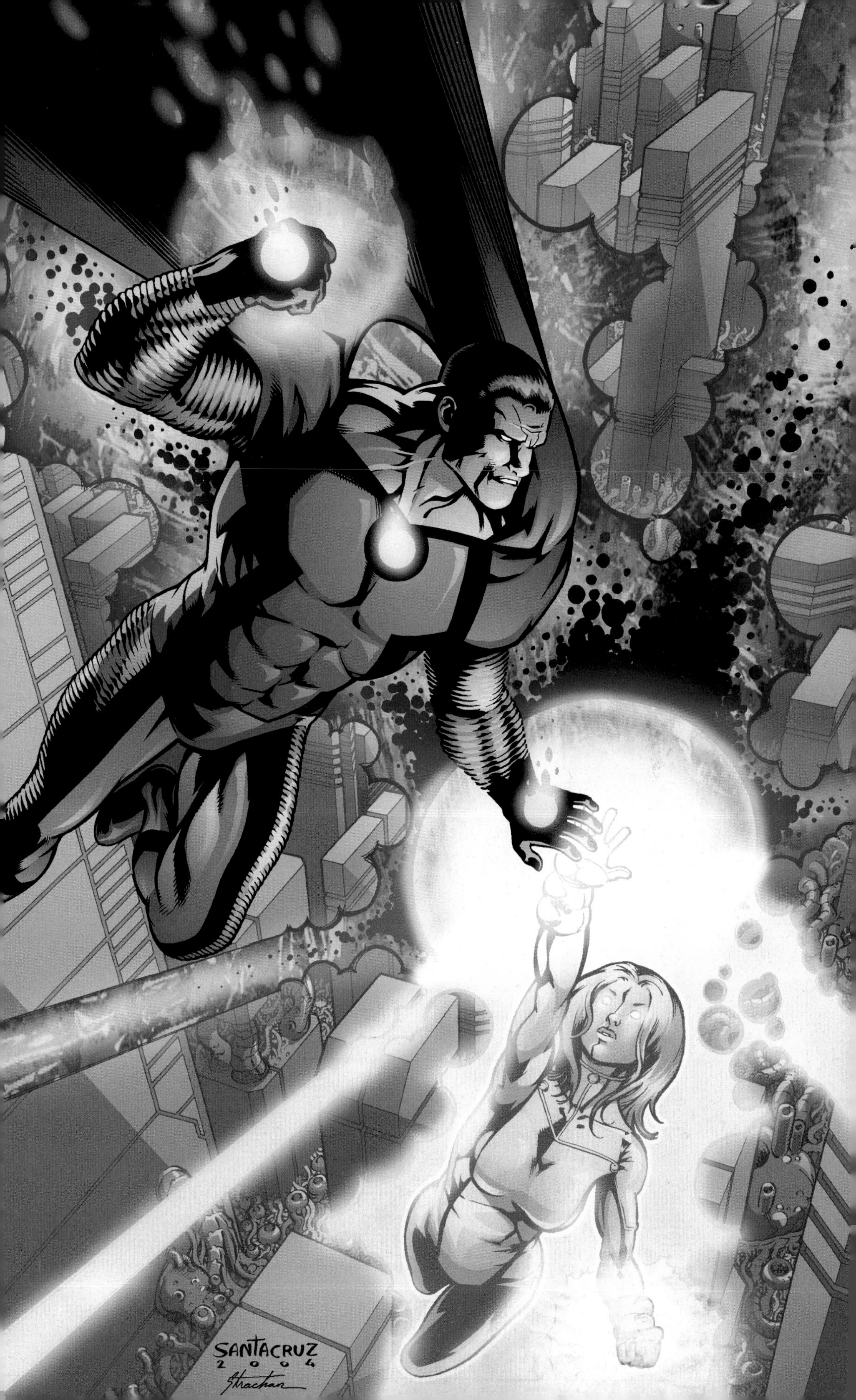
SANTACRUZ
2004
Strachan

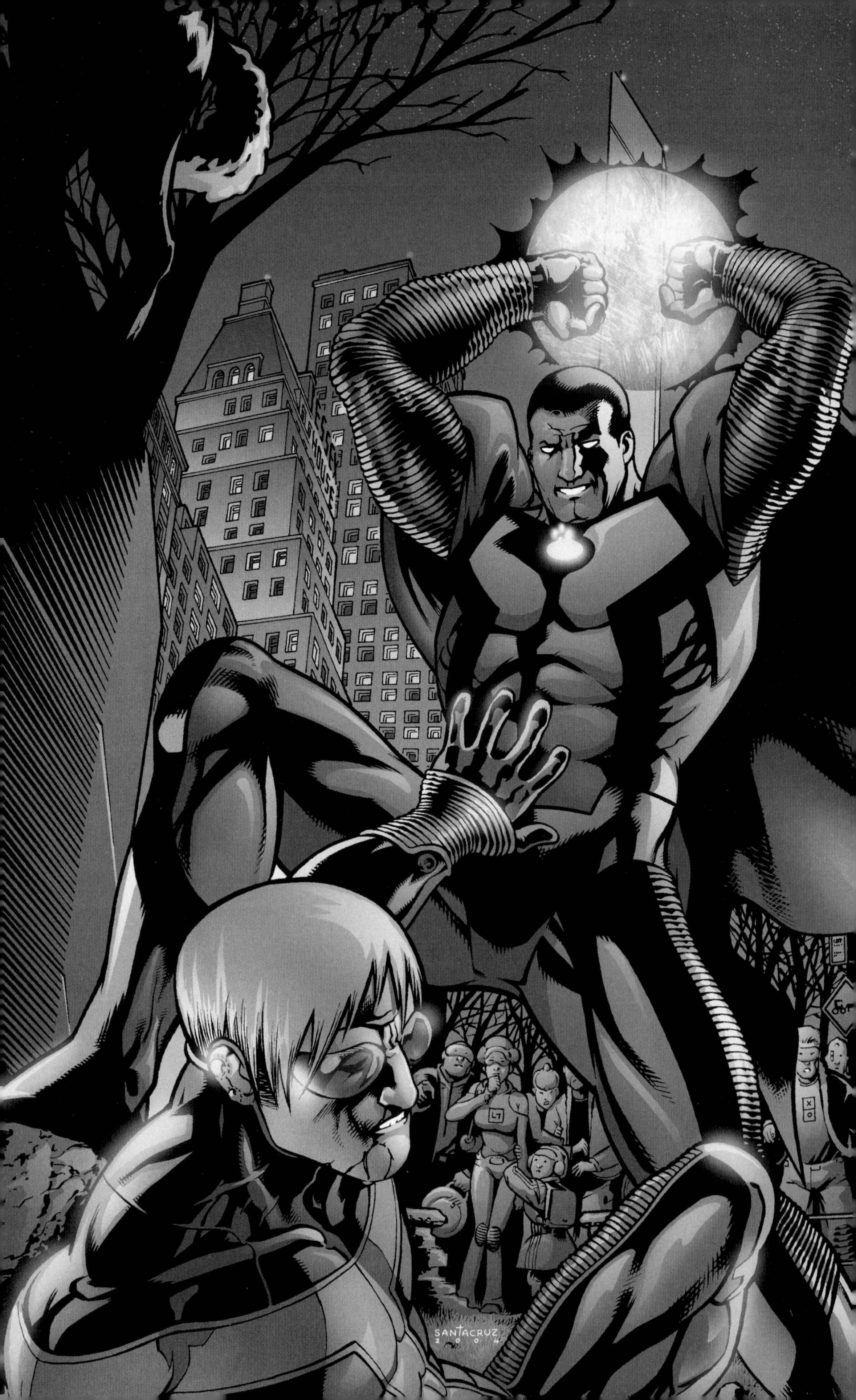
SANTACRUZ
2004

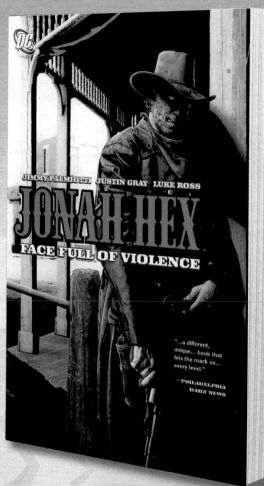
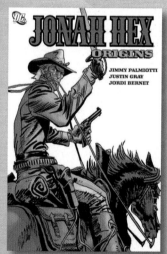
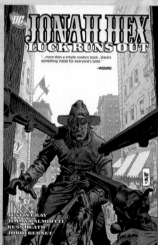
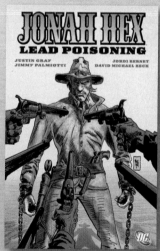

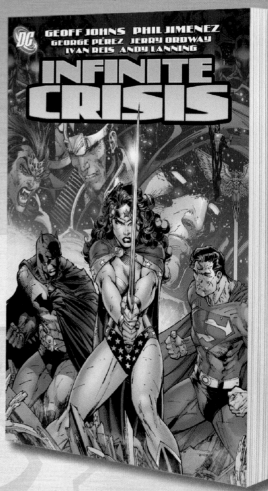

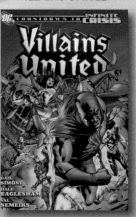